Essentials of Psychological Assessment Series

Series Editors, Alan S. Kaufman and Nadeen L. Kaufman

Essentials of WAIS®-III Assessment
by Alan S. Kaufman and Elizabeth O. Lichtenberger

Essentials of Millon Inventories Assessment
by Stephen N. Strack

Essentials of CAS Assessment
by Jack A. Naglieri

Essentials of Forensic Psychological Assessment
by Marc J. Ackerman

Essentials of Bayley Scales of Infant Development–II Assessment
by Maureen M. Black and Kathleen Matula

Essentials of Myers-Briggs Type Indicator® Assessment
by Naomi Quenk

Essentials of WISC-III® and WPPSI-R® Assessment
by Alan S. Kaufman and Elizabeth O. Lichtenberger

Essentials of Rorschach® Assessment
by Tara Rose, Nancy Kaser-Boyd, and Michael P. Maloney

Essentials of Career Interest Assessment
by Jeffrey P. Prince and Lisa J. Heiser

Essentials of Cross-Battery Assessment
by Dawn P. Flanagan and Samuel O. Ortiz

Essentials of Cognitive Assessment with KAIT and Other Kaufman Measures
by Elizabeth O. Lichtenberger, Debra Broadbooks, and Alan S. Kaufman

Essentials of Nonverbal Assessment
by Steve McCallum, Bruce Bracken, and John Wasserman

Essentials of MMPI-2™ Assessment
by David S. Nichols

Essentials of NEPSY® Assessment
by Sally L. Kemp, Ursula Kirk, and Marit Korkman

Essentials of Individual Achievement Assessment
by Douglas K. Smith

Essentials of TAT and Other Storytelling Techniques Assessment
by Hedwig Teglasi

Essentials of WJ III™ Tests of Achievement Assessment
by Nancy Mather, Barbara J. Wendling, and Richard W. Woodcock

Essentials of WJ III™ Cognitive Abilities Assessment
by Fredrick A. Schrank, Dawn P. Flanagan, Richard W. Woodcock, and Jennifer T. Mascolo

Essentials of WMS®-III Assessment
by Elizabeth O. Lichtenberger, Alan S. Kaufman, and Zona C. Lai

Essentials of MMPI-A™ Assessment
by Robert P. Archer and Radhika Krishnamurthy

Essentials of Neuropsychological Assessment
by Nancy Hebben and William Milberg

Essentials

of Individual

Achievement

Assessment

Douglas K. Smith

John Wiley & Sons, Inc.
NEW YORK · CHICHESTER · WEINHEIM · BRISBANE · SINGAPORE · TORONTO

Library of Congress Cataloging-in-Publication Data:
Smith, Douglas K.
        Essentials of individual achievement assessment / Douglas K. Smith.
            p. cm. — (Essentials of psychological assessment series)
        Includes bibliographical references and index.
        ISBN 0-471-32432-9 (paper : alk. paper)
            1. Achievement tests—United States   2. Achievement tests—United States—Evaluation.
I. Title.   II. Series

LB3060.3 .S62 2001
371.26′2′0973—dc21

                                                                                    2001026074

Printed in the United States of America

10   9   8   7   6   5   4   3   2   1

To my parents, Beth and Claude Smith,
for their unconditional love, unfailing support,
and continual encouragement

DOUGLAS K. SMITH
1947–2001

CONTENTS

SERIES PREFACE

I n the *Essentials of Psychological Assessment* series, our goal is to provide the reader with books that will deliver key practical information in the most efficient and accessible style. The series features instruments in a variety of domains, such as cognition, personality, education, and neuropsychology. For the experienced clinician, books in the series offer a concise yet thorough way to master utilization of the continuously evolving supply of new and revised instruments, as well as a convenient method for keeping up to date on the tried-and-true measures. The novice will find here a prioritized assembly of all the information and techniques that must be at one's fingertips to begin the complicated process of individual psychological diagnosis.

Wherever feasible, visual shortcuts to highlight key points are utilized alongside systematic, step-by-step guidelines. Chapters are focused and succinct. Topics are targeted for an easy understanding of the essentials of administration, scoring, interpretation, and clinical application. Theory and research are continually woven into the fabric of each book, but always to enhance clinical inference, never to sidetrack or overwhelm. We have long been advocates of "intelligent" testing—the notion that a profile of test scores is meaningless unless it is brought to life by the clinical observations and astute detective work of knowledgeable examiners. Test profiles must be used to make a difference in the child's or adult's life, or why bother to test? We want this series to help our readers become the best intelligent testers they can be.

In *Essentials of Individual Achievement Assessment,* Dr. Doug Smith examines five popular tests of achievement that are used in both school and clinical settings. Based on Dr. Smith's thirty years of experience as a practitioner, university trainer, and workshop presenter, he offers readers practical tips on the selection and evaluation of achievement tests as well as the administration, scoring, and interpretation of each test. Whenever possible, pertinent research and practice issues are assimilated. A unique feature of this book is the chapter on developing appropriate testing accommodations for students with disabilities.

Alan S. Kaufman, PhD, and Nadeen L. Kaufman, EdD, Series Editors
Yale University School of Medicine

One

The academic assessment of individuals from preschool to post-high school has increased greatly over the past few years. In the area of individually administered achievement tests, we have seen both the development of new tests and the revision of older instruments. Psychometric properties of the tests have increased on the whole and standardization samples have become more representative of the population. In addition, the purposes of these tests have changed from being primarily norm-based comparisons with peers, now including the analysis of deficit academic skills and of ability-achievement discrepancies through conorming or linking samples with individual tests of ability.

The academic areas of assessment have also expanded beyond reading decoding, spelling, and arithmetic to encompass reading comprehension, arithmetic reasoning, arithmetic computation, listening comprehension, oral expression, and written expression. These changes make it difficult for practitioners to remain current on the instruments available, as well as on how to administer, score, and interpret them.

Essentials of Individual Achievement Assessment is designed to simplify the process of remaining up to date in this area, with a chapter devoted to each of the most frequently used achievement tests. The structure of each chapter is similar, with a test overview and sections describing administration, scoring, interpretation, and application of the test in clinical and educational settings. Chapters are supplemented with case reports and *Test Yourself* questions. The case reports are based on real cases, but the names and identifying information have been changed to protect the confidentiality of the students.

A unique feature of this book is a chapter on testing accommodations for students with disabilities; in this chapter the need for accommodations is reviewed and a process for developing appropriate accommodations is described. Finally, each test we have covered is analyzed and recommendations are made for appropriate testing accommodations and disability populations for which the test is suitable.

CRITERIA FOR INCLUSION OF TESTS IN THIS VOLUME

There are dozens of achievement tests designed for use with the preschool through adult population. To provide in-depth coverage of each instrument is, therefore, impossible. Consequently, the most frequently used measures of achievement have been selected for coverage.

In order to determine the tests to be included in this book, a review of recent studies of test usage was conducted. Numerous studies were located that were national in scope (e.g., Archer & Newsom, 1999; Archer, Maruish, Imfhof, & Piotrowski, 1991; Hammill, Fowler, Bryant, & Dunn, 1992; Hutton, Dubes, & Muir, 1992; Laurent & Swerdlik, 1992; Stinnett, Havey, & Oehler-Stinnett, 1994; Watkins, Campbell, Nieberding, & Hallmark, 1996; Wilson & Reschly, 1996); international in scope (e.g., Chan & Lee, 1995; Oakland & Hu, 1992); and regional in scope (e.g., Zaske, Hegstrom, & Smith, 1999). Based on these studies and on feedback from practitioners, a list of the most frequently used achievement tests was developed. The following achievement tests were selected for inclusion: Kaufman Test of Educational Achievement/Normative Update (K-TEA/NU; Kaufman & Kaufman, 1997); Peabody Individual Achievement Test–Revised/Normative Update (PIAT-R/NU; Markwardt, 1997); Wechsler Individual Achievement Test (WIAT; The Psychological Corporation, 1992); and the Wide Range Achievement Test 3 (WRAT3; Wilkinson, 1993). The Woodcock-Johnson III Tests of Achievement were not included as they are the subjects of another volume in this series.

SELECTING AN ACHIEVEMENT TEST

Selecting the appropriate achievement test to use in a specific situation depends on a number of factors. The test should be reliable, valid, and used only for the purposes for which it was developed. The *Code of Fair Testing Practices in Education* (1988) outlines the responsibilities of both test developers and test users. You are encouraged to refer to the *Code* (see Appendix) and become familiar with its content.

First, we should consider the purpose of the testing. At this point we can discern whether a comprehensive measure (covering the areas of achievement specified in the Individuals with Disabilities Education Act Amendments of 1997) is needed or whether a less specific screening measure is appropriate. Another issue is whether we need to examine an ability-achievement discrepancy. If so, the achievement test should be conormed or linked with an ability test. If we are seeking diagnostic information and level of skill development in academic areas then we should consider a test with skills analysis procedures.

Second, the test should be designed to answer the specific questions that are being asked in the referral. The specificity of those referral questions will guide our decisions.

Third, we need to be thoroughly familiar with the test and need to have used it before. Familiarity with the test includes not only administration but also scoring and interpretation.

Fourth, we should consider the appropriateness of the test's standardization. How recent are the norms? Is the standardization sample appropriate? Were students with disabilities included in the standardization sample? (This is of utmost importance if we are assessing a student suspected of having a disability.) Were the appropriate stratification variables used in the standardization process?

Fifth, we should examine the psychometric properties of the test. Common problem areas for students at the extremes of the test's age and ability ranges are inadequate floors and ceilings. Are there enough easy items for younger students with below average ability? Are there enough difficult items for older students with above average ability? Is the standard score range appropriate at the age level of the student?

Finally, we should closely examine the reliability and validity data for the test. Important considerations are internal consistency, usually determined by split-half reliability or coefficient alpha; test-retest reliability; correlations with other achievement tests; and the match between the skills measured by the test and the student's current curriculum. The latter characteristic is usually addressed by test authors by basing item selection on suggestions from curriculum experts or by aligning the test with representative textbooks or curriculum guides in the specific subject area.

The chapters on each test are designed to provide you with this information. The many "Rapid Reference," "Caution," and "Don't Forget" boxes summarize this information so that it is easily accessible. Table 1.1 summarizes key

Table 1.1   Key Points in Test Selection

1. Indicate the purpose(s) of the assessment.
   a. Comprehensive assessment   _____
   b. Screening assessment   _____
   c. Ability-achievement discrepancy analysis   _____
   d. Skills analysis   _____

2. Indicate the test you have selected based on your answers to question 1, and the specific referral information.

---

3. Indicate your experience with the following aspects of the selected test.

	None	*Some*	*Extensive*
Administration	_____	_____	_____
Scoring	_____	_____	_____
Interpretation	_____	_____	_____

4. Assess the adequacy of the test's standardization.

Are the norms recent?	Yes _____	No _____
Was the standardization sample appropriate?	Yes _____	No _____
Were students with disabilities included?	Yes _____	No _____

   Indicate the stratification variables:
   Age _____   Gender _____   Geographic region _____   Ethnicity _____
   Socioeconomic status (parent educational level) _____

5. Is the floor of the test adequate?[a]   Yes _____   No _____

6. Is the ceiling of the test adequate?[a]   Yes _____   No _____

7. Is the standard score range appropriate?[a]   Yes _____   No _____

8. Is the evidence of reliability appropriate?

Internal consistency (split-half reliability)	Yes _____	No _____
Internal consistency (coefficient alpha)	Yes _____	No _____
Test-retest reliability	Yes _____	No _____

9. Is the evidence of validity appropriate?

Correlations with other achievement tests	Yes _____	No _____
Match between skills measured and curriculum	Yes _____	No _____

10. Additional comments:

---

[a]Will vary by age and ability of the particular student.

points in test selection and provides a checklist to use when selecting an appropriate instrument.

EVALUATING AN ACHIEVEMENT TEST

As tests are continually revised and updated and new instruments developed, it is important that we evaluate them critically. The dimensions for evaluation, of course, vary from individual to individual. Published reviews of tests are a good source for suggested criteria. In addition to reviews that appear in the professional journals, other sources include the *Mental Measurements Yearbook of the Buros Institute* and such major assessment textbooks as those by Salvia and Ysseldyke (2001).

Table 1.2 presents a form outlining the dimensions of various achievement

Table 1.2 Dimensions for Evaluating an Achievement Test

Test:_____

Author:_____

Publisher:_____

Date of Publication:_____

Purpose:_____

_____

_____

Administration Time:_____

Age Range:_____

Format:_____

_____

_____

Scores:_____

_____

Norms:_____

_____

Reliability:_____

_____

_____

Validity:_____

_____

_____

Reviews:_____

_____

_____

≡Rapid Reference 1.1

Dimensions for Evaluating an Achievement Test: WIAT

Test: Wechsler Individual Achievement Test (WIAT)

Author: The Psychological Corporation

Publisher: The Psychological Corporation

Date of Publication: 1992

Purpose: The WIAT is a comprehensive, individually administered achievement battery. The complete battery assesses skills in oral expression, listening comprehension, written expression, reading decoding, reading comprehension, spelling, mathematics reasoning, and mathematics computation.

Administration Time: 30 to 50 minutes

Age Range: 5 years 0 months through 19 years 11 months

Format: The WIAT consists of two stimulus books utilizing an easel format for the presentation of subtest items. Record forms consist of the Comprehensive Battery Record Form and the Screener Record Form. A separate response booklet is provided for the Numerical Operations and Written Expression subtests. Starting points are based on grade, and discontinue rules vary across subtests. Reverse rules are used if a student scores 0 on initial items that are administered.

Scores: Responses are dichotomously scored, excepting those for Written Expression. Raw scores are converted to a variety of derived scores, including standard scores (mean of 100, standard deviation of 15, and range of 40 to 160), percentile ranks (age and grade), age and grade equivalent scores, normal curve equivalents, and stanines.

Norms: The standardization sample consisted of 4,252 students (2,160 females, 2,092 males) in 13 age groups designed to match 1988 census data. A stratified random-sampling plan was used for the following variables: age, grade, gender, race/ethnicity, geographic region, and parent education. Students with disabilities who were mainstreamed into regular classes were included in the sample (7.4%), as were gifted and talented students (4.3%). A linking sample of 1,284 students was administered the Wechsler Intelligence Scale for Children–Third Edition (WISC-III; 1,118), the Wechsler Adult Intelligence Scale–Revised (WAIS-R; 82), or the Wechsler Preschool and Primary Scale of Intelligence–Revised (WPPSI-R; 84). For the WISC-III sample, "a small adjustment to the distribution of WISC-III Full Scale IQ (FSIQ) scores was made by employing case weighting of a small percentage of the sample. The weighting procedures resulted in a mean FSIQ score near 100.0 for the linking sample, which matched the mean FSIQ score of the WISC-III normative sample" (The Psychological Corporation, 1992, p. 130 of WIAT manual).

Reliability: Split-half reliability estimates corrected by the Spearman-Brown formula range from .69 to .95 for subtests, and from .83 to .97 for composites. Mean reliability estimates range from .81 (Written Expression) to .92 (Basic Reading) for the subtests and from .90 (Language and Writing) to .97 (Total) for composites. Average test-retest reliabilities for 367 students across five grade levels range from .68 (Oral Expression) to .94 (Basic Reading and Spelling) for subtests and from .78 (Language) to .96 (Total) for composites. The interval between testings ranged from 12 to 52 days, with a median retest interval of 17 days. Interscorer reliability for the Oral Expression and Written Expression subtests ranged from .79 to .93.

Validity: Evidence for content validity and construct validity of the WIAT is discussed in the manual for the WIAT. Criterion-related validity was examined by administering the WIAT and other achievement tests, including the K-TEA, Wide Range Achievement Test–Revised (WRAT-R), Woodcock-Johnson Psycho-Educational Battery–Revised (WJ-R), Differential Ability Scales (DAS), and Peabody Picture Vocabulary Test–Revised (PPVT-R). Significant correlations among the scores on reading, mathematics, and spelling subtests were reported.

tests. This form can assist in evaluating an instrument for a particular assessment. Rapid Reference 1.1 is an example of the completed form.

ADMINISTERING ACHIEVEMENT TESTS

All of the tests discussed in this book require graduate-level training in psychoeducational assessment to insure appropriate interpretation of test results. It is essential that test administration follow standardized procedures. Although the tests are easy to administer, it is imperative that you become very familiar with the test directions and practice administration of the test before it is used "for real." Examiners should be familiar with the testing procedures in general and have experience working with students of similar age to those being evaluated. Each test presents specific test administration procedures as well as discussions of such issues as establishing and maintaining rapport, observing student behaviors, and the importance of following standardized testing procedures.

In general, achievement testing should take place in a quiet room that is free of distractions. It should be furnished with a table and chairs of appropriate size for the student and the examiner. The seating arrangement should enable the examiner to see the student's side of the test easel (for those tests using an easel format). I prefer to sit at a right angle to the student with the student on my left and my test materials on a chair or small table to my right. With this arrangement I can use the test easel to shield the record form from the student's view. For those tests without test easels I usually use a clipboard for the record form and in that way keep it from the student's view. An alternative arrangement is for the examiner to sit across from the student. The arrangement you select should be the one with which you are most comfortable.

Two

KAUFMAN TEST OF EDUCATIONAL ACHIEVEMENT/NORMATIVE UPDATE

OVERVIEW

The Kaufman Test of Educational Achievement/Normative Update (K-TEA/NU; Kaufman & Kaufman, 1997) is a restandardization of the original K-TEA, which was first published in 1985. While the individual subtest items remained the same, the standardization sample was designed to match U.S. Bureau of the Census estimates of the population in 1994. As with the original test, two forms, the Comprehensive Form and the Brief Form, were retained. The main focus of this chapter is the Comprehensive Form of the test. The Brief Form of the test, an abbreviated three-subtest version, is used primarily for academic screening and is addressed at the end of this chapter.

The K-TEA and K-TEA/NU are used frequently in both clinical and educational settings, as shown by numerous studies of test usage (e.g., Archer et al., 1991; Hammill et al., 1992; Hutton et al., 1992; Laurent & Swerdlik, 1992; Stinnett et al., 1994; Wilson & Reschly, 1996). In addition, they are frequently used in research studies. A recent literature search, for example, produced more than 75 publications on the K-TEA over the last 10 years. Clinical use of the K-TEA/NU is discussed later in this chapter.

Description of the K-TEA

The K-TEA and K-TEA/NU are individually administered, normative tests of school achievement in children and adolescents, and encompass the age range of 6 years 0 months to 22 years 11 months. Both age-based norms and grade-based norms are provided. The Brief Form of the test consists of three subtests and provides global scores in Reading, Spelling, and Mathematics, as well as a battery composite. There is no overlap in items between the two forms of the test. The Comprehensive Form consists of five subtests providing more specific scores in Reading Decoding, Reading Comprehension, Spelling, Mathematics Applications, and Mathematics Computation. In addition, Reading composite, Mathematics composite, and battery composite scores are available. Both forms of the K-TEA and K-TEA/NU utilize standard scores with a mean of 100 and standard deviation (SD) of 15. An analysis of student errors is provided only in the Comprehensive Form.

The Reading composite score is based on the scores on Reading Decoding and Reading Comprehension, whereas the Mathematics composite score is based on the scores on Mathematics Applications and Mathematics Computation. The battery composite score is based on all five subtests; Rapid Reference 2.1 describes each of the subtests.

≋Rapid Reference 2.1

Description of the K-TEA/NU Subtests

Reading Decoding
Measures the ability to identify letters and pronounce words (both phonetic and nonphonetic).

Reading Comprehension
Measures literal and inferential comprehension, with students reading passages along with one or two questions about the passage and responding orally to them. Items 1–8 require the student to respond gesturally and items 46–50 require the student to do what the sentence says.

Spelling
Measures spelling ability using words read aloud by the examiner and used in sentences and requiring the student to write the word. Students who cannot write adequately are permitted to spell the word orally.

Mathematics Applications
Measures a wide variety of arithmetic concepts and extensive applications of mathematical principles and reasoning skills to real-life situations using items presented orally by the examiner along with visual stimuli (pictures, graphs, and the words spoken by the examiner).

Mathematics Computation
Measures the student's skills in solving written computational problems using paper and pencil.

Note. Adapted from Kaufman & Kaufman (1985, 1997).

Standardization of the K-TEA and K-TEA/NU

Standardization of the K-TEA/NU took place in two distinct phases. The initial phase was in 1983 and 1984. The second phase took place in 1997 and was part of a renorming project involving four achievement batteries.

The Original Standardization

The K-TEA was standardized on 2,476 students ranging in age from 6 years through 18 years. The sample was chosen to match U.S. Bureau of the Census population estimates for 1983 and 1984. Within each grade level, the sample was stratified on the basis of gender, geographic region, socioeconomic status (as measured by the highest educational level of the parents or caregivers), and race or ethnic group. The match between the sample and census data is generally within 2 to 3 percentage points. The greatest discrepancy is with parent educational level, with the divergence ranging up to 5 percentage points at both the lowest and highest educational levels. Students with disabilities were included in the standardization sample. Kamphaus, Slotkin, and DeVincentis (1990) note that the inclusion of such students, "a procedure not commonly used, gives additional strength to the representativeness of the standardization sample" (p. 560). Standardization took place in the spring of 1983 (for spring norms) and fall of 1983 (for fall norms). As Witt, Elliott, Kramer, and Gresham (1994) state, "The standardization process is exemplary in its attention to detail" (p. 169).

The Renorming Project

Renorming for the 1997 edition of the K-TEA/NU took place during 1995 and 1996, and was part of a coordinated norming program that included the K-TEA (Brief and Comprehensive Forms), the Peabody Individual Achievement Test–Revised (PIAT-R), KeyMath–Revised (KeyMath-R), and the Woodcock Reading Mastery Tests–Revised (WRMT-R). The five instruments were linked by their common measurement for five achievement domains: word reading, reading comprehension, spelling, mathematics applications, and mathematics computation. Each student was administered one of the primary batteries (K-TEA Brief, K-TEA Comprehensive, PIAT-R, KeyMath-R, or WRMT-R) along with subtests from the other instruments. Thus, each of the primary batteries was administered to approximately one-fifth of the standardization sample.

The sample was stratified within age and grade level by gender, geographic region, parent educational level, educational placement (special education, non-special education, or gifted/talented), and race or ethnicity group based on 1994 census estimates of the population. The overall match between the sample and the population estimates was very good with overall differences generally less than 3%. The greatest disparity was with geographic region, with the northeastern and western United States somewhat underrepresented and the north-central and southern regions somewhat overrepresented. Grade norms were based on 3,184 students; age norms, including the 18–22-year-old group, were based on 3,429 individuals. On average, there were 245 students per grade level. The 18–22-year-old group consisted of students (from high school, 2-year colleges, and 4-year colleges) and nonstudents.

A comparison of the updated norms with the original norms documents that there was little change in average scores. Scores at the 50th percentile (grade-level or age-level norms) are slightly higher for first graders and slightly lower for high school students at the upper grade levels. A greater range of scores (from high to low) is present at most levels.

Psychometric Characteristics of the K-TEA /NU

Detailed reliability and validity data are presented in the K-TEA/NU Comprehensive Form *Manual* (Kaufman & Kaufman, 1997) and are based on original K-TEA norms. The reader is encouraged to study these data before using the test. In the meantime, I have attempted to summarize some of the more important features of those data.

Reliability

The average internal consistency coefficients, for the age and grade samples, respectively, are .97 and .96 for the Reading composite, .95 and .94 for the Mathematics composite, and .98 and .98 for the battery composite. Internal consistency coefficients for the subtests range from .83 to .97 for the age norms and from .87 to .96 for the grade norms. As Doll (1989) writes, in a review of the K-TEA, the subtest and composite reliabilities "can be reported with confidence and are well suited for diagnosing strengths or deficits between individual subtests" (p. 411). Test-retest correlations for the composites range from .93 to .97 for a sample of students in grades 1 to 6 and from .94 to

≡Rapid Reference 2.2

Average K-TEA/NU Reliability

Composites and Subtests	Split-Half Reliability Grades 1–12	Test-Retest Reliability Grades 1–6	Grades 7–12
Reading Composite	.96	.96	.94
Mathematics Composite	.94	.93	.96
Battery Composite	.98	.97	.97
Reading Decoding	.95	.95	.91
Reading Comprehension	.92	.92	.90
Spelling	.93	.95	.96
Mathematics Applications	.91	.90	.94
Mathematics Computation	.90	.83	.92

.97 for a sample of students in grades 7 to 12, and thus demonstrate that the K-TEA/NU is a stable measure of achievement. See Rapid Reference 2.2 for specific test-retest reliabilities.

Validity

K-TEA validity is demonstrated through a multistage format beginning with item development, empirical analyses of tryout versions of the test leading to final item selection, and analyses of the relationships among items and test scores in the final version and validation studies with other measures of achievement. As Salvia and Ysseldyke (1998) note, the "content of subtests on the CF [Comprehensive Form] appears well selected" (p. 460). With the exception of Mathematics Computation for grade 3, all correlations between subtests and the battery composite were .70 or above at all grade levels. Validation studies also compared the K-TEA with the Wide Range Achievement Test (WRAT; Jastak & Jastak, 1978), Peabody Individual Achievement Test (PIAT; Dunn & Markwardt, 1970), Kaufman Assessment Battery for Children (K-ABC; Kaufman & Kaufman, 1983) and the Peabody Picture Vocabulary Test–Revised (PPVT-R; Dunn & Dunn, 1981). These data are reported in detail in the K-TEA Comprehensive Form *Manual* and support the validity of the

Rapid Reference 2.3

Kaufman Test of Educational Achievement/ Normative Update

Authors: Alan S. Kaufman and Nadeen L. Kaufman

Publication Dates: 1985 (K-TEA); 1997 (K-TEA/NU)

What the Test Measures: Reading decoding, reading comprehension, spelling, mathematics application and computational skills

Age Range: 6 years 0 months through 22 years 11 months

Administration Time: 25 to 65 minutes, depending on the age of the student

Qualification of Examiners: Training in educational or psychoeducational testing

Publisher: American Guidance Service
4201 Woodland Road
Circle Pines, MN 55014-1796
(800) 328-2560
www.agsnet.com

Prices: Complete test kit $211.95 (2001 catalog price); $296.95 for combination Comprehensive and Brief forms
Computer scoring program $199.95 (2001 catalog price)

instrument. Rapid Reference 2.3 provides basic information on the test and its publisher.

HOW TO ADMINISTER THE K-TEA/NU

As with any standardized test, the K-TEA/NU examiner should follow closely the test administration instructions contained in the test manual. General testing procedures are reviewed in chapter 2 of the test manual, and the examiner should study them in detail. These include establishing and maintaining rapport, following standardized procedures, making clinical observations of student behaviors, and providing feedback to students and parents.

The K-TEA/NU utilizes an easel format in which test items are presented on the student's side of the easel and the directions for administration and scoring guidelines are presented on the examiner's side. In addition to the test easel and record form, a pencil with an eraser and blank paper (for use during the math subtests) are needed. A separate booklet is provided for the Mathematics Computation and Spelling subtests. Subtests are administered in the order of their presentation on the easel and this order should be followed closely.

For each subtest, the first page of the easel outlines the general proce-

> **DON'T FORGET**
> ....
>
> ### Order of Subtest Administration
>
> 1. Mathematics Applications
> 2. Reading Decoding
> 3. Spelling
> 4. Reading Comprehension
> 5. Mathematics Computation

dure for administering the subtest and lists any additional materials that are needed. The second page is known as the Remember Page and lists reminders and pointers for administering the subtest, along with starting points for testing based on the student's grade level. The K-TEA/NU utilizes starting points and a discontinue rule to make test administration more efficient. Items are also grouped into item units. Rapid Reference 2.4 summarizes these features.

Before administering the K-TEA/NU you should address several details. First, complete the biographical information on the front page of the Individual Test Record. This includes the student's and parents' names, home address, telephone, grade, teacher, school, and your name as the examiner. Second, record the student's birth date and the test date in the next section. Calculate the chronological age, which you will need to determine the appropriate starting points. Always double-check your calculations, which are the most common source of error. When you have to borrow from the months column to the days column, always use 30 days. As a third check, I usually ask the student his or her age while we are establishing rapport. Sometimes discrepancies occur and school records can be incorrect. Rapid Reference 2.5 summarizes the steps in completing the inside of the Individual Test Record.

Subtest-by-Subtest Notes on Administration

Mathematics Applications

This subtest is relatively easy to administer. The student's side of the easel contains the visual stimulus; the examiner's side of the easel contains the question

≡ Rapid Reference 2.4

Item Units, Starting Points, and Discontinue Rule

Item Units   Groups of items identified by heavy horizontal lines on the Individual Test Record Form. Used to facilitate use of starting points and the discontinue rule.

Starting Points   Based on the grade level of the student (chronological age can be substituted if the student is in an ungraded setting) and marked with start arrows on the Individual Test Record Form. *If the student passes at least two items* in the first unit given, keep testing until the discontinue rule is met. *If the student passes one item* in the first unit, (1) continue testing until the discontinue rule is met if you began with item 1; (2) if you began with any other item, return to item 1 and keep testing until the discontinue rule is met. If the discontinue rule is not met when the original starting point is reached, keep testing until all items in a unit are failed. If the discontinue rule is met before you reach the original starting point, stop testing but give the student credit for the one correct item in the original starting-point unit. *If no items are passed* in the first unit given, (1) stop testing and go to the next subtest *if you began with item 1*; (2) *if you began with an item other than item 1*, return to item 1 and keep testing up to the original starting item (unless the discontinue rule is met first).

Discontinue Rule   *Stop testing if the student fails every item in one unit.* The only exception to this occurs if the starting point is beyond item 1. In this case, return to item 1. *Do not give credit for items the student might have passed after failing a complete unit*, except as noted under Starting Points (above).

Note. Adapted from Kaufman & Kaufman (1985, 1997).

the examiner will read. Blank paper and a pencil with an eraser should be available for the student to use. Item 32 requires the student to use the paper and pencil while items 17 and 32 prohibit their use. On the other items, use of the paper and pencil is optional depending on the student's preference. No other aids such as calculators are allowed. The student must respond orally to all questions. Most items have only one part; however, items 7 and 8 have two parts and item 11 has four parts. The student must respond correctly to each part to receive credit for the item.

≡Rapid Reference 2.5

Test Administration Pointers

1. Complete the biographical information on the front page of the Individual Test Record. **The student's age is particularly important** and should be verified when establishing rapport, because miscalculating age is the most common source of error.

2. **Write the student's response** in the response column of the Record Form for all subtests except Spelling (in which the student writes the response). I always write the student's response even if it is incorrect, so that I don't give nonverbal cues that a response is incorrect. This also allows me to recheck my initial scoring.

3. **Verbal probing of a response** usually is not needed. The only exceptions are for ambiguous responses (those you are unable to score without additional information) and incomplete responses. This is most likely to occur on the Reading Comprehension subtest. Neutral statements should be used to encourage the student to elaborate upon the response. I frequently use "I'm not sure that I understand what you said" or "Tell me more about that." Do not use leading questions. Often, students interpret verbal probes as an indication of an incorrect response. Therefore, I try to put the student at ease by placing the emphasis on *my* not understanding the response rather than on any shortcomings of the response.

4. **Verbal items can be repeated** if the student indicates the need for this either verbally or nonverbally.

5. Unlike many tests, **the K-TEA/NU allows the examiner to read-minister easy items** to students who answer a series of more difficult items. This should be used only when you suspect that the student's shyness, lack of motivation, initial uneasiness in the testing situation, or similar factor resulted in an incorrect response or, most likely, a failure to respond. This procedure should be used cautiously. When this procedure is used, the student receives credit for the correct responses to the items that were initially failed.

6. **If the student gives more than one response to a test item, you must determine which response is the one to score.** The K-TEA/NU assumes that the final response is the one to be scored. In the case of multiple responses you must determine which is the final response. In some cases you may need to ask the student which is the final response.

7. **Responses to items requiring a verbal response (except Reading Decoding) may be in English, sign language, or another language.** Of course, you must be able to understand the response in order

(continued)

to score it. Therefore, it is imperative that the examiner be familiar with the student's background (both cultural and linguistic) prior to testing.

8. **Sometimes items that should not have been given are administered.** Such items should be ignored in scoring. The only exception to this is outlined in Rapid Reference 2.4 in discussing the discontinue rule. When the student correctly answers all items in the unit corresponding to the grade-level starting point, all items below the starting-point item should be ignored. This is true even if you begin with item 1. Items administered beyond the discontinue point should also be ignored, with the exception noted above. In the unlikely event that a "double basal" occurs, with one unit of responses that are all correct prior to the unit containing the starting point, ignore the earlier basal. The student receives credit for passing all items below the basal containing the original starting point item. Likewise, if a "double ceiling" occurs, always use the lower ceiling and disregard the additional items because they should not have been administered anyway.

Note. Adapted from Kaufman & Kaufman (1985, 1997).

Reading Decoding

In this subtest the student is shown letters and words on the student side of the easel, and he or she must name the letter or pronounce the word. For items 1–5, the student must name the letter rather than give the sound it makes. For the remainder of the items the student must pronounce words that are shown. In order to utilize the error analysis system the examiner must record the student's incorrect responses. Students should be encouraged to respond to provide for a more accurate analysis of error patterns. A response of "I don't know" provides little information as to the exact skill deficits that may exist. The examiner may use verbal cue "What word is this?" as needed.

Spelling

For this subtest the examiner says a word, uses it in a sentence, and repeats the word. Be sure to pronounce the word clearly and correctly (a pronunciation guide is provided for the more difficult items). The word and sentence may be repeated at the student's request. Be sure to use the Spelling Sheet and provide the student a pencil with an eraser. Students who are unable to write may spell the words orally. In such cases, write "responded orally" at the top of the Spelling Sheet.

Reading Comprehension

The format of items 1–8 and 46–50 is somewhat different from that of traditional measures of reading comprehension. The student reads a sentence and does what it says, or reads a paragraph and responds orally to the item. Some students may need encouragement to complete items 1–8 and 46–50; consequently, you may need to convey to the student that play-acting is necessary for some items. The student may read the sentences and paragraphs silently or aloud. Be sure to remind the student to respond to all parts of each item.

Item 1 requires the student to stand. If this is not physically possible, do not administer the item, but score it correct if item 2, 3, or 4 is passed. For items 9–45 the student reads a paragraph and answers the question. *The examiner does not read the question aloud.*

Mathematics Computation

This subtest measures computational skills with printed problems on a worksheet. Be sure to fold the booklet to show only the page containing the appropriate starting items. Give the student a pencil with an eraser and indicate that

CAUTION

Common Errors in Administering the K-TEA/ NU

- Recording an incorrect birth date
- Calculating the chronological age incorrectly
- Not establishing a basal
- Not establishing a ceiling
- Failure to have the separate Spelling Sheet and Mathematics Computation Worksheet
- Not having paper and pencil with eraser available for Mathematics Applications
- Skipping test items—e.g., easel pages sticking together, turning two pages instead of one
- Inappropriate questioning of ambiguous responses; asking leading questions
- Failure to question ambiguous responses
- Not recording student responses for use in error analysis on Reading Decoding
- Mispronouncing difficult words in Spelling
- Not allowing students who are unable to write to respond orally to the Spelling and to note this on the Spelling Sheet
- Failure to ask about letter reversals on Spelling

it is acceptable to erase at any time. No other aids, such as calculators, are allowed, although counting with one's fingers is acceptable.

When the student completes the page, scan the page for errors to determine whether to continue testing forward, return to item 1, or discontinue. Then proceed with testing, giving the student the folded booklet so that only one page of problems is visible. Unless the student becomes frustrated or indicates that he or she cannot do the problems, continue testing until all items in a unit are missed. Score the items after testing has ended.

HOW TO SCORE THE INDIVIDUAL TEST RECORD FORM

The K-TEA yields two types of scores: raw scores and standard scores. Raw scores reflect the number of points earned by the student on each subtest. These scores, by themselves, are meaningless because they are not norm-based scores. They are converted to standard scores, which are norm-based and allow us to compare the student's performance with that of others. The K-TEA standard scores have a mean of 100 and SD of 15. The range of standard scores for the subtests and composites is 40 to 160. We assume that achievement-test performance is distributed on a normal curve, with the majority of students scoring within +/− 1 SD of the mean. Thus, about two-thirds (66%) of students score in the range of 85 to 115. Less than 3% of students score above 130 or below 70.

Step-by-Step Scoring of the K-TEA/NU

Scoring the K-TEA/NU test items is facilitated by the dichotomous nature of the items. Each item is either correct (scored as 1) or incorrect (scored as 0). The examiner should enter the correct score for each item in the score column of the test record form. If you score the items as you are testing, double-check the accuracy of each score prior to calculating the raw score. My preference is to record the student's response, tentatively score items as we approach the ceiling, and finalize my scoring after the test session.

Raw Scores

All subtest raw scores are computed in the same way. In the box at the end of the subtest, record the ceiling item (highest-numbered item administered), add the number of errors (responses scored 0), enter this number in the box, and subtract the errors from the ceiling item to obtain the raw score. This score reflects the number of items passed by the student and assumes that all items below the starting point are passed and that all items above the ceiling are failed.

Transfer the raw scores to their appropriate columns on the front page of the record form. Note that the raw scores for Mathematics Applications and Mathematics Computation are placed in two boxes—one under the heading "Mathematics Composite" and the other under "Battery Composite." Similarly, the raw scores for Reading Decoding and Reading Comprehension are recorded in the Reading Composite column and the Battery Composite column. The Spelling raw score is transferred to the Battery Composite column only.

The raw score totals for each column are obtained by adding the relevant scores. Enter these values in the semicircles under each column.

Standard Scores

The conversion of raw scores to standard scores involves two decisions: The first is whether to use age-based or grade-based norms. This decision depends on whether you want to compare the student's test performance with that of same-age peers or same-grade peers. In most cases the resulting standard scores will be similar. However, important differences can occur if the student has been retained or has received an accelerated grade placement, or if the stu-

DON'T FORGET

Subtests Making Up the K-TEA Composites

Reading Composite	Mathematics Composite	Battery Composite
	Mathematics Applications	Mathematics Applications
Reading Decoding		Reading Decoding
		Spelling
Reading Comprehension		Reading Comprehension
	Mathematics Computation	Mathematics Computation

dent began school earlier or later than is typical. In these cases, the age-based norms are probably more relevant. If you are comparing the student's performance on the K-TEA/NU with performance on an ability measure, *always* use age-based norms because they are the basis for standard scores on ability measures.

The second decision involves the use of fall and spring norms. With the NU the age-based norms are not subdivided by season. Thus, the choice of fall or spring norms occurs only with the use of grade-based norms. If testing took place any time during August through January, the fall norms are used; if testing took place during February through July, the spring norms are used. Indicate your decision(s) on the front page of the record form by circling "age" or "grade" and, for grade-based norms, "fall" or "spring." You should also indicate whether you are using the updated norms or the original ones. The best practice is to use the updated norms; Rapid Reference 2.6 depicts the type of norms produced by each table.

Standard scores are obtained by entering the appropriate table with the student's raw score and age/grade (depending on norm type). The procedure is the same for the subtests and composites, with the exception of using the respective sum of subtest raw scores for the composites.

Since all scores have error associated with them, it is standard practice to create bands of error or confidence intervals around individual scores. The K-TEA/NU allows you great flexibility in creating such bands. Tables 5 and 6 in the test manual present this information and allow you to choose from 68%, 85%, 90%, 95%, and 99% confidence levels. My recommendation is to use the 95% confidence level. To use these tables, enter the table with the student's

≡Rapid Reference 2.6

Types of Norms Available

	Type of Norm	
Date of Testing	**Age-Based**	**Grade-Based**
August–January (fall norms)	Table 1	Table 2
February–July (spring norms)	Table 3	Table 4

chronological age in years, select the confidence level, and read across the table for subtests and then on the right side of the double line for composites.

Percentiles, Normal Curve Equivalents, and Age / Grade Equivalents

Percentile rank equivalents are obtained from Table 7 in the test manual. Enter this table with the student's standard scores on the subtests and composites. Then read across the table for the percentile rank equivalent and the normal curve equivalent, if needed. Descriptive categories can also be indicated for the composite scores. Rapid Reference 2.7 presents the suggested categories.

The column labeled "Other Data" may be used to record other information. Examples are stanines, age equivalents, grade equivalents, descriptive categories for subtests, previous scores on the K-TEA, or local norms. Although age and grade equivalents are frequently used to explain test performance, they are also frequently misunderstood. They lack the precision of standard scores and percentiles and often suggest large differences in performance when, in fact, the differences are insignificant. For example, a raw score of 44 on Mathematics Applications yields an age equivalent score of 14 years 0 months, and a raw score of 48 on the same subtest yields an age equivalent score of 17 years 0 months. For a student aged 15 years 1 month, the respective standard scores are 98 and 104. Thus, age and grade equivalents should be used very cautiously.

≡Rapid Reference 2.7

Descriptive Categories for Standard Scores

Range of Standard Scores	Descriptive Category
130 and above	upper extreme
120–129	well above average
110–119	above average
90–109	average
80–89	below average
70–79	well below average
60 and lower	lower extreme

Global and Specific Skill Comparisons

The next step in scoring the test record is to compare the student's reading, spelling, and mathematics performances to one another to determine any relative strengths or weaknesses. Therefore, you need to complete the lower portion of the front page of the record form. In the appropriate ovals record the composite standard scores and the subtest standard scores. The table is designed to facilitate comparisons among global skills and specific skills within the reading and mathematics areas.

For each comparison, subtract the lower standard score from the higher standard score and record the result in the standard-score difference column. Enter Table 10 (age norms) and Table 11 (grade norms) in the test manual by the student's age or grade to determine whether the difference in scores is statistically significant at the .05 or .01 level. If the standard score difference equals or exceeds the tabled value then the difference is statistically significant at either the .05 or .01 level. Circle the significance level. If it is not significant, circle "NS." Finally, go back to the column between the two sets of standard scores and enter the appropriate sign for greater than (>) or less than (<) if the difference is significant, and the appropriate sign for about equal (~) otherwise. The completed summary page of an Individual Test Record is shown in Figure 2.1.

Completing the Score Profile

The final step in scoring is to complete the score profile on the back page of the Test Record form. The profile presents the results graphically and is useful in explaining test results to teachers, parents, and students. The top of the graph depicts the standard score range (40–160); percentile ranks and standard deviations are shown on the bottom of the graph. To begin the process, transfer the standard scores and band of errors to the appropriate boxes. The test manual outlines one method of plotting the results, in which a bar graph to depict the test score is used in the upper or larger part of the graph; the band of error is depicted on the lower or smaller part of the graph, with the graph darkened between the lowest value in the range and the highest value in the range. This method is illustrated in Figure 2.2. An alternative method (and my preference) is to plot the range of scores in the confidence interval and to mark the obtained score with a large X. A computer scoring program that converts raw scores to standard scores is also available from the test publisher.

Comprehensive Form

K·TEA NU

KAUFMAN TEST of EDUCATIONAL ACHIEVEMENT
by Alan S. Kaufman &
Nadeen L. Kaufman

INDIVIDUAL TEST RECORD

Student's Name: TED Sex: M
Parent's Name:
Home Address: Home Phone:
Grade: 5
Teacher: DOUGLAS K. SMITH
School: Examiner:

	Year	Month	Day
Test Date	99	11	12
Birth Date	88	12	16
Chronological Age	10	10	26

COMPREHENSIVE FORM SUBTESTS Mean=100; SD=15	Reading Composite	Mathematics Composite	Battery Composite	Standard Score Table 1	Band of Error 95% Confidence Table 5 or 6	%ile Rank Table 7	Other Data GRADE EQUIV.
Mathematics Applications		26	26	88	±8	21	3.8
Reading Decoding	32		32	90	±7	25	3.8
Spelling			7	71	±6	3	1.8
Reading Comprehension	12		12	78	±8	7	2.3
Mathematics Computation		13	13	68	±9	2	2.1
Sum of Subtest Raw Scores	44	39	90				

Transfer sums to Composite Scales, Sum of Subtest Raw Scores column.

*Standard Scores Derived from (Circle the table used): AGE Table 1 / GRADE Table 2
Fall Norms (August–January) Table 1 / Table 2
Spring Norms (February–July) Table 3 / Table 4
Norms used: ☒ Updated ☐ Original

COMPREHENSIVE FORM COMPOSITE SCALES Mean=100; SD=15	Sum of Subtest Raw Scores	Standard Score* Table 1	Band of Error 95% Confidence Table 5 or 6	%ile Rank Table 7	Descriptive Category	Other Data GRADE EQUIV.
Reading Composite	44	84	±6	14	BELOW AVERAGE	3.1
Mathematics Composite	39	76	±6	5	WELL BELOW AVERAGE	2.7
Battery Composite	90	75	±4	5	WELL BELOW AVERAGE	2.7

Indicate >, <, or ≈   Standard Score Difference   Circle the Significance Level

GLOBAL SKILL COMPARISONS
84 Reading Composite > 76 Mathematics Composite | 8 | NS .05 .01
84 Reading Composite > 71 Spelling Subtest | 13 | NS .05 .01
76 Mathematics Composite > 71 Spelling Subtest | 5 | NS .05 .01

SPECIFIC SKILL COMPARISONS
90 Reading Decoding > 78 Reading Comprehension | 12 | NS .05 .01
88 Mathematics Applications > 68 Mathematics Computation | 20 | NS .05 .01

AGS®

Figure 2.1 Completed Summary Page of a K-TEA/NU Individual Test Record

Note: Kaufman Test of Educational Achievement/Normative Update (K-TEA/NU): Comprehensive Individual Test Record © 1985 AGS

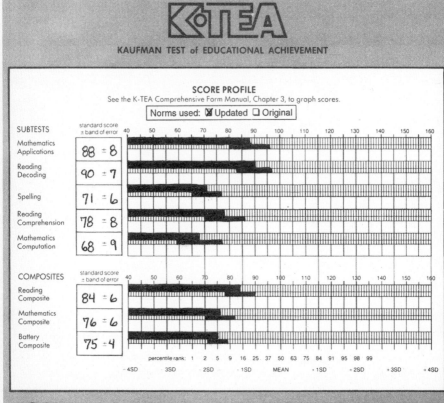

Figure 2.2 Completed Score Profile of a K-TEA/NU Record Form

Note: Kaufman Test of Educational Achievement/Normative Update (K-TEA/NU): Comprehensive Individual Test Record © 1985 AGS

HOW TO INTERPRET THE K-TEA/NU

Interpretation of the K-TEA/NU test results is a multilevel process. Initially, the examiner focuses on global scale comparisons and comparisons with peers. Then, since the purpose of many academic assessments is to compare achievement level with cognitive level, the examiner briefly focuses on such

CAUTION

Common Errors in Scoring

- Calculating the raw score incorrectly
- Transferring the raw score to the front page of the record form incorrectly
- Adding raw scores incorrectly for the sum of subtest raw scores
- Using the wrong tables for standard score conversions and bands of error
- Misreading the norms tables—e.g., using the wrong line or wrong column
- Errors in transferring scores from the upper portion to the lower portion of the score summary
- Subtraction errors in comparing composites and subtest scores
- Errors in transferring scores from the score summary (front page of record form) to the score profile (back page of the record form)

comparisons. The final level of interpretation is to examine the student's relative strengths and weaknesses through subtest comparisons and an error analysis system unique to the K-TEA/NU.

The goal of interpretation is twofold: first, to provide a comparison with the performance of peers, and second, to provide information on the individual student's academic strengths and weaknesses. In the latter process emphasis is placed on examining the skills measured by the individual subtests and generating hypotheses to explain the student's pattern of scores. These hypotheses can then be explored further through other test data, classroom products, teacher observations, and classroom observations.

Global Skill Comparisons

We begin the interpretive process with the battery composite. This score is the most reliable and valid measure of the student's overall achievement level in reading, spelling, and mathematics since it is composed of all five subtests. It provides information on how the student compares to peers. Is the student functioning at an average level? above average level? below average level?

Often comparisons are made with the student's level of intellectual functioning as measured by an individual IQ test. While the K-TEA/NU was not conormed with an ability test, the correlation of the K-TEA/NU has been explored with many popular ability tests. Such information is needed to determine if differences in scores are statistically significant. Many states use a regression formula to make such comparisons in determining eligibility for programs for students with learning disabilities. A table of correlations between the K-TEA/NU and selected intelligence tests is presented in Rapid Reference 2.8.

≡Rapid Reference 2.8

Correlations between the K-TEA/ NU and Selected Intelligence Tests

Intelligence Test	K-TEA/NU Ages 6/0 through 7/11	K-TEA/NU Ages 8/0 through 22/11
K-ABC Mental Processing Composite	.63	.73
K-ABC Nonverbal Scale	.29	.68
KAIT Fluid Scale	—	.63
KAIT Composite	—	.73
DAS General Conceptual Ability	.68	.73
DAS Special Nonverbal Composite	.58	.63
Stanford-Binet Intelligence Test: Fourth Edition Composite	.68	.73
WJ-R Broad Cognitive Ability Composite	.68	.73
WISC III Verbal Scale IQ	.68	.73
WISC III Performance Scale IQ	.58	.63
WISC III Full Scale IQ	.68	.73
WAIS-III Verbal Scale IQ	—	.73
WAIS-III Performance Scale IQ	—	.63
WAIS-III Full Scale IQ	—	.73

Note. K-ABC = Kaufman Assessment Battery for Children; KAIT = Kaufman Adolescent and Adult Intelligence Test; DAS = Differential Ability Scales; WJ-R = Woodcock-Johnson Psychoeducational Battery–Revised; WISC III = Wechsler Intelligence Scale for Children–Third Edition; WAIS-III = Wechsler Adult Intelligence Scale–Third Edition. Long dash indicates that tests are not available for this age range.

Source. AGS.

These data are incorporated into the computer scoring program and were made available by the test publisher.

Next, we compare the Reading composite score with both the Mathematics composite score and the Spelling subtest score, and the Mathematics composite score with the Spelling subtest score. By making these comparisons we can determine whether the student's academic skills in these three major areas are evenly developed. We are interested only in statistically significant differences—those large enough that they are unlikely to have occurred by chance. This is the reason we establish confidence levels at either the .05 or .01 level; if a statistically significant difference occurs, we can say with 95% or 99% confidence, respectively, that the scores represent true differences in levels of skill development. Rapid Reference 2.9 presents the range of difference scores that are significant at the .05 and .01 levels for the possible comparisons of the Reading composite, Mathematics composite, and Spelling subtest. If a difference score falls in the ranges indicated, then Table 10 of the test manual should be consulted for the exact value. The values vary by age and grade of student for the age-level norms and grade-level norms, respectively.

≡ Rapid Reference 2.9

Range of Differences Required for Making Global Comparisons

Range of Standard Score Differences Required for Significance

	Age-Level Norms		Grade-Level Norms	
	.05	.01	.05	.01
Reading composite vs. Mathematics composite	8–12	11–15	11–12	13–15
Reading composite vs. Spelling	9–14	11–17	10–13	12–16
Mathematics composite vs. Spelling	10–16	13–19	12–15	14–18

Note. Actual standard score difference required for significance varies by age, and Table 10 in the test manual should be consulted for the exact value.

Comprehensive Form

K·TEA NU

KAUFMAN TEST of EDUCATIONAL ACHIEVEMENT
by Alan S. Kaufman &
Nadeen L. Kaufman

Student's Name: MICHAEL   Sex: M

Parent's Name:

Home Address:

Grade: 3

School: Teacher/Examiner: DOUGLAS K. SMITH

INDIVIDUAL TEST RECORD

	Year	Month	Day
Test Date	2000	02	17
Birth Date	1990	10	15
Chronological Age	9	4	2

COMPREHENSIVE FORM SUBTESTS Mean = 100; SD = 15	RAW SCORES Reading Composite	RAW SCORES Mathematics Composite	RAW SCORES Battery Composite	Standard Score* Table 1	Band of Error 95% Confidence Table 5 or 6	%ile Rank Table 7	Other Data GRADE EQUIV.	
Mathematics Applications		27	27	101	± 8	53	4.0	
Reading Decoding	19		19	82	± 5	12	2.2	
Spelling			16	92	± 6	30	3.2	
Reading Comprehension	12		12	85	± 7	16	2.3	
Mathematics Computation		27	27	105	± 7	63	4.2	
Sum of Subtest Raw Scores	31	54	101					

Transfer sums to Composite Scales, Sum of Subtest Raw Scores column.

*Standard Scores Derived from (Circle the table used):
- Fall Norms (August–January): (AGE) Table 1 / GRADE Table 2
- Spring Norms (February–July): Table 3 / Table 4

Norms used: ☒ Updated ☐ Original

COMPREHENSIVE FORM COMPOSITE SCALES Mean = 100; SD = 15	Sum of Subtest Raw Scores	Standard Score* Table 1	Band of Error 95% Confidence Table 5 or 6	%ile Rank Table 7	Descriptive Category	Other Data GRADE EQUIV.
Reading Composite	31	84	± 5	14	BELOW AVERAGE	2.1
Mathematics Composite	54	103	± 6	58	AVERAGE	4.1
Battery Composite	101	89	± 3	23	BELOW AVERAGE	3.0

Indicate >, <, or =

					Standard Score Difference	Circle the Significance Level		
GLOBAL SKILL COMPARISONS	84 Reading Composite	<	103 Mathematics Composite		19	NS	.05	(.01)
	84 Reading Composite	<	92 Spelling Subtest		8	(NS)	.05	.01
	103 Mathematics Composite	>	92 Spelling Subtest		11	NS	(.05)	.01
SPECIFIC SKILL COMPARISONS	82 Reading Decoding	<	85 Reading Comprehension		3	(NS)	.05	.01
	101 Mathematics Applications	<	105 Mathematics Computation		4	(NS)	.05	.01

AGS®

Figure 2.3 Michael's Score Summary

Note: Kaufman Test of Educational Achievement/Normative Update (K-TEA/NU): Comprehensive Individual Test Record © 1985 AGS

Let's consider an example. Michael was administered the K-TEA/NU on February 17, 2000, and his score summary is presented in Figure 2.3. His overall battery composite of 89 is at the upper end of the below average range, while his Reading composite score of 84 is significantly lower than his Mathematics composite score of 103. In this case, the battery composite masks the significant variability among the composite scores. Michael's overall reading skills are significantly lower than his mathematics skills and fall in the middle of the below average range. His mathematics skills indicate average development.

The finding of a significant discrepancy between composite scores, as Michael exhibits, provides useful but limited information. If we are considering a possible learning disability, this information helps pinpoint the general area of academic deficiency. This area can then be compared with overall ability to determine whether there is a significant difference between ability and academic achievement.

Michael was administered the Wechsler Intelligence Scale for Children–Third Edition (WISC-III) as part of the assessment process. He obtained a Verbal Scale IQ (VIQ) score of 108, a Performance Scale IQ (PIQ) score of 108, and a Full Scale IQ (FSIQ) score of 109. The difference between the FSIQ and the K-TEA/NU Battery Composite is 20 points, with differences of 25 points and 6 points in comparison with the Reading composite and Mathematics composite, respectively. Many states use regression tables to determine whether the difference between ability and achievement scores represents a severe discrepancy. In Minnesota, for example, Michael's discrepancy between the FSIQ and K-TEA/NU Reading composite represents a severe discrepancy based on the correlation of .73 between the two measures (Rapid Reference 2.8). Thus, he meets this particular criterion for learning disabilities eligibility. However, we need more specific information to pinpoint the deficit skills.

Specific Skills Comparisons

For this information we focus on the specific skills comparisons. This allows us to determine whether there are any significant differences in skill development within the word recognition and reading comprehension skills for reading; and between the understanding of mathematical concepts and the actual solution of a wide range of arithmetic problems. The latter activity resembles closely the classroom task of completing a page of arithmetic problems, and the former is similar to solving word problems.

In the reading area, we focus on comparing the standard scores on Reading Decoding and Reading Comprehension. While in mathematics we compare the standard scores on Mathematics Applications and Mathematics Computation. We are interested only in those comparisons that are statistically significant. The range of differences required for making these comparisons by age and grade is presented in Rapid Reference 2.10.

After completing this comparison we can make one of the following statements about the student's reading skills:

- The student's word recognition (reading decoding) skills are developed to the same degree as his or her ability to understand what is read.
- The student's word recognition (reading decoding) skills are better developed than his or her ability to understand what is read.
- The student's ability to understand what is read is better developed than his or her ability to recognize words (decode words).

In addition, we can discuss the level of development (average, above average, below average), compare it with that of peers, and provide examples of the skills.

Similarly, in the mathematics area, we compare the standard scores on Mathematics Applications and Mathematics Computation. Again, we are interested in only those comparisons that are statistically significant. After com-

≡Rapid Reference 2.10

Range of Differences Required for Making Specific Skills Comparisons

Range of Standard Score Differences Required for Significance

	Age-Level Norms		Grade-Level Norms	
	.05	.01	.05	.01
Reading Decoding vs. Reading Comprehension	9–15	11–19	11–15	14–18
Mathematics Applications vs. Mathematics Computation	10–18	13–22	14–16	17–20

Note. Actual standard score difference required for significance varies by age, and Table 12 in the test manual should be consulted for the exact value.

pleting this comparison we can make one of the following statements about the student's mathematics skills:

- The student's ability to solve word problems and reason through math problems is as well developed as his or her ability to solve a variety of math problems requiring calculation skills.
- The student's ability to solve word problems and reason through math problems is better developed than his or her ability to solve a variety of math problems requiring calculation skills.
- The student's ability to solve a variety of math problems requiring calculation skills is better developed than his or her ability to solve word problems and reason through math problems.

As with reading, we can discuss the level of development, compare it with that of peers, and give examples of the skills.

In Michael's case, his reading decoding skills and his reading comprehension skills show similar levels of development. In addition, his mathematics application skills and his mathematics computation skills show similar levels of development. Mathematics skills, in fact, demonstrate grade-level development, while both reading decoding and reading comprehension skills are less well developed and represent a relative weakness for him. Thus, intervention should focus on developing his reading skills (both decoding and comprehension). For more specific information we need to analyze Michael's specific errors on the K-TEA/NU.

In Sarah's case (Figure 2.4), the composite scores are quite consistent, ranging from 76 to 83, and indicate well-below average to below average performance. In comparison to her peers she is functioning at the lower 15% of students her age; it is unlikely that more than three or four other students in her classes are functioning as low as she is. In terms of grade equivalents, she is at the 5th- to 6th-grade level in spelling, reading, and arithmetic skills overall. However, the global skill and specific skill comparisons reveal a very uneven pattern of development. Reading decoding and spelling skills show strong development with scores of 124 and 117, respectively. This suggests an effective use of phonics skills to spell words and pronounce them correctly. The Reading Comprehension score of 67, however, reflects great difficulty in understanding the meaning of what is read. This indicates difficulties in understanding the meaning of words and perhaps in verbal reasoning skills as well. While Sarah may be able to recognize, pronounce, and use many words on an everyday basis, she is less skilled at knowing their meanings and the concepts

Comprehensive Form

K·TEA NU

KAUFMAN TEST of EDUCATIONAL ACHIEVEMENT
by Alan S. Kaufman &
Nadeen L. Kaufman

Student's Name: SARAH   Sex: F
Parent's Name:
Home Address:
Grade: 10   Home Phone:
School: Teacher/Examiner: DOUGLAS K. SMITH

INDIVIDUAL TEST RECORD

	Year	Month	Day
Test Date	1999	01	27
Birth Date	1981	11	17
Chronological Age	17	2	10

COMPREHENSIVE FORM SUBTESTS Mean = 100; SD = 15	Reading Composite	Mathematics Composite	Battery Composite	Standard Score* Table 1	Band of Error 95% Confidence Table 5 or 6	%ile Rank Table 7	Other Data GRADE EQUIV.
Mathematics Applications		31	31	75	± 10	5	4.8
Reading Decoding	59		54	124	± 9	84	>12.9
Spelling			46	117	± 9	87	>12.9
Reading Comprehension	14		14	67	± 10	1	2.5
Mathematics Computation		34	34	76	± 9	5	5.5
Sum of Subtest Raw Scores	73	65	184				

Transfer sums to Composite Scales, Sum of Subtest Raw Scores column.

*Standard Scores Derived from (Circle the table used):

	AGE	GRADE
Fall Norms (August-January)	Table 1	Table 2
Spring Norms (February-July)	Table 3	Table 4

Norms used:
☒ Updated
☐ Original

COMPREHENSIVE FORM COMPOSITE SCALES Mean = 100; SD = 15	Sum of Subtest Raw Scores	Standard Score* Table 1	Band of Error 95% Confidence Table 5 or 6	%ile Rank Table 7	Descriptive Category	Other Data GRADE EQUIV.
Reading Composite	73	83	± 7	13	BELOW AVERAGE	6.6
Mathematics Composite	65	76	± 7	5	WELL BELOW AVERAGE	5.3
Battery Composite	184	81	± 5	10	BELOW AVERAGE	6.3

Indicate >, <, or ≈

GLOBAL SKILL COMPARISONS			Standard Score Difference	Circle the Significance Level
83 Reading Composite	>	76 Mathematics Composite	7	(NS) .05 .01
83 Reading Composite	<	117 Spelling Subtest	34	NS .05 (.01)
76 Mathematics Composite	<	117 Spelling Subtest	41	NS .05 (.01)
SPECIFIC SKILL COMPARISONS 124 Reading Decoding	>	67 Reading Comprehension	57	NS .05 (.01)
75 Mathematics Applications	<	76 Mathematics Computation	1	(NS) .05 .01

AGS®

Figure 2.4 Sarah's Score Summary

Note: Kaufman Test of Educational Achievement/Normative Update (K-TEA/NU): Comprehensive Individual Test Record © 1985 AGS they represent. In the mathematics area, both computational and applications skills show impaired development. Difficulties exist not only in determining how to solve problems but also in the basic skills of addition, subtraction, multiplication, and division. In Sarah's case, the subtest comparisons reveal more useful information than does comparing composite scores alone.

Clinical Analysis of Errors

This step in profile analysis focuses on the types of errors that students make in decoding skills, reading comprehension, understanding and applying mathematics principles, and actually solving mathematics problems. In order to proceed with this step in the interpretive process we must analyze the types of errors made on the student's incorrect responses to the subtests.

Subtest Error Analysis

In the reading decoding area there are 10 categories used to analyze errors on Reading Decoding and Spelling; these categories are defined with examples in Rapid Reference 2.11. On Reading Comprehension only two skill categories are utilized: literal comprehension and inferential comprehension. *Literal comprehension* is defined as the student's paraphrasing the passage only—in other words, simply giving back to the examiner what was read without elaboration or interpretation. *Inferential comprehension* requires the student to "deduce the central thought of the passage, make an inference about passage content or the purpose or point of view of the writer, recognize the tone and mood of the passage or the literary devices used by the writer, or follow the organization of the passage" (Kaufman & Kaufman, 1997, p. 112). Inferential comprehension is more complex and involves the application of reasoning skills.

In the mathematics area, two sets of categories are used for each of the two mathematics subtests. The categories for Mathematics Applications are defined with examples in Rapid Reference 2.12, while the categories for Mathematics Computation are defined with examples in Rapid Reference 2.13. Items involving more than one skill are classified under each skill utilized. The Applications subtest assesses knowledge of mathematical concepts and skills to solve real-life problems. The Computation subtest emphasizes the use of mathematical operations and techniques to complete computation exercises.

A thorough explanation of the analysis of errors (including the rationale, method for selecting the skills categories, procedure for completing this portion of the record form, examples, reliability data, interpretation guidelines,

⟞Rapid Reference 2.11

Definitions and Examples of Skill Categories for Reading, Decoding, and Spelling

Skill Category	Frequently Occurring Words	Infrequently Occurring Words
Prefixes, Word Beginnings	Common prefixes (*in-*, *un-*, *pre-*); word beginnings from Greek and Latin (*tele-*, *micro-*, *hyper-*, *octa-*) Examples: *pro*gressive, *ob*jection	
Suffixes, Word Endings	Common suffixes (*-ite*, *-ing*, *-able*), word endings that are the last morphological unit of a word (*-tial* in *initial*; *-cial* in *special*; *-gious* in *contagious*) Examples: harrass*ment*, indo*lence*	
Closed-Syllable (short) Vowels	Vowel within a closed syllable has short vowel sound Examples: tw*e*nty; w*e*nt	Vowel within a closed syllable has other than short vowel sound Examples: break*fast*, defini*tion*
Open-Syllable (long) Vowels	Vowel within an open syllable has long vowel sound Examples: h*e*llo, sh*e*	Vowel within an open syllable has other than long vowel sound Examples: m*a*nipulator, *a*nticipate
Final e–related (long) Vowels	Vowel of a final e–pattern has the long vowel sound, final e is not sounded Examples: kn*ife*, tele*phone*	Vowel of a final e–pattern has other than long vowel or final e is sounded Example: camou*flage*
Vowel Digraphs	First letter of vowel pair in syllable has long vowel and second vowel not sounded Examples: d*ee*p, r*ea*ch	Vowel pair is a sound or sounds other than the long vowel sound of first letter in pair Examples: s*ue*de, s*ai*d

Definitions and Examples

Skill Category	Frequently Occurring Words	Infrequently Occurring Words
Vowel Diphthongs	Vowel pairs *oi, oy* have /oi/ sound (oil, boy); vowel pairs *ou, ow* have the /ou/ sound (out, cow) Examples: do*u*bt, emplo*y*ed	Vowel pairs *oi, oy, ou, ow* have sounds other than /oi/ and /ou/ Example: couple
r-controlled Vowels	Sound of vowel before *r* in a syllable with a modified /r/ sound Examples: po*w*der, mother	Sound of vowel before *r* in a syllable does not have modified /r/ sound Examples: so*rr*y, infe*r*ior
Consonant-*le* Vowels	Final e of a *Cle* pattern has a schwa sound immediately preceding an /l/ sound Example: ap*ple*	
Single Consonants, Double Consonants, Consonant Digraphs, Consonant Clusters	Consonant or consonants of a syllable have the predicted consonant or consonant blend sounds Examples: *o*pen, *w*agon	Consonant letter or letters of a syllable do not have the predicted consonant or consonant blend sounds Examples: dou*b*t, o*c*ean (*sh*)

Note. Adapted from Kaufman & Kaufman (1985, 1997).

procedures for recommending teaching strategies, and case studies) are included in chapter 4 of the test manual. Error analyses for the Reading Decoding and Spelling subtests are based on the specific errors made by the student. Error analyses of Reading Comprehension, Mathematics Applications, and Mathematics Computation is based on the items with incorrect responses and skills measured by them. The unique response of the student is not examined individually, as in Reading Decoding and Spelling. The development of norms for the error analysis procedure is also described in detail. This component of the K-TEA/NU is a valuable resource. Error analysis is best suited to student scores of less than 100.

≡Rapid Reference 2.12

Definitions of Skill Categories for Mathematics Applications

Skill Category	Definitions
Elementary Number Concepts	Basic counting, numeration, one-to-one correspondence, geometric shape, quantity
Reading Tables and Graphs	Problems requiring only basic fact knowledge of tables or graphs
Addition	Problems requiring only basic fact knowledge
Subtraction	Problems requiring only basic fact knowledge
Multiplication	Problems requiring only basic fact knowledge
Division	Problems requiring only basic fact knowledge
Fractions	Problems requiring only basic fact knowledge
Decimals and Percents	Problems requiring only basic fact knowledge of decimals or percents
Advanced Number Concepts	Place value of numbers, converting fractions to decimals, finding averages, probability, prime numbers
Measurement	Problems requiring only basic fact knowledge
Money	Problems requiring only basic fact knowledge
Estimation	Problems requiring only basic fact knowledge
Two-Step Problems	Problems requiring two distinct steps in order to solve

The starting point for error analysis is to record the student's incorrect responses to the stimulus words in Reading Decoding, writing them so that you can understand the incorrect pronunciation. The spelling responses are already recorded by the student on the Spelling Sheet as well as the Mathematics Computation Worksheet. As you complete the test, record the student's incorrect responses to Reading Comprehension and Mathematics Applications.

Error analysis should be completed *only after testing has been completed*. While we may be tempted to begin the process during testing, it is best to avoid this temptation. The specific procedures for subtest error analysis are presented in Rapid Reference 2.14.

≡Rapid Reference 2.13

Definitions of Skill Categories for Mathematics Computation

Skill Category	Definitions
Basic Addition	Problems requiring only basic fact knowledge
Regrouping Addition	Problems requiring carrying
Advanced Addition	Problems requiring either basic fact or regrouping knowledge used in combination with other higher-order concepts and skills, such as rational and integer number systems, standard measurement units, or algebraic equations
Basic Subtraction	Problems requiring only basic fact knowledge
Regrouping Subtraction	Problems requiring borrowing
Advanced Subtraction	Problems requiring basic fact knowledge or regrouping with higher-order concepts and skills
Multiplication	Problems requiring only basic fact knowledge
Division	Problems requiring only basic fact knowledge
Fractions	Problems requiring only basic fact knowledge
Algebraic Equations	Problems requiring only basic fact knowledge
Square Roots and Exponents	Problems requiring only basic fact knowledge

Completing the Error Analysis Summary

Now that we have completed the subtest analysis of errors, we must complete the Error Analysis Summary. This involves transferring data to pages 12 and 13 of the Individual Test Record Form and reading some additional tables in the test manual appendix. Rapid Reference 2.15 outlines this procedure. Figure 2.5 shows a completed Error Analysis Summary.

Interpreting the Error Analysis Summary

The purpose of the Error Analysis Summary is to provide a concise picture of the individual student's strong and weak points in specific areas of reading,

═Rapid Reference 2.14

Procedures for Completing Clinical Analysis of Errors

Reading Decoding and Spelling Subtests

Step 1: After the test session is completed, use the record of incorrect pronunciations from Reading Decoding and the student's Spelling Sheet to complete the Word Parts categorization of errors. The open boxes with word parts in them indicate the types of errors that pertain to the particular word. For each incorrect response check the boxes that correspond to the error or errors. (An individual word may involve several error categories. Also, some boxes contain more than one word part. Chapter 4 of the test manual explains this process in more detail.)

Step 2: Count the number of checks in each category and record the total in the Total Errors by Skill Category boxes.

Reading Comprehension

Step 1: After the test session is completed, place a check mark in the appropriate skill classification column for each error.

Step 2: Count the number of checks in the two categories and record the total in the Total Errors by Skill Category boxes.

Mathematics Applications and Mathematics Computation

Step 1: After the test session is completed, place a check mark in the appropriate skill classification column or columns for each error. Some items represent skills in more than one category. Use the completed student worksheet for the Mathematics Computation subtest.

Step 2: Count the number of checks in the categories and record the total in the Total Errors by Skill Category boxes.

---

spelling, and arithmetic. The profile is based both on the student's unique pattern of responses and on the number of errors made and number of test items administered. In addition, the normative comparison allows us to compare this picture with that of an average student of similar age or grade level. Students may have very similar composite and subtest scores and yet differ significantly in the specific reading and math skills they have. This procedure allows us to uncover that information.

To demonstrate this interpretive approach, let's consider the example of

≡ Rapid Reference 2.15

Completing the Error Analysis Summary

Step 1: Record the student's grade level and the ceiling item for each of the subtests on the Error Analysis Summary on pages 12 and 13 of the Individual Test Record.

Step 2: For Reading Comprehension, Mathematics Applications, and Mathematics Computation record the number of items attempted by the student. These data are found in Tables 21, 18, and 22 of the test manual, respectively, and are based on the ceiling item for the student on each subtest. The tables are arranged by the student's grade level, so be careful to use that correct table! (The tabled values give the student credit for all items below the starting point that were not given but were assumed to have been passed.) Next, enter the tables based on the ceiling item for each subtest; the first column under the ceiling item indicates the number of items attempted. Each error category is listed on the left side of the tables.

Step 3: For Reading Comprehension, Mathematics Applications, and Mathematics Computation continue using Tables 21, 18, and 22 in the test manual, respectively, and record the average number of errors, which is in the second column under the ceiling item. The average number of errors for skill categories with three or fewer items at the ceiling are not provided. Draw a dash on the Error Analysis Summary to indicate this.

Step 4: For Reading Decoding and Spelling, use Tables 19 and 20 in the test manual, respectively. These tables are arranged similarly to the ones we have just used with the exception of not having the number-of-items-attempted column. Record the average number of errors, which is in the column under the ceiling item. These tables, too, are arranged by grade.

Step 5: Transfer the student's number of errors for each subtest (from inside the Individual Test Record) to the appropriate column for each subtest on the Error Analysis Summary.

Step 6: The last column to complete is Skill Status. Compare the student's number of errors with the average number of errors. If the student's errors are more than the average number, circle W (weak). If the student's errors equal or are in the range of the average number of errors, circle A (average). If the student's number of errors is less than the average, circle S (strong).

Error Analysis Summary

Margaret
Grade __2__
Ceiling Item __20__

Mathematics Applications SKILL CATEGORY	Number of Items Attempted Table 18	Average Number of Errors Table 18	Student's Number of Errors Page 3	Skill Status Weak[a] Average[b] Strong[c]		
Elementary Number Concepts	9	1	2	Ⓦ	A	S
Reading Tables & Graphs	3	1	2	Ⓦ	A	S
Addition	5	1-2	4	Ⓦ	A	S
Subtraction	2	–	0	W	A	S
Multiplication	1	–	1	W	A	S
Division	0	–	0	W	A	S
Fractions	0	–	0	W	A	S
Decimals & Percents	0	–	0	W	A	S
Advanced Number Concepts	0	–	0	W	A	S
Measurement	1	–	1	W	A	S
Money	1	–	1	W	A	S
Estimation	1	–	1	W	A	S
Two-Step Problems	0	–	0	W	A	S

Grade __2__
Ceiling Item __10__

Mathematics Computation SKILL CATEGORY	Number of Items Attempted Table 22	Average Number of Errors Table 22	Student's Number of Errors Page 11	Skill Status Weak[a] Average[b] Strong[c]		
Basic Addition	6	0-1	3	Ⓦ	A	S
Regrouping Addition	1	–	1	W	A	S
Basic Subtraction	3	0	3	Ⓦ	A	S
Regrouping Subtraction	0	–		W	A	S
Multiplication	0	–		W	A	S
Division	0	–		W	A	S
Fractions	0			W	A	S
Advanced Addition	0			W	A	S
Advanced Subtraction	0			W	A	S
Algebraic Equations	0			W	A	S
Square Roots & Exponents	0			W	A	S

[a]Student's Number of Errors is greater than the Average Number of Errors.
[b]Student's Number of Errors is equal to (or within the range of) the Average Number of Errors.
[c]Student's Number of Errors is less than the Average Number of Errors.

Figure 2.5 Completed Error Analysis Summary for Margaret

Note: Kaufman Test of Educational Achievement/Normative Update (K-TEA/NU): Comprehensive Individual Test Record © 1985 AGS

Margaret, whose Error Analysis Summary is presented in Figure 2.6. Margaret is a 2nd-grade student with a chronological age of 7 years 8 months. The figure shows the front page of her Individual Test Record. Her composite scores range from 72 to 80 and are in the well-below-average range. Her Spelling Subtest score is 94 and represents a relative strength as compared to the other subtest scores. Reading Decoding and Reading Comprehension

Margaret

Grade **2**

Ceiling Item **20**

Reading Decoding	Average Number of Errors	Student's Number of Errors	Skill Status		
			Weak[a]	Average[b]	Strong[c]
WORD PART	Table 19	Page 5			
Prefixes & Word Beginnings	–	0	W	A	S
Suffixes & Word Endings	–	1	W	A	S
Closed Syllable (Short) Vowels	0	2	(W)	A	S
Open Syllable (Long) & Final e Pattern Vowels	0	4	(W)	A	S
Vowel Digraphs & Diphthongs	0	3	(W)	A	S
r-Controlled Patterns	–	1	W	A	S
Consonant-le Patterns	–	1	W	A	S
Consonant Clusters & Digraphs	0	1	(W)	A	S
Single & Double Consonants	0	3	(W)	A	S

Grade **2**

Ceiling Item **15**

Spelling	Average Number of Errors	Student's Number of Errors	Skill Status		
			Weak[a]	Average[b]	Strong[c]
WORD PART	Table 20	Page 7			
Prefixes & Word Beginnings	–	0	W	A	S
Suffixes & Word Endings	–	1	W	A	S
Closed Syllable (Short) Vowels	0	0	W	A	S
Open Syllable (Long) & Final e Pattern Vowels	–	0	W	A	S
Vowel Digraphs & Diphthongs	1–2	3	(W)	A	S
r-Controlled Patterns	–	1	W	A	S
Consonant Clusters & Digraphs	0	2	(W)	A	S
Single & Double Consonants	0–1	2	(W)	A	S

Grade **2**

Ceiling Item **10**

Reading Comprehension	Number of Items Attempted	Average Number of Errors	Student's Number of Errors	Skill Status		
				Weak[a]	Average[b]	Strong[c]
SKILL CATEGORY	Table 21	Table 21	Page 9			
Literal Comprehension	2	–	2	W	A	S
Inferential Comprehension	0	–	0	W	A	S

[a]Student's Number of Errors is greater than the Average Number of Errors.
[b]Student's Number of Errors is equal to (or within the range of) the Average Number of Errors.
[c]Student's Number of Errors is less than the Average Number of Errors.

Figure 2.5 (Continued)

scores show uniform development; although her mathematics scores are less uniform than her reading scores, they are not significantly different from each other.

As a result of Margaret's below average scores, the error analysis focuses on skills that are considered weak as compared to those of peers. In the reading area, five areas of weakness are indicated in Reading Decoding and three in Spelling, with the three in Spelling overlapping the Reading Decoding weak-

Comprehensive Form

K·TEA NU

KAUFMAN TEST of EDUCATIONAL ACHIEVEMENT
by Alan S. Kaufman & Nadeen L. Kaufman

INDIVIDUAL TEST RECORD

Student's Name: MARGARET Sex: F
Parent's Name:
Home Address: Home Phone:
Grade: 2 Teacher:
School: Examiner: DOUGLAS K. SMITH

	Year	Month	Day
Test Date	1999	12	6
Birth Date	1992	4	4
Chronological Age	7	8	2

COMPREHENSIVE FORM SUBTESTS Mean = 100; SD = 15	RAW SCORES Reading Composite	Mathematics Composite	Battery Composite	Standard Score* Table ___	Band of Error 95 % Confidence Table 5 or 6	%ile Rank Table 7	Other Data	
Mathematics Applications		11	11	83	± 9	13	< 1.0	
Reading Decoding	9		9	84	± 5	14	1.1	
Spelling			7	94	± 6	34	1.8	
Reading Comprehension	2		2	81	± 6	10	1.0	
Mathematics Computation		3	3	70	± 8	2	< 1.0	
Sum of Subtest Raw Scores	11	14	32					

Transfer sums to Composite Scales, Sum of Subtest Raw Scores column.

*Standard Scores Derived from (Circle the table used):	AGE	GRADE
Fall Norms (August-January)	Table 1	Table 2
Spring Norms (February-July)	Table 3	Table 4

Norms used: ☒ Updated ☐ Original

COMPREHENSIVE FORM COMPOSITE SCALES Mean = 100; SD = 15	Sum of Subtest Raw Scores	Standard Score* Table ___	Band of Error 95 % Confidence Table 5 or 6	%ile Rank Table 7	Descriptive Category	Other Data
Reading Composite	11	78	± 4	7	WELL BELOW AVERAGE	< 1.0
Mathematics Composite	14	72	± 6	3	WELL BELOW AVERAGE	< 1.0
Battery Composite	32	80	± 3	9	WELL BELOW AVG./BELOW AVG.	1.2

		Indicate >, <, or ≈		Standard Score Difference	Circle the Significance Level
GLOBAL SKILL COMPARISONS	78 Reading Composite	>	72 Mathematics Composite	6	(NS) .05 .01
	78 Reading Composite	<	94 Spelling Subtest	16	NS .05 (.01)
	72 Mathematics Composite	<	94 Spelling Subtest	22	NS .05 (.01)
SPECIFIC SKILL COMPARISONS	84 Reading Decoding	>	81 Reading Comprehension	3	NS .05 (.01)
	83 Mathematics Applications	>	70 Mathematics Computation	13	(NS) .05 .01

AGS®

Figure 2.6 Completed Score Summary for Margaret

Note: Kaufman Test of Educational Achievement/Normative Update (K-TEA/NU): Comprehensive Individual Test Record © 1985 AGS

nesses. Her pattern of errors indicates great difficulty with vowel digraphs and diphthongs, consonant clusters and digraphs, and single and double consonants. Words containing these word parts are difficult for Margaret to pronounce and spell. Examples include *ea* as in *each, br* as in *brown, kn* as in *knight,* and the single consonants *c, s, n,* and *p.* Additionally, weakness is shown in pronouncing words with a silent final *e* and with a short vowel between two consonants. In the mathematics area, weakness is shown in basic addition and subtraction. Margaret was able to complete single-digit addition problems as long as regrouping was not required. If the sum of the numbers added was in double digits, as in "6 + 4 = 10," she was unable to solve the problem. Likewise, she was unable to complete any subtraction problems, continuing to add the numbers together rather than subtracting them. Reading calendars and clocks was also beyond Margaret's skills.

As you can see, the error analysis adds important information to the test analysis. This information may confirm what the classroom teacher has already noted or it may be new information. Regardless, intervention activities can then be developed.

STRENGTHS AND WEAKNESSES OF THE K-TEA/NU

The K-TEA and K-TEA/NU have been in use for 15 years. Consequently, there have been many reviews of the test and many studies of its relationship to other measures of achievement. Rapid Reference 2.16 presents a list of reviews of the K-TEA and K-TEA/NU. In this section I summarize my own views of the major strengths and weaknesses of the K-TEA/NU, drawing from the formal reviews listed in Rapid Reference 2.16 as well as from my own experience with the instrument as a practitioner and university trainer. Feedback from practitioners in a variety of areas has also contributed to my analysis of the instrument. I focus my summary on the areas of test development, standardization, administration and scoring, reliability, validity, and interpretation; this information is summarized in Rapid References 2.17–2.19.

There are many strengths of the K-TEA/NU: the theoretical base for the test and the subsequent va-

═Rapid Reference 2.16

Reviews of the K-TEA and K-TEA/NU

Dickenson (1986)
Doll (1989)
Henson & Bennett (1985)
Lewandowski (1986)
Miller (1998–99)
Radencich (1986)
Salvia & Ysseldyke (1998, 2001)
Sattler (1989)
Witt, Elliott, Kramer, & Gresham (1994)
Worthington (1987)

≡ Rapid Reference 2.17

Strengths and Weaknesses of the K-TEA/NU

Strengths	Weaknesses
Test Development	
The rationale for item selection using curriculum consultants, and basing item selection on content of widely used textbooks	Entry level is grade 1 rather than kindergarten or prekindergarten
Extensive tryout data using samples with approximate proportional representation by sex and race/ethnicity	Insufficient number of test items for 1st-graders with below average academic skills
Easel format for presenting subtest items	Error analysis procedures may be difficult for examiners lacking a background in curriculum
Innovative item types, especially in Reading Comprehension	
Use of extensive item analysis procedures to eliminate biased items (sex or race) and items with poor psychometric properties	
Error analysis procedures	
Standardization	
Inclusion of students receiving special education services	All students in the normative update standardization did not take all five batteries
Very detailed information on standardization procedures and sample	Number of students in normative update sample less than in original standardization
Overall standardization procedures considered a strength by test reviewers	Test items not updated in normative update
Both the original and normative update samples are appropriate match to U.S. census data	
Expanded age range to 22 years	

Strengths	Weaknesses
Administration and Scoring	
Layout of test protocol is user friendly	Need to write Reading Decoding responses phonetically to use error analysis
Clear and consistent starting and stopping points for all subtests	Complex error analysis procedures
Use of item units	Error analysis for mathematics uses items and not the exact student response as with the Reading and Spelling subtests
Easel format of test	
Administration time is appropriate (no more than 60–75 minutes)	
Inclusion of key administration points on Remember Page for each subtest	
Dichotomous scoring	
Both age and grade norms	
Reliability	
High mean split-half reliabilities of subtests and composites (.85 and above)	Reliability studies were not updated with the updated norms
Acceptable interrater reliabilities for error analysis (.65 to .85)	Limited number of students in test-retest reliability studies
Test-retest reliabilities exceed .93 for composites and .90 for subtests, except Mathematics Computation (.83 at grades 1–6)	
Validity	
Moderate correlations (.75 to .85) between K-TEA and other achievement measures for concurrent reliability	Lack of current validity studies with updated norms
Strong face validity based on use of textbook content and skill development in reading and mathematics	
Construct validity indicated by increasing scores across grades and ages	

(continued)

Strengths	Weaknesses
Interpretation	
Both composites and subtests can be interpreted due to high reliability data	Insufficient floor for 1st-graders with below average academic skills
Error analysis procedures pinpoint specific skill deficits	Tables presenting average differences for significance when comparing pairs of subtests and for comparing subtests with means of the other subtests based on original standardization
Yields much diagnostic information	
Norms tables present subtest and battery composite intercorrelations by age and grade, as well as p-values for subtests	
	Error analysis norms based on original standardization
Cross-linking with K-TEA Brief form, PIAT-R, WRMT-R, KeyMath-R	
Successive-level approach to interpretation is familiar to examiners	

lidity data; the original standardization sample, with its inclusion of students with disabilities; the reliabilities of the composites and subtests; the error analysis procedures and their implications for instruction; the ease of administration; the linking of the test with other achievement measures in the updated standardization; and the comprehensiveness of the test manual. As with any test there are also weaknesses; these include the limited floor at the 6 years–11 months age range; the lack of current validity studies with the updated norms; the reduced number of students at each age range completing the entire battery as part of the updated standardization process; and the lack of subtests in certain achievement areas, such as written expression.

As with most tests, the K-TEA/NU is not as precise in measuring its constructs at the youngest and oldest age ranges, particularly with individuals considerably below average or above average in achievement; Rapid References 2.18 and 2.19 document this. Although the standard score range is designed to be from 40 to 160 at all ages, a perusal of Rapid References 2.18 and 2.19 shows that this score range occurs for the middle age ranges of the test and not for the extremes. For the student considerably below average in achievement, the floor of the test is insufficient at ages 6 years 0 months through 6 years 11 months. In addition, the Spelling and Reading Comprehension subtests have a limited floor in the 6–9-year age range. The ceiling of the test for students considerably above average in achievement is much better. Only for the oldest

Rapid Reference 2.18

Strengths and Weaknesses of the K-TEA/NU: Effective Range of Subtest and Composite Scores, by Age (based on raw score of 0)

Age (year/month)	Subtests					Composites		
	Math App	Rdg Dcdg	Spell	Rdg Comp	Math Comp	Rdg	Math	Total Battery
6/0–6/2	42	58	85	92	61	71	66	58
6/3–6/5	42	53	82	87	60	66	62	57
6/6–6/8	40	49	78	82	58	62	59	57
6/9–6/11	40	48	75	78	57	61	57	56
7/0–7/2	40	47	72	75	56	61	56	56
7/3–7/5	40	46	70	73	54	60	54	56
7/6–7/8	40	45	68	70	56	60	52	55
7/9–7/11	40	44	66	69	50	59	51	55
8/0–8/2	40	41	65	68	48	58	51	55
8/3–8/5	40	40	64	67	46	57	50	54
8/6–8/8	40	40	63	66	44	57	49	54
8/9–8/11	40	40	62	65	43	56	48	54
9/0–9/2	40	40	60	65	42	56	48	53

(continued)

Age (year/month)	Subtests					Composites		
	Math App	Rdg Dcdg	Spell	Rdg Comp	Math Comp	Rdg	Math	Total Battery
9/3–9/5	40	40	58	64	41	55	47	53
9/6–9/8	40	40	55	62	40	55	47	53
9/9–9/11	40	40	54	60	40	54	45	57
10/0–10/2	40	40	52	57	40	54	44	50
10/3–10/5	40	40	50	53	40	53	42	49
10/6–10/8	40	40	48	51	40	53	42	48
10/9–10/11	40	40	47	50	40	52	41	47
11/0–11/2	40	40	45	47	40	52	41	46
11/3–11/5	40	40	44	48	40	51	40	46
11/6–11/8	40	40	43	47	40	51	40	45
11/9–11/11	40	40	43	45	40	50	40	44
12/0–12/2	40	40	42	44	40	49	40	43
12/3–12/5	40	40	42	43	40	48	40	42
12/6–12/8	40	40	41	42	40	47	40	40
12/9–12/11	40	40	41	42	40	47	40	40
13/0–13/2	40	40	41	42	40	46	40	40

	Subtests					Composites		
Age (year/month)	Math App	Rdg Dcdg	Spell	Rdg Comp	Math Comp	Rdg	Math	Total Battery
13/3–13/5	40	40	40	41	40	46	40	40
13/6–13/8	40	40	40	41	40	46	40	40
13/9–13/11	40	40	40	41	40	45	40	40
14/0–14/2	40	40	40	40	40	45	40	40
14/3–14/5	40	40	40	40	40	44	40	40
14/6–14/8	40	40	40	40	40	44	40	40
14/9–14/11	40	40	40	40	40	43	40	40
15/0–15/2	40	40	40	40	40	43	40	40
15/3–15/5	40	40	40	40	40	42	40	40
15/6–15/8	40	40	40	40	40	41	40	40
15/9–21/11	40	40	40	40	40	40	40	40

Note. Math App = Mathematics Applications; Rdg Dcdg = Reading Decoding; Spell = Spelling; Rdg Comp = Reading Comprehension; Math Comp = Mathematics Computation.

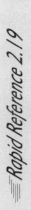

Rapid Reference 2.19

Strengths and Weaknesses of the K-TEA/NU:
Effective Range of Subtest and Composite Scores, by Age (based on maximum raw score)

Age (year/month)	Subtests						Composites		
	Math App	Rdg Dcdg	Spell	Rdg Comp	Math Comp	Rdg	Math	Total Battery
6/0–9/8	160	160	160	160	160	160	160	160
9/9–9/11	160	159	160	160	160	159	160	160
10/0–10/2	160	159	160	160	160	159	160	160
10/3–10/5	160	159	160	160	160	158	160	160
10/6–10/8	160	158	160	160	160	158	159	160
10/9–10/11	160	158	160	160	160	157	157	160
11/0–11/2	159	158	160	160	160	157	154	160
11/3–11/5	158	158	160	160	160	156	152	159
11/6–11/8	157	157	160	157	160	156	150	159
11/9–11/11	157	156	160	156	160	155	149	159
12/0–12/2	157	155	160	156	160	153	148	158
12/3–12/5	156	154	160	155	160	151	147	158
12/6–12/8	156	152	160	153	160	149	147	158
12/9–12/11	156	151	160	152	160	148	146	157

Age (year/month)	Subtests					Composites		
	Math App	Rdg Dcdg	Spell	Rdg Comp	Math Comp	Rdg	Math	Total Battery
13/0–13/2	155	148	160	151	160	147	146	157
13/3–13/5	155	147	160	151	160	146	146	157
13/6–13/8	155	145	159	150	157	145	146	157
13/9–13/11	154	143	156	150	152	144	146	156
14/0–14/2	153	142	153	148	149	143	146	156
14/3–14/5	152	140	151	147	146	142	146	156
14/6–14/8	149	139	150	146	145	142	145	155
14/9–14/11	147	137	149	145	145	141	143	154
15/0–15/2	145	136	147	144	145	140	141	153
15/3–15/5	143	135	148	143	144	139	139	151
15/6–15/8	142	134	147	142	144	139	137	150
15/9–15/11	141	134	147	140	144	138	136	150
16/0–16/2	141	133	146	138	143	137	136	149
16/3–16/5	140	133	145	137	142	136	135	149
16/6–16/8	140	133	144	137	142	136	135	149
16/9–16/11	140	133	144	136	142	135	134	143

(continued)

Age (year/month)	Subtests					Composites		
	Math App	Rdg Dcdg	Spell	Rdg Comp	Math Comp	Rdg	Math	Total Battery
17/0–17/2	139	133	144	136	142	135	134	148
17/3–17/5	139	133	143	136	142	134	133	147
17/6–17/8	139	132	142	136	141	133	133	147
17/9–17/11	139	131	141	136	141	133	132	147
18/0–18/2	138	130	141	135	140	132	132	146
18/3–18/5	138	129	140	135	139	131	131	146
18/6–18/8	138	128	139	135	138	130	131	146
18/9–18/11	138	128	132	135	137	130	131	146
19/0–19/11	137	127	138	134	136	129	131	146
20/0–20/11	135	126	137	133	133	128	130	145
21/0–21/11	133	125	137	131	131	128	130	145
22/0–22/11	131	123	136	129	130	127	129	144

Note. Math App = Mathematics Applications; Rdg Dcdg = Reading Decoding; Spell = Spelling; Rdg Comp = Reading Comprehension; Math Comp = Mathematics Computation age ranges (20 years and above) is the ceiling limited for individual subtests, and the battery composite remains strong even at this age level.

CLINICAL APPLICATIONS OF THE K-TEA/NU

Since the original publication of the K-TEA, numerous studies have compared performance on the test with performance on other measures of achievement, including the PIAT-R, WRAT-R/WRAT3, WIAT, and Woodcock-Johnson Psycho-Educational Battery–Revised Tests of Achievement (WJ-R TA; Woodcock & Johnson, 1989). Rapid Reference 2.20 provides references for some of these studies.

≡ Rapid Reference 2.20

References Comparing Performance on the K-TEA with That on Other Achievement Measures

Peabody Individual Achievement Test–Revised

Bookman & Peach (1988)
Hultquist & Metzke (1993)
Prewett & Giannuli (1991)
Shapiro & Derr (1987)
Webster & Braswell (1991)

Wide Range Achievement Test–Revised
Wide Range Achievement Test 3

Bell, Lentz, & Graden (1992)
Prewett, Bardos, & Fowler (1991)
Prewett & Giannuli (1991)
Prewett, Lillis, & Bardos (1991)
Shapiro & Derr (1987)
Webster & Braswell (1991)

Wechsler Individual Achievement Test

Gentry, Sapp, & Daw (1995)

Woodcock-Johnson Psycho-Educational Battery–Revised Tests of Achievement

Hultquist & Metzke (1993)
Posey, Sapp, & Gladding (1989)
Prewett & Giannuli (1991)
Shull-Senn, Weatherly, Morgan, Kanouse, & Bradley-Johnson (1995)

The majority of studies with the K-TEA have examined its relationships with other achievement tests as well as the use of the K-TEA with students referred for possible special-education services. In the latter category, the emphasis has been on students referred for possible learning disabilities. Some of these studies have also examined the relationship of the K-TEA to measures of intelligence because the discrepancy between ability and achievement is one of the criteria for eligibility for learning disabilities services.

The K-TEA and Achievement Measures

The majority of studies with the K-TEA have examined its relationship with other achievement tests. For example, Prewett, Bardos, and Fowler (1991) compared the K-TEA and WRAT-R with 91 elementary-age children referred for possible special-education eligibility. They found that scores on the Comprehensive and Brief forms of the K-TEA were similar while those on the WRAT-R were significantly lower than those on the two forms of the K-TEA. Using a sample of 50 incarcerated delinquents, Prewett, Lillis, and Bardos (1991) compared performance on the K-TEA Brief Form and the WRAT-R and found similar scores that were highly correlated with each other.

Kamphaus, Schmitt, and Mings (1986) compared performance on the K-TEA with that on group-administered achievement tests in three samples of students. They found that mean scores were similar across measures and that the correlations of the K-TEA with the group measures were high.

Demaray and Elliot (1999) examined the relationship between teachers' judgments of students' academic achievement and the students' performance on the K-TEA Brief Form. Moderately high correlations were found, and the teachers seemed to be better predictors of higher-achieving students than of lower-achieving students. In an earlier study, Webster, Hewett, and Crumbacker (1989) compared teacher estimates of academic functioning for 134 3rd- and 4th-graders with the students' performance on the WRAT-R and K-TEA. They found that teacher estimates and scores on the two achievement tests were consistent, and that the WRAT-R and K-TEA were equal to one another in predictiveness of classroom functioning levels.

The K-TEA and Intelligence Measures

One line of research with the K-TEA has been to explore its relationship to tests of intelligence. These studies have found moderate but usually not significant correlations between the K-TEA battery composite and the overall ability measure. For example, Lavin (1996) used the K-TEA and the Wechsler Intelligence Scale for Children–Third Edition (WISC-III) with a sample of 72 students with emotional disabilities, who ranged in age from 7 to 16 years.

The K-TEA and Program Evaluation

The K-TEA has also been used as a measure in program evaluation studies, the majority of which have used it to measure the effectiveness of instructional methods on students' academic performance. For example, Knapp and Winsor (1998) used the Reading Comprehension subtest in a pretest/posttest design to show that an apprenticeship method of assisting delayed readers develop reading skills produced significantly larger gains in reading comprehension as compared to a control group. However, the K-TEA has also been used to show the effectiveness of support groups on the academic achievement of chronically ill students (e.g., Rynard, Chambers, Klinck, & Gray [1998]).

Test-Retest Reliability and Stability

As noted earlier, some reviewers had expressed concern over the limited number of test-retest reliability studies with the K-TEA. Since the test's publication, this topic has been explored by several researchers. Shull-Senn, Weatherly, Morgan, Kanouse, and Bradley-Johnson (1995) examined test-retest reliability of the K-TEA and the WJ-R TA in two samples of elementary-age students, and found that K-TEA composites and subtests produced correlations of .90 and higher. In a stability study of the K-TEA Brief Form over a 3-year period with a sample of 52 students with learning disabilities, Hewett and Bolen (1996) obtained stability coefficients ranging from .69 to .88. There was, however, significant individual variation in scores.

AN ILLUSTRATIVE CASE REPORT

In this section, our focus turns to a psychoeducational report for a student referred for possible special education placement. We will be interpreting Michael's

<table>
<tr><td>

CAUTION
....

Information to Include
in Reports

• Name of the student
• Student's date of birth
• Date of testing
• Student's chronological age
• Grade in school
• Date of report
• Examiner's name

</td></tr>
</table>

K-TEA/NU results along with additional test data (Michael's score summary was presented in Fig. 2.3).

This section integrates the levels of interpretation previously presented for the K-TEA/NU and supplements the K-TEA/NU data with additional test information, background information, and behavioral observations. Each report that you write should include some basic information about the student, such as age, grade in school, testing date, and so forth.

Reason for Referral

Michael M. was referred for evaluation by his 3rd-grade teacher, Ms. H. She expressed concern over Michael's difficulty with reading skills, memory, and language skills. Inattention and distractibility were also reported. Specifically, Ms. H. wanted to know if Michael was achieving at a level consistent with his abilities and whether any specific learning problem were present.

An interview with Ms. H. provided additional information. She described Michael as having difficulty in both reading decoding and reading comprehension with performance at the 2nd-grade level. According to Ms. H., Michael has great difficulty with phonics. In addition, his performance in reading is quite variable, with "okay" performance on occasion but mostly below average. Ms. H. reported that Michael has difficulty completing assignments and that he is "terribly disorganized." She further described Michael as being "off-task" much of the time.

Background Information

Michael is currently a 3rd-grade student in a regular education classroom of 29 students. He is working with the Title I teacher in a small group setting with an emphasis on developing his reading skills. He lives with his mother and an older sister, who is in the 7th grade and is doing well academically.

Michael's school history indicates concerns over his slow academic progress and skills deficits with reading and with written language. These concerns were initially noted in the 1st grade. Results of the California Achievement Test, which was taken last year, revealed overall reading and language scores approximately one year below those of other students his age. His spelling skills and reading skills were at the 1.2 to 1.4 grade-equivalent level, as compared to his grade placement of 2.7 at that time.

Michael has been receiving Title I services for reading since the beginning of 1st grade. In 1st and 2nd grades his Title I programming was in a small-group setting; this year he is seen daily for 30 minutes during his language arts class.

Behavioral concerns have also been noted since the 1st grade. Specifically, these concerns focused on his inattention, distractibility, off-task behavior, and impulsive behavior. Ms. H. reports that he received a medical evaluation for Attention-Deficit Hyperactivity Disorder (ADHD) last year, with results being "inconclusive." Currently, Ms. H. reports that Michael has difficulty remembering directions and staying on task. Impulsive behavior is also reported by the Title I teacher. These behaviors first became a concern during 2nd grade.

An interview with Michael's mother, Ms. M., prior to the evaluation revealed no concerns regarding his behavior in the home setting. She reported that Michael participated in both the prekindergarten program and the kindergarten program prior to entering 1st grade. She did note that Michael was "a little slower" than his sister, Jean. Developmental milestones were described as average with no serious childhood illnesses or injuries. The evaluation for ADHD was initiated by Ms. M. in response to the school's concern about his distractibility during 2nd grade.

Behavioral Observations

Prior to evaluation, Michael was observed in his classroom during instruction in reading and spelling. Both time-sample and event-recording procedures were utilized. Michael was on task approximately 70% of the time while a randomly selected "average" peer was on task 80% of the time. Michael's off-task behavior was primarily gazing away from his classwork or the teacher's presentation. No reinforcement of his off-task behavior by peers or his teacher was noted. When the teacher came over to his desk and redirected him to the task at hand, he was able to remain on task. He also was on task more often when the teacher was physically near his desk. In summary, his overall behavior during this observation was not significantly different from that of his other classmates.

During testing Michael was very friendly and talkative. He talked about school, himself, and particularly hockey. He was relaxed and comfortable with the various tasks that were presented. He frequently asked how he was doing and if his answers were correct. He continually sought feedback from the examiner and became frustrated when feedback was not provided. He seemed much more relaxed during the cognitive abilities portion of the assessment as compared to the achievement portion. He seemed especially concerned about his performance on reading-related tasks and required much encouragement to complete the word recognition and spelling items. He eagerly approached the mathematics items and was eager to continue with the computation problems. Michael was able to focus his attention on the tasks at hand and did not display impulsive or distractible behavior.

On the basis of these observations, Michael's results are believed to be a valid and accurate estimate of his current levels of cognitive and academic functioning.

Evaluation Procedures/Instruments

Review of school records
Interviews with teachers and parents
Classroom observation
Wechsler Intelligence Scale for Children–Third Edition (WISC-III)
Kaufman Test of Educational Achievement/Normative Update
  (K-TEA/NU) Comprehensive Form

Test Results

WISC-III Results

Scale/Index	IQ	95% Confidence Interval	Percentile Rank
Verbal Scale	108	101–114	70
Performance Scale	106	97–113	66
Full Scale	107	101–112	68
Verbal Comprehension Index	108	101–114	70
Perceptual Organization Index	104	95–112	61
Freedom from Distractibility Index	106	96–114	66
Processing Speed Index	111	100–119	77

Verbal Subtests	Scaled Score	Performance Subtests	Scaled Score
Information	09	Picture Completion	09
Similarities	15S	Coding	12
Arithmetic	11	Picture Arrangement	15S
Vocabulary	09	Block Design	09
Comprehension	13	Object Assembly	09
(Digit Span)	11	(Symbol Search)	12

Note. "S" represents a significant relative strength, $p < .05$.

K-TEA/NU

Composites/Subtests	Standard Score	95% Confidence Interval	Percentile Rank
Reading composite	84	79–89	14
Mathematics composite	103	97–109	58
Battery composite	89	86–92	23
Reading Decoding subtest	82	77–87	12
Reading Comprehension subtest	85	78–92	16
Spelling subtest	92	86–98	30
Mathematics Applications subtest	101	93–109	53
Mathematics Computation subtest	105	98–112	63

Note. Michael's complete score summary was presented earlier in Figure 2.3. Error analysis results for the K-TEA/NU are presented in Figure 2.7.

Error Analysis Summary

Grade: 3
Ceiling Item: 40

Mathematics Applications SKILL CATEGORY	Number of Items Attempted (Table 18)	Average Number of Errors (Table 18)	Student's Number of Errors (Page 3)	Skill Status Weak[a]	Average[b]	Strong[c]
Elementary Number Concepts	9	0	0	W	A	S
Reading Tables & Graphs	4	0-1	0	W	A	S
Addition	5	0	1	(W)	A	S
Subtraction	7	1-2	1	W	(A)	S
Multiplication	9	4-5	5	W	(A)	S
Division	4	2	2	W	(A)	S
Fractions	6	4	5	(W)	A	S
Decimals & Percents	1	—	1	W	A	S
Advanced Number Concepts	4	3	3	W	(A)	S
Measurement	3	1	0	W	A	(S)
Money	5	2-3	2	W	(A)	S
Estimation	3	1-2	1	W	(A)	S
Two-Step Problems	2	—	1	W	A	S

Grade: 3
Ceiling Item: 35

Mathematics Computation SKILL CATEGORY	Number of Items Attempted (Table 22)	Average Number of Errors (Table 22)	Student's Number of Errors (Page 11)	Skill Status Weak[a]	Average[b]	Strong[c]
Basic Addition	6	0	0	W	A	S
Regrouping Addition	5	0	0	W	A	S
Basic Subtraction	6	0	0	W	A	S
Regrouping Subtraction	4	1-2	0	W	A	(S)
Multiplication	7	1-2	3	(W)	A	S
Division	4	3	2	W	A	(S)
Fractions	2	—	2	(W)	A	S
Advanced Addition	1	—	1	W	A	S
Advanced Subtraction	0	—	0	W	A	S
Algebraic Equations	2	—	2	(W)	A	S
Square Roots & Exponents	0	—	0	W	A	S

[a]Student's Number of Errors is greater than the Average Number of Errors.
[b]Student's Number of Errors is equal to (or within the range of) the Average Number of Errors.
[c]Student's Number of Errors is less than the Average Number of Errors.

Figure 2.7 Error Analysis Results for Michael

Note: Kaufman Test of Educational Achievement/Normative Update (K-TEA/NU): Comprehensive Individual Test Record © 1985 AGS

Analysis of Results

The WISC-III is an individually administered test of cognitive abilities covering the age range of 6–16 years. It consists of six subtests emphasizing verbal content and six subtests emphasizing nonverbal content. The Full Scale IQ (FSIQ) combines both sets of subtests and produces the most valid overall score. Michael's performance on the WISC-III falls solidly within the average

Reading Decoding

Grade __3__
Ceiling Item __30__

WORD PART	Average Number of Errors (Table 19)	Student's Number of Errors (Page 5)	Weak[a]	Skill Status Average[b]	Strong[c]
Prefixes & Word Beginnings	—	1	W	A	S
Suffixes & Word Endings	0	1	(W)	A	S
Closed Syllable (Short) Vowels	0	0	W	A	S
Open Syllable (Long) & Final e Pattern Vowels	0	0	W	A	S
Vowel Digraphs & Diphthongs	0-1	1	W	(A)	S
r-Controlled Patterns	0	1	(W)	A	S
Consonant-le Patterns	0	1	(W)	A	S
Consonant Clusters & Digraphs	0	0	W	A	S
Single & Double Consonants	0-1	3	(W)	A	S

Spelling

Grade __3__
Ceiling Item __25__

WORD PART	Average Number of Errors (Table 20)	Student's Number of Errors (Page 7)	Weak[a]	Skill Status Average[b]	Strong[c]
Prefixes & Word Beginnings	0-1		W	A	S
Suffixes & Word Endings	0	1	(W)	A	S
Closed Syllable (Short) Vowels	0		W	A	S
Open Syllable (Long) & Final e Pattern Vowels	0		W	A	S
Vowel Digraphs & Diphthongs	1-2	4	(W)	A	S
r-Controlled Patterns	—		W	A	S
Consonant Clusters & Digraphs	0	1	(W)	A	S
Single & Double Consonants	0-1	1	W	(A)	S

Reading Comprehension

Grade __3__
Ceiling Item __20__

SKILL CATEGORY	Number of Items Attempted (Table 21)	Average Number of Errors (Table 21)	Student's Number of Errors (Page 9)	Weak[a]	Skill Status Average[b]	Strong[c]
Literal Comprehension	7	1-2	3	(W)	A	S
Inferential Comprehension	5	1-3	5	(W)	A	S

[a]Student's Number of Errors is greater than the Average Number of Errors.
[b]Student's Number of Errors is equal to (or within the range of) the Average Number of Errors.
[c]Student's Number of Errors is less than the Average Number of Errors.

Figure 2.7 (Continued)

range of intellectual functioning. His overall score of 107 +/− 5.5 places him at the 68th percentile, indicating that he is functioning at a level equal to or greater than that of 68% of students of the same age. Furthermore, his Verbal, Performance, and Index scores are quite consistent, ranging from 104 to 111, and are all in the average range. Thus, Michael's verbal/language skills as well as his nonverbal reasoning skills and ability to organize visual information are uniformly developed. It should be noted that *all* subtests scores were in the average range or above. Thus, deficits in memory as well as language skills were not indicated.

A closer examination of Michael's results shows relative strengths on two subtests, Similarities and Picture Arrangement, with scores in the high average range and at the 95th percentile. This pattern of scores in conjunction with his performance on the other subtests indicates well-developed verbal reasoning skills, social comprehension skills, and visual sequencing skills as compared to his overall cognitive profile *and* in comparison to the skills of his peers. Michael demonstrated strong language skills and the ability to reason through situations that were presented verbally. He showed an ability to handle abstractions as well. Specifically, he was able to verbalize how two objects or concepts were alike and to resolve various social situations that were presented to him. These results are consistent with his talkative and verbal nature during the test session. Although his ability to define words was slightly below his level of verbal reasoning, the difference was not statistically significant. He also demonstrated strengths in organizing visual information, especially when sequence or order (temporal or serial) was emphasized.

Michael's performance on the K-TEA/NU was more variable and at a lower level, with subtest scores ranging from below average to average. His Reading, Mathematics, and battery composites of 84, 103, and 89, respectively, are 6 to 25 points lower than his WISC-III FSIQ. Using the state discrepancy criteria in comparing ability and achievement, the 25-point discrepancy between the Reading composite and the WISC-III Full Scale score is not only statistically significant but also considered a severe discrepancy. Thus, Michael meets this criterion for possible placement in a special education program for students with learning disabilities.

Michael's overall battery composite score of 89 is at the upper end of the below average range, while his Reading composite score of 84 is significantly lower than his Mathematics composite score of 103. Thus, his overall reading skills are at a significantly lower level than his mathematics skills. His reading skills indicate below average development, which is consistent with the reports of his teachers and the results of the California Achievement Test. Mathematics skills, however, are in the average range, and again consistent with teachers' reports.

A further analysis of the K-TEA/NU results reveals that Michael's word recognition skills (reading decoding) and reading comprehension skills are equally developed in the below average range at approximately the 2nd-grade level or one year below current grade placement. An analysis of Michael's pattern of errors (error analysis) in Reading Decoding and Spelling indicates considerable difficulty with phonics skills. Two skills categories show average development and no categories show strong development. Specific areas of weakness include single/double consonants, especially in reading decoding, and vowel digraphs/diphthongs in spelling. For example, he was unable to pronounce such words as *knife* (*k nif*) and *powder* (*power*) and to spell such words as *because* (*be cuse*) and *ocean* (*o cen*). Difficulties are also indicated in both literal and inferential comprehension of reading passages. Thus, Michael is experiencing difficulty in pronouncing new words as well as in understanding the meaning of the words he does read.

In the mathematics area his understanding of arithmetic problems, including arithmetic reasoning and his computational skills, show average development, which is consistent with his performance on the WISC-III Arithmetic subtest and the comments of his teachers. The error analysis reveals average development in six skills categories and strong development in three other categories. Areas of weakness include solving problems requiring the use of fractions and problems requiring multiplication. In both areas, Michael's class has only recently been introduced to these concepts, so his weaker performance on such problems is to be expected.

Behavioral observations in the classroom and during the testing session were consistent. Although Michael was off task on occasion, he was not off task excessively. In addition, these occurrences were usually when the subject matter focused on tasks that were somewhat difficult for him (reading and spelling). Based on these observations and on interviews with Michael's teachers and mother, a further examination of possible ADHD does not seem warranted.

Summary

Michael M. was referred for evaluation by his 3rd-grade teacher. Major referral questions included: Is Michael performing at an academic level consistent with his cognitive ability? Are learning problems present, specifically in the areas of reading, memory, and language skills? Is his level of distractibility and off-task behavior excessive?

Michael was observed in the classroom and was evaluated with the WISC-III and K-TEA/NU. While some off-task behavior was observed, it was not excessive and did not deviate significantly from that of his peers. During the test session Michael was very talkative and cooperative. His overall level of cognitive functioning is solidly in the average range with strengths in verbal reasoning and visual sequencing skills. All subtest scores were in the average range or higher. Academically, Michael is performing at a level consistent with grade-level placement in arithmetic. His reading skills, both decoding skills and comprehension skills, are considerably less well developed and reflect a severe discrepancy between cognitive ability and reading performance. Thus, Michael meets one of the criteria for possible placement in a program for students with learning disabilities. His memory and language skills show average development.

Recommendations

1. Since Michael does meet one criterion for possible learning disabilities placement, the child study team should consider this option.
2. Regardless of program placement, Michael needs specialized intervention focusing on his less well-developed reading decoding and reading comprehension skills. Michael exhibited deficits in several phonics areas, including pronouncing words with single and double consonants and words with vowel digraphs and diphthongs. In addressing these areas of weakness, both a visual and a verbal presentation of material is suggested. Michael's visual sequencing skills are well developed. Combining this strength with a traditional verbal/ auditory approach to phonics instruction may be more effective. The use of color-coding techniques in presenting word parts may also be of benefit.
3. Michael, like most students, seems to perform at a higher level in one-on-one or small-group settings. Therefore, these settings should be utilized as much as possible. An example of this is having an older student provide tutoring in specific reading areas (with appropriate supervision).

4. Michael's off-task behavior occurred most often when he was engaged in tasks that were difficult for him. He also returned to task when his teacher was in close proximity or redirected him to the task at hand. When difficult subject matter is being presented, it would be helpful for the classroom teacher to monitor his behavior closely and to be nearby when possible. These strategies may help prevent the occurrence or escalation of off-task behavior.

Douglas K. Smith, PhD, NCSP
Examiner

THE K-TEA/NU BRIEF FORM

The K-TEA/NU Brief Form is an individually administered measure of academic achievement for students in grades 1 through 12 (ages 6 years 0 months through 22 years 11 months). It is best used as a screening test and provides global scores for Reading, Mathematics, and Spelling, as well as a battery composite.

The Reading subtest consists of 52 items that measure both reading decoding and reading comprehension. The first 23 items assess letter identification skills (items 1–4) and word identification skills (items 5–23), and the next 29 items (items 24–52) assess reading comprehension skills. The reading comprehension items require the student to read a printed statement containing a command and to respond orally or gesturally.

The Spelling subtest consists of 40 items. The examiner reads each word and uses it in a sentence. The student writes the word (or spells it orally if unable to write).

The Mathematics subtest consists of 52 items that measure mathematics application skills and mathematics computation skills. The computation items (1–25) are the easier part of the subtest; the applications and concepts items (items 26–52) are presented orally with visual stimuli.

The K-TEA/NU Brief Form was conormed with the Comprehensive Form and the PIAT-R, WRMT-R, and the KeyMath-R. The content is totally separate from the Comprehensive Form, while the mean correlation between the two instruments is .92. Thus, they could be used in a test-retest format (e.g., in student reevaluations). There is, however, considerable overlap in content

≡Rapid Reference 2.21

Average K-TEA/NU Brief Form Reliability

Subtests and Battery Composite	Split-Half Reliability (grades 1–12)	Test-Retest Reliability	
		Grades 1–6	Grades 7–12
Mathematics	.87	.88	.85
Reading	.91	.84	.85
Spelling	.89	.90	.84
Battery composite	.95	.94	.92

with the Kaufman Assessment Battery for Children (K-ABC; Kaufman & Kaufman, 1983). Thus, the K-TEA Brief Form *should not* be used with students who are also being administered the K-ABC.

Since the K-TEA/NU Brief and Comprehensive forms were developed in tandem with each other, the original standardization procedures as well as the renorming project are the same. Likewise, the two tests are administered in similar ways. The Brief Form, however, does not offer error analysis procedures. The process for converting raw scores to standard scores is the same for both tests. The Brief Form allows for a comparison of subtest scores in the same way that the Comprehensive Form does; consequently, that procedure is not repeated here. The comparison of reading decoding skills with reading comprehension skills and the comparison of mathematics applications skills and mathematics computation skills are not possible because the two reading subtests of the Comprehensive Form are combined into one, as are the mathematics subtests.

A summary of the reliability data for the Brief Form is presented in Rapid Reference 2.21.

K-TEA Brief Form validity is demonstrated through a multistage format beginning with item development; empirical analyses of tryout versions of the test leading to final item selection; and analyses of the relationships among items and test scores in the final version and validation studies with other measures of achievement. Validation studies compared the test with the WRAT,

≡*Rapid Reference 2.22*

K-TEA/NU Brief Form

Authors: Alan S. Kaufman and Nadeen L. Kaufman
Publication Dates: 1985 (K-TEA); 1997 (K-TEA/NU)
What the Test Measures: Reading, spelling, and mathematics skills
Age Range: 6 years 0 months through 22 years 11 months
Administration Time: 10 to 35 minutes, depending on the age of the student
Qualifications of Examiners: training in educational or psychoeducational testing
Publisher: American Guidance Service
4201 Woodland Road
Circle Pines, MN 55014-1796
(800) 328-2560
www.agsnet.com
Price: Complete test kit $137.95 (2001 catalog price); $296.95 for combined Brief and Comprehensive forms

PIAT, K-ABC, and PPVT-R. Results of these studies are reported in detail in the manual for the K-TEA Brief Form and support the validity of the instrument. Rapid Reference 2.22 provides basic information on the test and its publisher.

A PREVIEW OF THE K-TEA–REVISED

The K-TEA Comprehensive Form is currently being revised and is in the tryout stage of development. Consequently, the final design of the instrument may differ from the preview presented here. The age range of the test is likely to be ages 4 years 6 months through 22 years 11 months. There will also be two forms of the test. The original five subtests will have completely new items and several new subtests will be added. The reading area will be divided into four areas: Letters, Word Reading (reading decoding for sight words), Decoding (decoding nonsense words), and Reading Comprehension. The Spelling subtest remains with all new items, and three new subtests are added: Phonological Awareness, Listening Comprehension, and Written Expression. Another new subtest, Oral Expression, will be included on Form A only. Mathematics Applications and Mathematics Computation round out the subtest array.

The error analysis feature of the K-TEA will be retained with some modification of the error categories for both reading and mathematics. In developing the test blueprint, curriculum experts were consulted in an effort to insure that the scope and sequence of items reflected the scope and sequence of skills actually taught in reading and mathematics curricula. Various domains were identified in each area and items were then developed to sample the most important domains.

The K-TEA is also being conormed with the revision of the K-ABC. Thus, it will be possible to make ability-achievement comparisons for students based on the same standardization sample. Projected release date of the revised K-TEA is 2002; as with all test development projects, the release date is tentative and may change.

📌 TEST YOURSELF 📌

1. **The K-TEA includes a subtest measuring written expression.** True or False?
2. **Subtests can be administered in any order.** True or False?
3. **Subtest starting points are based on**
   (a) grade level.
   (b) age level.
   (c) raw score on Reading Decoding.
   (d) raw score on Reading Comprehension.
4. **The discontinue rule is**
   (a) five consecutive errors.
   (b) 10 consecutive errors.
   (c) five errors in seven consecutive items.
   (d) failing every item in one unit.
5. **Responses to items requiring a verbal response (except Reading Decoding) may be in English, sign language, or another language.** True or False?
6. **Students with disabilities were included in the standardization sample.** True or False?

7. Error analysis categories for_____and_____are the same.

8. Error analysis is based on the individual student's response for
   (a) Reading Decoding.
   (b) Reading Comprehension.
   (c) Mathematics Applications.
   (d) Mathematics Computation.

9. Error analysis is based on the individual test items for Mathematics Applications and Mathematics Computation. True or False?

10. Error analysis categories for Reading Comprehension are _____ and _____.

Answers: 1. False; 2. False; 3. a; 4. d; 5. True; 6. True; 7. Reading Decoding, Spelling; 8. a; 9. True; 10. literal, inferential

Three

PEABODY INDIVIDUAL ACHIEVEMENT TEST–REVISED/NORMATIVE UPDATE

OVERVIEW

The Peabody Individual Achievement Test–Revised/Normative Update (PIAT-R/NU; Markwardt 1997) is a restandardization of the original PIAT-R, which was first published in 1989. The PIAT-R was a revision of the original PIAT, which was published in 1970 (Dunn & Markwardt 1970). Thus, the PIAT-R/NU has a 30-year history in the measurement of academic achievement. With the 1997 restandardization, the individual subtest items remained the same from the 1989 revision. The standardization sample was designed to match U.S. Bureau of the Census estimates of the population in 1994.

Description of the PIAT-R/NU

The PIAT-R and PIAT-R/NU are individually administered, normative tests of school achievement in children and adolescents and encompass the age range of 5 years 0 months to 18 years 11 months. The restandardization extended the age range to 22 years 11 months. Both age-based and grade-based norms are provided. The PIAT-R/NU consists of six subtests: General Information, Reading Recognition, Reading Comprehension, Mathematics, Spelling, and Written Expression. In addition to subtest scores, a Total Reading score and Total Test score are provided along with an optional Written Language composite. Standard scores with a mean of 100 and SD of 15 are provided for all subtests except Written Expression and for the Total Reading, Written Language, and Total Test composites. Grade equivalents, age equivalents, percentile ranks, and normal curve equivalents are also available. The Written Expression subtest produces developmental scaled scores and grade-based stanines.

The Total Reading composite is based on the scores on Reading Recognition and Reading Comprehension, while the Written Language composite is based on the scores on Spelling and Written Expression. The Total Test composite is based on the scores for all subtests except Written Expression. Rapid Reference 3.1 describes each of the subtests.

Standardization of the PIAT-R/NU

Standardization of the PIAT-R/NU took place in two distinct phases. The initial phase began in 1980 with a survey of users and led to the national stan-

≡Rapid Reference 3.1

Description of the PIAT-R/ NU Subtests

General Information	This subtest measures the student's knowledge of basic facts and his or her range of information by having the student respond orally to a question read by the examiner.
Reading Recognition	This subtest measures the student's oral reading skills, with initial items involving the recognition of sounds associated with printed letters and later items requiring the student to read words aloud.
Reading Comprehension	This subtest measures the student's understanding of what is read by having the student read a sentence silently and then choose from four pictures the one picture that best illustrates the sentence.
Mathematics	This subtest measures knowledge and application of mathematical concepts and facts through multiple-choice items.
Spelling	This subtest measures the student's ability to recognize letters from their names or sounds, and then his or her ability to recognize standard spellings by choosing the correct spelling of a word spoken by the examiner.
Written Expression	This subtest measures the student's written language skills at two levels: prewriting skills (copying and writing letters, words, and sentences from dictation) and writing skills (writing a story in response to a picture format).

Note. Adapted from Markwardt (1989, 1998).

dardization in 1986. The second phase took place in 1997 and was part of a renorming project involving four achievement batteries.

The Original Standardization

The PIAT-R was standardized on 1,563 students ranging in age from 5 years through 19 years and ranging in grade from kindergarten through grade 12. The sample was chosen to match population estimates from the U.S. Bureau of the Census in 1985. More than 90% of the students were selected from public schools; special education classes were excluded. Within each geographic region, the sample was stratified on the basis of sex, socioeconomic status, and race. The match between the sample and census data is generally within 3 percentage points. The greatest discrepancy is with parent educational level, with the divergence ranging up to 3.5% at the highest educational level. (The standardization sample was underrepresented at this level).

The Renorming Project

Renorming for the PIAT-R/NU took place during 1995 and 1996 and was part of a coordinated norming program that included the PIAT-R, Kaufman Test of Educational Achievement (K-TEA) Brief and Comprehensive Forms, KeyMath–Revised (KeyMath-R), and Woodcock Reading Mastery Tests–Revised (WRMT-R). The five instruments were linked by their common measurement for five achievement domains: word reading, reading comprehension, spelling, mathematics applications, and mathematics computation. Each student was administered one of the primary batteries (PIAT-R, K-TEA Brief, K-TEA Comprehensive, KeyMath–R, WRMT-R) along with subtests from the other instruments. Thus, each of the primary batteries was administered to approximately 20% of the standardization sample.

The sample was stratified within age/grade level by gender, geographic region, parent educational level, educational placement (non-special education, special education, gifted/talented), and race or ethnic group, based on 1994 census estimates of the population. The general match between the sample and the population estimates is very good with overall differences generally less than 3%. The greatest disparity is with geographic region, with the northeastern and western United States somewhat underrepresented and the north-central and southern areas somewhat overrepresented. Grade norms are based on 3,184 students, and age norms, including the 18–22-year-old group, are based on 3,429 individuals. On average there were 245 students per grade level. The 18–22-year-old group consisted of students (high school, 2-year colleges and 4-year colleges) and nonstudents.

A comparison of the updated norms with the original norms shows that average level of performance tends to have fallen at grades 1–3 and remained constant or increased at the high school level. Scores are more variable within each grade as compared to the PIAT-R norm sample. Below-average student performance on most subtests declined at all grade levels except kindergarten. At the same time, the greatest improvement in scores occurred on Reading Comprehension and Mathematics. These changes are discussed in much greater detail in the manual for the PIAT-R/NU.

Psychometric Characteristics

Detailed reliability and validity data are presented in the PIAT-R/NU *Manual* and are based on original PIAT-R norms. The reader is encouraged to study these data before using the test. In the meantime, I have attempted to summarize some of the more important features of those data.

Reliability

Median split-half reliability estimates and median Kuder-Richardson reliability coefficients are identical—specifically, they are by age and grade (respectively): .97 and .97 for the Total Reading composite and .99 and .98 for the Total Test composite. Split-half reliability coefficients for the subtests range from .83 to .98 by age and from .84 to .98 grade. Median Kuder-Richardson reliability coefficients for the subtests range from .87 to .98 by both age and grade. Median test-retest correlations for the composites range from .97 to .99 for a sample of students in grades K, 2, 4, 6, 8, and 10 and for a sample of students at ages 6, 8–10, 12, and 14–16. Median item response-theory coefficients for the composites by age and grade are the same: .98 and .99 for the Total Reading and Total Test composites. Median item response-theory coefficients for the subtests by age and grade, respectively, range from .96 to .98 and from .96 to .97. These data demonstrate that the PIAT-R is a stable measure of achievement. See Rapid Reference 3.2 for specific test-retest reliabilities.

≡Rapid Reference 3.2

Median PIAT-R Reliability

Composites and Subtests	Split-Half Reliability		Test-Retest Reliability		Item Response-Theory Reliability	
	Age	Grade	Age	Grade	Age	Grade
Total Reading	.97	.97	.96	.95	.98	.98
Total Test	.99	.98	.96	.96	.99	.99
General Information	.94	.94	.90	.91	.97	.96
Reading Recognition	.97	.96	.96	.96	.98	.97
Reading Comprehension	.93	.92	.90	.88	.96	.96
Mathematics	.94	.94	.90	.84	.96	.96
Spelling	.95	.94	.90	.88	.97	.96

Validity

A multistage process was used to establish PIAT-R validity. This process began with a survey of users and "a formal critique of the PIAT by a panel of content experts and minority reviewers" (Markwardt 1989, p. 31). Two changes resulted: increasing the number of items per subtest and adding a measure of written expression. The content of each subtest was specified in subtest blueprints, which were developed with the assistance of subject-matter consultants. Empirical analyses of tryout versions of the test led to final item selection. Validation studies, comparing performance on the PIAT-R with the PIAT and the PPVT-R, as well as factor analytic studies, were completed. An extensive discussion of the construct and content validity of the test is included in the test manual. As Witt and colleagues (1994) note: "The reliability and validity information is impressive, although more data assessing concurrent validity need to be collected. The vast amount of research with the original edition of this test suggests that this test does what it purports to: provide a rough measure of academic competence across a number of important academic skill areas" (p. 172). Rapid Reference 3.3 provides basic information on the test and its publisher.

≡Rapid Reference 3.3

Peabody Individual Achievement Test–Revised/ Normative Update

Author: Frederick C. Markwardt Jr.

Publication Dates: 1989 (PIAT-R), 1998 (PIAT-R/NU)

What the Test Measures: Knowledge of general information, reading decoding, reading comprehension, mathematics, spelling, and written expression skills

Age Range: 5 years 0 months through 22 years 11 months

Administration Time: Approximately 60 minutes, depending on age of student

Qualification of Examiners: Training in educational or psychoeducational testing and an understanding of curricula, such as the training and understanding held by psychologists, teachers, learning specialists, counselors, social workers, and others in related professions

Publisher: American Guidance Service
4201 Woodland Road
Circle Pines, MN 55014-1796
(800) 328-2560
www.agsnet.com

Prices: Complete test kit, $309.95 (2001 catalog price)
Computer scoring program $199.95 (2001 catalog price)

HOW TO ADMINISTER THE PIAT-R/NU

As with any standardized test, the PIAT-R/NU examiner should follow closely the test administration instructions contained in the test manual. While the test is quite easy to administer, it is imperative that the examiner become familiar with the test directions and practice administration of the test before it is used in the clinical setting. Examiners should be familiar with testing procedures in general and should have experience working with students of similar age to those being evaluated. General testing procedures are reviewed in part 2 of the test manual and the examiner should study them in detail. These include establishing and maintaining rapport; following standardized procedures, including verbatim administration of subtests; providing appropriate student encouragement; avoiding cues; clinical observations of student behaviors; and providing feedback to students and parents.

The PIAT-R/NU utilizes an easel format in which test items are presented

DON'T FORGET

Order of Subtest Administration

Subtest	Easel
General Information	I
Reading Recognition	I
Reading Comprehension	II
Mathematics	III
Spelling	IV
Written Expression, Levels I and II	IV

on the student's side of the easel (except for General Information) and directions for administration and scoring guidelines are presented on the examiner's side. There are four easels used in test administration. Supplementary materials such as calculators, paper, and pencil are not permitted on the subtests; the only exception is Written Expression. For this subtest the student is supplied with a pencil, and additional lined paper can also be provided. Subtests are administered in the order of their presentation in the easels and this order should be followed closely.

For each subtest, the first page outlines the general procedure for administering the subtest, including information on the starting point and administration guidelines specific to the particular subtest. The second page gives the

≡Rapid Reference 3.4

Training Exercises, Starting Points, Basal and Ceiling Items, and Critical Range

Training Exercises Set of three sample items at the beginning of each subtest (except Level II of Written Expression) designed to teach what will be required on that subtest. *Must* be administered if starting point is item 1; *may* be administered to others if necessary to teach the expected response or to build confidence.

Starting Points The initial item to be administered in a subtest; determined by the student's raw score on the preceding subtest. For General Information *only*, the initial item is based on the student's grade level.

Basal Item The *lowest* item of the five *highest* consecutive responses.

Ceiling Item The *highest* item of the seven *lowest* consecutive responses containing five errors.

Critical Range Range of items yielding the maximum discrimination among students at a similar level of achievement. The basal item is the lower limit of the range and the ceiling item is the upper limit of the range. Only Written Expression does not utilize this procedure.

≡Rapid Reference 3.5

Procedures for Establishing Basals and Ceilings

Step 1: Test forward from the starting point item until the student makes an error.

Step 2: If the student has answered *five* consecutive items correctly, the basal has been established.

Step 3: If the student has *not* answered *five* consecutive items correctly, drop back to the item preceding the starting point and test backward until the student has answered five consecutive items correctly.

Step 4: Return to the item following the first error and resume testing forward.

Step 5: If the student makes an error on the starting point item, drop back five items and administer that item. If the student makes an error, drop back another five items until the student answers an item correctly. Then continue forward until the basal is established.

Step 6: Test forward until the student makes *five* errors in *seven* consecutive items.

Step 7: The ceiling item is the highest-numbered item in the lowest group of *seven* consecutive responses containing *five* errors.

Step 8: Use brackets ([ ]) to mark the basal and ceiling.

verbatim directions for the subtest and the *verbatim* directions for starting the subtest. The PIAT-R/NU utilizes starting points, training exercises, and basal and ceiling rules. Rapid Reference 3.4 summarizes these features, and Rapid Reference 3.5 describes the procedures for establishing basals and ceilings.

Before the PIAT-R/NU is administered, several clerical details must be handled. First, complete the biographical information on the front page of

DON'T FORGET

Subtest Starting Points

General Information Grade level of the student, indicated by the grade in a circle printed next to the starting point item

Reading Recognition Raw score on General Information

Reading Comprehension Raw score on Reading Recognition

Mathematics Raw score on Reading Comprehension

Spelling Raw score on Mathematics

Written Expression, Level I For kindergarten and 1st grade

Written Expression, Level II For grades 2–12

DON'T FORGET

Tips for Training Exercises

1. These are **always administered** if the student's suggested starting point is the **first item** in the subtest.

2. You must repeat the sequence of exercises until the student answers **all three items** correctly in **consecutive** order, or until a total of **three minutes** has passed.

3. Record the student's responses for each item and each trial.

4. When the student makes an error, you should give the correct response and say, "You made a good try, but this is the correct answer." Then explain why it is correct and repeat the item until the student responds correctly. Continue with the next item.

5. If the three minutes have elapsed and the student has not successfully completed a complete sequence of Training Exercises, move to the first subtest item. If the student did not answer any Training Exercises items correctly, do not administer the subtest and enter a raw score of zero.

6. If the student does not respond to any of the Training Exercises for a subtest (including the first subtest), go to the next subtest and administer the Training Exercises. If the student is successful on the Training Exercises for the next subtest, then administer the subtest. At the end of the test session, readminister the Training Exercises for the subtests that were skipped. If the student is successful at this point, then administer the subtest.

7. There are no Training Exercises for Written Expression, Level II.

the Combined Test Record and Written Expression Response Booklet (or more simply, the Test Record). This includes the student's name, address, telephone number, sex, grade placement or educational level, school or agency, teacher or counselor, and your name as examiner. Space is also provided for you to record the reasons for testing. Next, record the test date and student's birth date in the shaded box; enter these in order of year, month, and day. Calculate the chronological age, then round the chronological age to the year and nearest month. (If the number of days is greater than 15, add one month and drop the days. If the number of days is 15 or less, drop the days). Incorrect age calculation is the most common error made, so always double-check your calculations. When borrowing from the months column to the days column, always borrow 30 days. As a third check I usually ask the student his or her age or birthdate while we are establishing rapport, because discrepancies sometimes occur and school records may be in error or may contain conflicting information. Rapid Reference 3.6 offers pointers to completing the inside of the Record Form.

≡ Rapid Reference 3.6

Test Administration Pointers

1. **Record the student's response** for the items in each subtest except Written Expression (in which the student writes the response). In most cases, the student is giving the examiner the number of the response. Exceptions are all of the items in General Information and items 17–100 in Reading Recognition.

2. **Score responses as you go** because you must establish basal and ceiling items for each subtest.

3. **The starting point** for Reading Recognition, Reading Comprehension, Mathematics, and Spelling is the *ceiling item* for the previous subtest. See the Don't Forget box on page 79 for more details.

4. **Verbal probing of a response** is usually not needed due to the multiple-choice format of most subtests. The only exceptions are for ambiguous responses (those you are unable to score without additional information) and incomplete sentences. These are most likely to occur on General Information. Neutral statements should be used to encourage the student to elaborate upon the response. I frequently use "I'm not sure that I understand what you said," or "Tell me more about that." Do not use leading questions. Often students interpret verbal probes as an indication of an incorrect response. Therefore, I try to put the student at ease by placing the emphasis on my not understanding the response rather than any shortcomings of the response.

5. **Verbal items may be repeated** if the student indicates a need for this or does not respond. The item must be repeated in its entirety.

6. **Unlike many other tests,** the PIAT-R/NU permits the examiner to encourage students to guess on items if they are unsure of the answer. You are advised by the test author to use such comments as "Even if you aren't sure, give it a try," or "This is a hard question, but give me the best answer you can."

7. **If the student gives more** than one response to a test item or you are unsure to which test plate the student pointed, you must determine which response or plate is the one to score.

8. **You should mark the basals** and ceilings on the Record Form with brackets ([ ]) to indicate the five items forming the basal and the seven items forming the ceiling.

9. **If more than one basal or ceiling** is determined, use the highest basal and the lowest ceiling so that the critical range of items is the smallest. The additional basals or ceilings are considered false.

Subtest-by-Subtest Notes on Administration

General Information

This subtest is relatively easy to administer but differs from the others in that the student gives a verbal response, which I recommend writing in the space provided. Starting points are indicated in the margin of the Test Record and are based on the student's current grade level. Each question is read aloud and may be repeated as necessary. The response must be scored immediately in order to calculate the subtest ceiling correctly. A scoring guide is printed on the examiner's side of the easel. It gives examples of correct responses, incorrect responses, and responses to be questioned further. Although clarification of responses is permitted, I find it seldom necessary. After the ceiling is established, record the ceiling item in the shaded box on page 3, calculate the raw score, and go to the next subtest, Reading Recognition.

Reading Recognition

This subtest has two response formats. For items 1–16 the student chooses an answer from four choices either by pointing to the correct response or by saying the response number. For the remaining items the student pronounces a word aloud. The starting point for the subtest is the ceiling item from General Information; I find it helpful to circle this item prior to starting the subtest. If this starting point falls between items 1 through 16, it is suggested that you begin with item 1 because the nature of items 1–16 is different from the remainder of the items. On difficult items students may need some encouragement to respond, such as "Try it" or "Why don't you take a guess?"

I recommend recording the student's responses phonetically so that the errors can be analyzed later; the PIAT-R/NU Pronunciation Guide Cassette is included with the test materials. After the ceiling is established, record the ceiling item in the shaded box on page 4, calculate the raw score, and go to the next subtest, Reading Comprehension.

Reading Comprehension

This subtest is administered only to students receiving a raw score of at least 18 on Reading Recognition. For students with Reading Recognition raw scores of less than 18, go to the Mathematics subtest and administer it. The Reading Comprehension subtest begins with item 19, and all students starting with this item are administered the Training Exercises. Once again, I circle the starting point prior to beginning the subtest. On this subtest, each item consists of two test plates, the first showing a printed sentence and the second showing four pictures. The student is shown the first plate and reads the sentence silently. Then the examiner shows the second plate and the student points to the correct picture or says its number. The student is to read the sentence only once, so you will need to monitor this. Also, once the plate of pictures is shown, the student cannot return to the sentence plate. The examiner *does not read* the sentence to the student. After the ceiling is established, record the ceiling item in the shaded box on page 5, calculate the raw score, and proceed to the next subtest, Mathematics.

Mathematics

For this subtest you read aloud the questions for all items and the student points to the correct response or gives you its number. Although pointing instructions are provided for the first 30 items, students may point to the correct response on all items. The starting point for this subtest is the student's raw score on Reading Comprehension. After the ceiling is established, record the ceiling item in the shaded box on page 6, calculate the raw score, and proceed to the next subtest, Spelling.

Spelling

The starting point for this subtest is the student's raw score on Mathematics. For students whose starting point is between 1 and 15, it is recommended that you begin with item 1; in this case, you would also administer the Training Exercises. As with the previous subtest, you read aloud all items that are administered and the student points to the correct response or says its number. For items 16–100, you say the stimulus word, read the sentence aloud, and then repeat the stimulus word. The pronunciation for each stimulus word can be heard on the Pronunciation Guide Cassette that comes with the test materials. After the ceiling is established, record the ceiling item in the shaded box on page 7, calculate the raw score, and proceed to the next subtest, Written Expression (levels I and II).

Written Expression

Level I. Level I is given to students in kindergarten and grade 1. The starting point is having the student write his or her name. All responses are written in the Written Expression Response Booklet, pages 12–16 in the Record Form. Unlike the other subtests, this subtest does not utilize basals and ceilings. After the student writes his or her name, you must score the item in order to determine the next item to be given. If eight correct letters are written consecutively, the next item is item 4. If fewer than eight correct letters are written consecutively, the Training Exercises are administered next. Detailed scoring guidelines are presented on the examiner's side of the easel. Testing continues through the final item but may be discontinued if the student has excessive difficulty on items 9–18. Unlike other subtests, this subtest is scored after the testing is completed, using Appendix A.1 of the manual for this process.

Level II. Level II is given to students in grades 2–12. This subtest uses two picture prompts that are interchangeable. You show the prompt and the student writes a story about it. There is a time limit of 20 minutes. If the space in the Written Expression Response Booklet is insufficient, you will need to provide additional lined paper. Unlike other subtests, this subtest is scored after the testing is completed and uses Appendix A.2 of the manual for this process.

SCORING THE INDIVIDUAL TEST RECORD

The PIAT-R/NU produces raw scores for each subtest, the Total Reading composite, and the Total Test composite. Raw scores reflect the number of points earned by the student on each subtest. These scores are meaningless by themselves because they are not norm-based. They are, therefore, converted to a variety of derived scores, including grade equivalents, age equivalents, standard scores, stanines, and percentile ranks. Standard scores are norm-based scores and allow us to compare the individual student's performance with that of other students. The PIAT-R/NU standard scores have a mean of 100 and SD of 15. The range of standard scores for the subtests and composites is 55–145. The scores produced by the PIAT-R/NU are summarized on pages 10 and 11 of the Test Record.

Step-by-Step Scoring of the PIAT-R/NU

As you have seen, scoring the individual test items is facilitated by the dichotomous nature of the items. Since you have already scored the items on all subtests except Written Expression, I suggest that you double-check the scoring before transferring the raw scores to page 10 of the Record Form. Then score Written Expression and transfer the raw score to page 10 of the Record Form.

Raw Scores

Prior to transferring the raw scores to page 10 of the Test Record, enter the student's name and testing date at the top of the page. Then indicate the grade placement and chronological age on the left side of the page. Next, transfer the raw scores for each subtest to the appropriate box in the column under the heading "Raw Scores" on page 10. For the Total Reading raw score, add the Reading Recognition and Reading Comprehension raw scores and enter the total in the shaded box. For the Total Test raw score, add the raw scores for General Information, Reading Recognition, Reading Comprehension, Mathematics, and Spelling and enter the total in the shaded box.

All scores have error associated with them and it is standard practice to create bands of error or confidence interval around individual scores. The PIAT-R/NU allows flexibility in creating such bands, and you may choose from the 68%, 90%, and 95% confidence levels. My recommendation is to use the 95% confidence level. The PIAT-R/NU applies this principle not only to the derived scores but also to the raw scores.

To the left of the Raw Scores column is a column by subtest and composite that is used to construct the confidence level for raw scores. This column allows you to determine the standard error of measurement (SEM) value by confidence level (68%, 90%, or 95%) based on the student's age (5–13 or 14–18+) or grade (K–7 or 8–12+). The precise SEMs are found in Tables 6.14 and 6.15 of the manual. I find the values on the Scores page to be sufficient. Circle the SEM corresponding to the confidence level you select and the age or grade of the student you have evaluated. Then subtract this number from the subtest raw score for the –SEM value and add it to the subtest raw score for the +SEM value. Figure 3.1 shows the completion of this part of the Scores page.

Derived Scores

The next step in completing the Scores page is to complete the Derived Scores summary. You can determine either grade or age equivalents; standard scores by either grade (for fall, winter, or spring) or age; and percentile ranks. If comparisons are being made to a cognitive ability measure, you should choose age-based standard scores and not grade-based standard scores. Rapid References

Scores

Norms used: ☐ Updated ☐ Original

Student's name ___Sandra___

Testing date ___10|2|00___

	RAW SCORES	DERIVED SCORES		

Grade Placement __3.3__
Chronological Age __8-5__

95 % confidence

Derived Scores headers:
- Grade Equivalents ☒ / Age Equivalents ☐ (Table G.1 or G.3) — 95 % confidence
- Standard Scores ☐ Grade(G.2) F W S / ☒ Age(G.4) (circle one) — 95 % confidence [3]
- Percentile Ranks (Table G.5) — 95 % confidence

Written Expression
☐ Level I
☒ Level II, Prompt Ⓐ B (circle one)

Subtest	Raw Scores (68% / 90% / 95%)	Grade Equivalents (−SEM / / +SEM)	Standard Scores (−SEM / / +SEM)	Percentile Ranks (−SEM / / +SEM)
General Information (K–7/5–13: 3,3,④ ; 8–12/14–18: 2,3,4)	39 / 45 / 51	2.9 / 3.4 / 3.9	103 / 109 / 114	58 / 73 / 82
Reading Recognition (K–12/5–18: 2,3,④)	41 / 45 / 49	2.6 / 2.9 / 3.2	102 / 105 / 109	55 / 63 / 73
Reading Comprehension (/5–6: 4,7,8 ; K–12/7–18: 3,5,⑥)	47 / 53 / 59	3.1 / 3.3 / 4.7	102 / 111 / 118	55 / 77 / 88
TOTAL READING [1] (1–12/5–18: 4,7,⑧ ; K/16–18: 5,6)	90 / 98 / 106	2.8 / 3.1 / 3.4	104 / 108 / 111	61 / 70 / 77
Mathematics (K–4/5–9: 2,3,④ ; 5–12/10–18: 3,5,6)	41 / 45 / 49	3.8 / 4.1 / 4.3	113 / 116 / 119	81 / 86 / 90
Spelling (K–6/5–17: 2,3,④ ; 7–12/18: 3,5,6)	37 / 41 / 45	2.2 / 2.5 / 2.9	93 / 98 / 104	32 / 45 / 61
TOTAL TEST [2] (K–8/5–14: 8,10,⑫ ; 9–12/15–18: 5,8,9)	217 / 229 / 241	3.0 / 3.2 / 3.4	104 / 107 / 110	61 / 68 / 75

Written Expression box:
- **Raw Score** 30
- **Grade-based Stanine** 5 (Levels I and II) (Table G.6 or G.7)
- **Developmental Scaled Score** 6 (Level II only) (Table G.8)

WRITTEN LANGUAGE COMPOSITE

Spelling Raw Score	Written Expression Raw Score
41	30
↓	↓
4	6
Scaled Score (Table I.1 or I.7)	Scaled Score (Table I.1 or I.7)

4 + 6

Scaled Score Sum 10

Standard Score
☐ Grade (Table I.2 or I.8) F W S (circle one)
☒ Age (Table I.3 or I.9) 95 % confidence (I.4 or I.10)

90 / 98 / 106 (−SEM / / +SEM)

Percentile Rank
25 / 45 / 66 (−SEM / / +SEM) (Table G.5)

[1] The Total Reading composite raw score is the sum of the Reading Recognition and Reading Comprehension subtest raw scores.
[2] The Total Test composite raw score is the sum of the General Information, Reading Recognition, Reading Comprehension, Mathematics, and Spelling subtest raw scores. Do not include the Total Reading composite raw score.
[3] Values to be used in the standard score confidence intervals are given in Appendix H of the manual.

PERFORMANCE EVALUATION

Rapport:	(Excellent)	Average	Poor
Need for Praise:	Extreme	(Average)	Negligible
Attention Span:	Long	(Average)	Short
Anxiety:	(Relaxed)	Average	Tense

Cooperativeness:	Antagonistic	Average	(Obliging)
Persistence:	Minimal	(Average)	Persevering
Decisiveness:	(Confident)	Average	Indecisive
Assertiveness:	Timid	(Average)	Forceful

Record observations about the subject, incidents that occurred during testing, or other factors that might have an effect on the validity or the interpretation of these PIAT-R results:

_____
_____
_____
_____

Figure 3.1 Completed Scores Page for Sandra

Note: Peabody Individual Achievement Test-Revised/Normative Update (PIAT-R/NU): Combined Test Record & Written Expression Response Booklet © 1990 AGS

3.7, 3.8, and 3.9 outline the steps in obtaining derived scores. Figure 3.1 shows a completed Scores page for Sandra.

The final step in the process is to calculate the derived scores for the Written Expression subtest and the Written Language composite. This involves completing the Written Expression box on the right side of the Scores page.

Rapid Reference 3.7

Steps for Obtaining Grade and Age Equivalents

1. Select grade equivalents or age equivalents and check the appropriate box. Indicate the confidence interval, which should be the same as that used for raw scores.
2. Convert raw scores to grade equivalents using Table G.1 and to age equivalents using Table G.2.
3. Subtests and composites are listed across Tables G.1 and G.2 in order of their listing on the Scores page. Under each subtest or composite find the raw score. The shaded column on the left shows the appropriate grade equivalent or age equivalent. Record the appropriate score in the box on the Scores page.
4. Confidence intervals for grade and age equivalents are obtained from the raw score intervals. For each subtest or composite, take the raw score for the lower limit and the raw score for the upper limit and repeat step 3 for each score.

Rapid Reference 3.8

Steps for Obtaining Standard Scores

1. Decide whether you want grade-based standard scores or age-based standard scores and check the appropriate box.
2. If using grade-based standard scores, you will be using Tables G.2a for fall norms (September–November testing), G.2b for winter norms (December–February testing), and G.2c for spring norms (March–June testing). Check the Grade box and indicate the confidence interval (68%, 90%, or 95%).
3. If using age-based standard scores, you will be using Table G.4. Check the Age box and indicate the confidence interval (68%, 90%, or 95%).
4. The grade-based tables and age-based tables are set up the same way. Subtests and composites are listed across the table in the same order as on the Scores page. Under each subtest or composite, the raw scores are listed. Locate the raw score for each subtest and composite, read across to the shaded Standard Scores column on the left or right, and record this score in the appropriate box on the Scores page.
5. Confidence levels are constructed by using Table H.1 for grade-based standard scores and Table H.2 for age-based standard scores. For each grade or age level, the table provides the value from which you will subtract and then add to the score you recorded in step 4. Subtests and composites are listed across the table in the same order as on the Scores page. Locate the appropriate grade or age (listed in the first column), then read across on the line corresponding to the 68%, 90%, or 95% confidence level. For each subtest and composite subtract this value from the score in step 4 for the lower limit, and add this value to the score in step 4 for the upper limit.

≡ Rapid Reference 3.9

Steps for Obtaining Percentile Ranks

1. Indicate the confidence level in the space provided. This should be the same as that used for the standard scores.
2. You will be using Table G.5 for this score conversion. This table also provides stanines and normal curve equivalents.
3. The table has four columns: Standard Score, Percentile Rank, Stanine, and Normal Curve Equivalent. Enter the table with the standard scores previously obtained for each subtest and composite. Read across to the Percentile Rank column and record this number in the appropriate box on the Scores page.
4. Confidence intervals are calculated by taking the lower limit and upper limit standard scores for each subtest and composite and repeating step 3.

≡ Rapid Reference 3.10

Procedure for Calculating Stanines and Developmental Scale Scores for the Written Expression Subtest

1. Indicate level administered (I or II) and prompt used if Level II (A or B).
2. Record raw score in the appropriate box.
3. Determine grade-based stanine by using Table G.6 (Level I) or Table G.7 (Level II). The stanines are listed in the first column and the grade of the student is listed across the table. Enter the column corresponding to the grade of the student and season of testing if in kindergarten. Read down the column until you find the raw score. Then read across the row to the stanine score in first column.
4. For Level II, the procedure is the same as outlined in step 3. Use the Table for Prompt A or for Prompt B.
5. Developmental scaled scores are located in Table G.8. The scaled score is in the first column. Enter the table for Prompt A or Prompt B. Locate the raw score the student received and read across the row to the Developmental Scaled Score column on the left.

Indicate the level administered and which prompt was used for Level II, then record the raw score in the appropriate box. The derived scores obtained from the raw score and are grade-based stanines and developmental scaled scores.

Stanines range from 1 to 9 and have an SD of 2. The grade-based stanine scores for Written Expression are determined by grade (K or 1 through 12) and, for kindergarten only, time of testing (fall for September through January testing and spring for February through June testing). These scores provide a rough estimate of achievement levels.

Developmental scaled scores are provided for Level II only and are more precise and "describe the individual's performance in relation to the full range of scores in the standardization sample" (*PIAT-R/NU Manual*, p. 21). This metric uses a 15-point scale with a mean of 8 and SD of approximately 3. Performance equal to the mean or average of all students in the sample for Level II is a scaled score of 8. Rapid Reference 3.10 outlines the procedure for obtaining stanines and developmental scaled scores.

≋ Rapid Reference 3.11

Calculating the Written Language Composite

1. Transfer the raw scores for Spelling and Written Expression to the appropriate boxes.
2. Using Table I.1 for Spelling and I.7 for Written Expression, convert the raw scores to scaled scores and enter them in the appropriate boxes.
3. Add these two scaled scores and record the result in the appropriate box.
4. Determine whether you want the standard score for the composite to be grade based or age based. Your decision should be consistent with the other standard scores for subtests and composites. Check the box corresponding to your choice. For grade-based scores, also indicate the time of testing (fall, winter, or spring).
5. Determine the confidence interval. Again, this should be consistent with your choices on the other subtests and composites.
6. Convert the scaled score sum to a standard score for grade-based scores using Table I.2 (K–grade 1) or I.8 (grades 2–12).
7. Convert the scaled score sum to a standard score based on age using Table I.3 (K–grade 1) or I.9 (grades 2–12).
8. Construct the confidence intervals for grade-based scores using Table I.4 and for age-based scores using Table I.10. Round the value obtained based on the student's grade or age and the confidence level (68%, 90%, or 95%). Then subtract from the standard score for the lower limit and add to the standard score for the upper limit.
9. Table G.5 can be used to determine percentile rank and confidence interval or normal curve equivalent and confidence interval.

The Written Language composite is calculated from the Spelling and Written Expression raw scores; Rapid Reference 3.11 outlines this procedure.

At the bottom of the Scores page is a Performance Evaluation. This allows you to evaluate the student's behavior on a number of dimensions (rapport, need for praise, attention span, anxiety, cooperativeness, persistence, decisiveness, and assertiveness). I strongly recommend completing this rating scale and adding other specific behaviors you may have observed. It helps tremendously in interpreting the student's scores.

HOW TO INTERPRET THE PIAT-R/NU

Interpreting the PIAT-R/NU largely involves completing the Profiles page of the Test Record. This page allows for comparison of the Developmental Score Profile (grade equivalent or age equivalent scores) and the Standard Score Profile (either grade-based with fall, winter, or spring norms, or age-based). There is also a space to record data from other tests and to record recommendations.

Developmental Scores

The first decision you must make is whether to plot the developmental scores. These scores are less precise than standard scores but may be easier for parents to understand. If you choose to plot these scores, the next decision is whether to use grade or age equivalents. *You may plot only one type of score on the Profiles page.* For most students the two sets of scores will be similar—the only difference is when a student is significantly older or younger than other students in the same grade. The steps for plotting either set of scores are the same and are outlined in Rapid Reference 3.12.

Standard Scores

The second decision you must make is whether to complete the Standard Score Profile. Since these are the most precise scores and utilize the same metric as scores from ability tests, I recommend completing this profile. Once again there is a choice of grade-based or age-based standard scores; if comparisons are to be made with an ability test score, use the age-based standard scores because ability tests also utilize this type. As with the Developmental Score Profile, the use of grade-based or age-based scores will produce similar

☰ Rapid Reference 3.12

Steps for Plotting Developmental Scores

Step 1: Decide whether you will plot grade-based or age-based scores and indicate your decision in the appropriate box.

Step 2: For each subtest, shade the interval between the lower and upper limit confidence intervals.

Step 3: If using grade-based scores, locate the student's current grade placement on the grade scale line above the profile and draw a vertical line through the profile corresponding to the current grade placement.

Step 4: If using age-based scores, locate the student's chronological age on the age scale line below the profile and draw a vertical line through the profiles corresponding to the student's age.

Step 5: Shaded intervals above the grade-placement or age lines represent areas of performance above that of the average student at that grade or age level.

Step 6: Shaded intervals below the grade-placement or age lines represent areas of performance below that of the average student at that grade or age level.

results unless the student is significantly older or younger than other students in the same grade. Once again, *you can plot only one type of score—grade-based or age-based*. The steps for plotting both sets of scores are the same and are outlined in Rapid Reference 3.13.

Subtest and Composite Comparisons

The profiles you have generated allow for comparisons among the subtests and the composite scores. For both profiles, the confidence interval for each subtest and composite were shaded. This allows us to determine if there are real differences among scores. By comparing the degree of overlap between the scores we can determine the likelihood of significant differences. As the box on the Profiles page and the test manual indicate, a rough rule of thumb is that

• Score intervals overlapping by more than half are *unlikely* to show real differences.

≡ *Rapid Reference 3.13*

Steps for Plotting Standard Scores

Step 1: Decide whether you will be plotting age-based or grade-based standard scores and indicate your choice in the appropriate box.

Step 2: If you are using grade-based standard scores, indicate fall, winter, or spring norms.

Step 3: For each subtest score, shade the confidence interval between the lower and upper limits.

Step 4: If you are using age-based standard scores and an ability or IQ score is available, draw a vertical line through the profile corresponding to that score.

Step 5: Draw a vertical line through the profile corresponding to the norm-group mean of 100.

≡ *Rapid Reference 3.14*

Range of Scores that are Statistically Significant for Subtest Comparisons, by Grade Level

| | Significance Level | |
Grade Level	.05	.01
K	15–23	18–27
1	12–14	14–18
2	12–15	14–17
3	12–18	14–21
4	13–16	15–19
5	14–18	16–21
6	14–17	15–19
7	14–18	16–21
8	10–15	12–18
9	11–16	13–19
10	14–18	16–20
11	14–19	17–22
12	12–16	14–19

- Score intervals overlapping by half or less are *possibly* showing real differences.
- Score intervals with no overlap are *probably* showing real differences.

A much better approach, however, is to use Appendix H of the test manual to determine statistically whether standard scores are significantly different from each other, and if so, the frequency of such differences occurring in the standardization sample. Tables H.3 and H.4 in the test manual list the minimum score difference between pairs of subtests needed for statistical significance at the .05 and .01 levels by grade and age. For each comparison, subtract the lower score from the higher score and determine whether the resulting difference is equal to or larger than the value listed at the .05 or .01 level. If it is, then the difference is significant at that significance level and is unlikely to have occurred by chance. Rapid Reference 3.14 and 3.15 provide the range of scores that are significant by grade and age, respectively.

While a difference in pairs of scores may be statistically significant and important for the individual, the difference may not be unusual or infrequent. Many other students may have such a profile. Tables H.5 and H.6 in the test manual allow us to determine this. For each combination of subtests the tables provide the minimum value that occurred in 16% or less, 10% or less, 5% or less, 2% or less, and 1% or less of the standardization sample. Rapid Reference 3.16 shows the average value across all subtest combinations at the various frequency levels.

Which comparisons are the most relevant? I always compare the Reading Recognition and Reading Comprehension scores because these two subtests measure distinctly different

=Rapid Reference 3.15

Range of Scores that are Statistically Significant for Subtest Comparisons, by Age Level

	Significance Level	
Age Level	.05	.01
5	15–22	14–26
6	11–16	13–19
7	10–15	12–17
8	11–15	13–17
9	09–13	11–15
10	11–16	13–15
11	11–16	13–18
12	14–16	17–19

≡Rapid Reference 3.16

Average Minimum Score Difference Indicating Unusual Scatter in Subtest Comparisons, by Grade and Age Levels

	Average Minimum Score Difference	
Occurrence in Sample	By Grade Level	By Age Level
16% or less	17	16
10% or less	21	19
5% or less	26	23
2% or less	31	29
1% or less	35	32

aspects of the reading process. While some students are great at decoding skills and have a large basic sight vocabulary, other students excel at the understanding of what they read, and vice versa. Of course, some students show well-developed skills in both areas or weaknesses in both areas. I also compare the Spelling and Reading Recognition scores because both are heavily related to phonetic skills. To determine whether basic areas of achievement show equivalent or variable development, I compare General Information with the Reading subtests and the Mathematics subtest. Although the other comparisons are also important, I usually begin with those that I have described.

Comparisons with Ability Measures

In assessing possible learning problems in students, we often want to make comparisons with ability measures. While the PIAT-R/NU was not conormed with an ability test, the correlation of the PIAT-R/NU has been explored with many popular ability tests. Such information is needed to determine whether differences in scores are statistically significant. Many states use a regression formula to make such comparisons in determining eligibility for programs for students with learning disabilities. A table of correlations between the PIAT-R/NU and selected intelligence tests is presented in Rapid Reference 3.17; these data are in-

═Rapid Reference 3.17

Correlations between the PIAT-R/ NU and Selected Intelligence Tests

	PIAT-R/NU		
Intelligence Test	**Total Reading**	**Mathematics**	**Spelling**
K-ABC Mental Processing composite	.65	.58	.35
K-ABC Nonverbal Scale	.36	.40	.28
KAIT Fluid Scale	.36	.40	.28
KAIT composite	.65	.58	.35
DAS General Conceptual Ability	.65	.58	.35
DAS Special Nonverbal composite	.36	.40	.28
Stanford-Binet Intelligence Scale: Fourth Edition composite	.65	.58	.35
WJ-R Broad Cognitive Ability composite	.65	.58	.35
WISC-III Verbal Scale IQ	.65	.58	.35
WISC-III Performance Scale IQ	.36	.40	.28
WISC-III Full Scale IQ	.65	.58	.35
WAIS-III Verbal Scale IQ	.65	.58	.35
WAIS-III Performance Scale IQ	.36	.40	.28
WAIS-III Full Scale IQ	.65	.58	.35

Note. K-ABC = Kaufman Assessment Battery for Children; KAIT = Kaufman Adolescent and Adult Intelligence Test; DAS = Differential Ability Scales; WJ-R = Woodcock-Johnson Psychoeducational Battery–Revised; WISC-III = Wechsler Intelligence Scale for Children–Third Edition; WAIS-III = Wechsler Adult Intelligence Scale–Third Edition.

Source. AGS.

≡Rapid Reference 3.18

Reviews of the PIAT, PIAT-R, and PIAT-R/NU

Allinder & Fuchs (1992)

Bartels (1998–99)

Benes (1992)

Costenbader & Adams (1991)

Edwards (1989)

Lazarus, McKenna, & Lynch (1989–90)

Luther (1992)

Riccio (1992)

Rogers (1992)

Salvia & Ysseldyke (2001)

Witt, Elliott, Kramer, & Gresham (1994)

corporated into the computer scoring program for the PIAT-R/NU and were made available by the publisher.

STRENGTHS AND WEAKNESSES OF THE PIAT-R/NU

The PIAT, PIAT-R, and PIAT-R/NU have been in use for more than 30 years. Consequently, there have been many reviews of the test and many studies of its relationship to other measures of achievement. Rapid Reference 3.18 presents a list of reviews of the PIAT-R/NU and its earlier editions.

In this section I summarize my view of the major strengths and weaknesses of the test. In so doing I focus on these specific areas: test development, standardization, administration and scoring, reliability, validity, and interpretation. This information is summarized in Rapid References 3.19–3.21.

Summary of PIAT-R/NU Strengths and Weaknesses

This summary of the strengths and weaknesses of the PIAT-R/NU is drawn from the formal reviews listed in Rapid Reference 3.18 as well as from my own experience with the instrument as a practitioner and university trainer. Feedback from practitioners in a variety of areas has also contributed to my analysis of the instrument.

As with most tests, the PIAT-R/NU is not as precise in measuring its constructs at the youngest and oldest age ranges, particularly with individuals considerably above or below average in the construct; Rapid References 3.20 and 3.21 document this. The test is designed to cover the standard score range of 55 to 145 at all age ranges. As with most (if not all) tests, this coverage occurs in the middle age ranges rather than at the ends of the continuum. For the stu-

≡Rapid Reference 3.19

Strengths and Weaknesses of the PIAT-R/ NU

Strengths	Weaknesses
Test Development	
The rationale for item selection using curriculum consultants and feedback from users of the original PIAT	Insufficient number of "easy" items for five year olds
Easel format for presenting subtest items	Lack of formal error analysis procedures
Use of a multiple-choice format, minimizing reliance on verbal expression skills	
Representation of various gender, cultural, and socioeconomic backgrounds	
Standardization	
Inclusion of students receiving special-education services	Not all students in the normative update standardization took all five batteries
Very detailed information on standardization procedures and sample	Lower number of students in normative update sample than in original standardization
Overall standardization procedures considered a strength by test reviewers	Test items not updated in normative update
Both the original and normative update samples are appropriate match to census data	
Expanded age range to 22 years	

(continued)

dent considerably below average in achievement, the floor of the test is insufficient at ages 5 years 0 months through 6 years 5 months. At the other end of the continuum (i.e., for the student considerably above average in achievement), the ceiling of the test is insufficient for the General Information and Reading Comprehension subtests at ages 18 years 0 months through 22 years 11 months. Composite scores remain strong at these levels, however.

Strengths	Weaknesses
Administration and Scoring	
User-friendly layout of test protocol	Need to score each subtest in order to determine starting point for next subtest
Consistent starting points for all subtests (raw score from preceding subtest)	Two levels (depending on grade) for Written Expression subtest
Same basal and ceiling rules for all subtests	Written Expression not included in Total Test score
Training exercises on most subtests	Lack of formal error analysis system
Dichotomous scoring of test items	
Easel format of the test	
Both age and grade norms	
Reliability	
High median split-half reliabilities of subtests and composites	Reliability studies not updated with the updated norms
Test-retest reliabilities exceeding .95 for composites and .84 for subtests	Limited number of students in test-retest reliability studies
	Low interrater reliability estimates for Written Expression subtest
Validity	
Strong face validity based on use of curriculum consultants and subtest blueprints	Lack of current validity studies with updated norms
Factor analytic data supportive of test's validity	Limited number of validity studies with other achievement tests

There are many strengths with the PIAT-R/NU: the theoretical base for the test; the Normative Update standardization sample, with its inclusion of students with disabilities; the multiple-choice format of the test, which lends itself to use with students with certain types of disabilities; the reliabilities of the subtests and composites; the ease of administration; and the linking of the test with other achievement measures in the updated standardization. As with any test, there are also weaknesses, and these include the lack of current validity studies with the updated norms as well as the PIAT-R edition; the relatively low

Strengths	Weaknesses
Interpretation	
Interpretability of both composites and subtests due to high reliability data	Insufficient floor for 5-year-olds with below average academic skills
Includes tables showing statistically significant differences between subtests	Lack of formal error analysis procedures and norms
Includes tables showing percentage of occurrence in standardization sample of statistically significant differences between subtest scores	
Cross linking with K-TEA/NU, WRMT-R/NU, KeyMath–R/NU	
Successive-level approach to interpretation is familiar to examinees	

interrater reliability of the Written Expression subtest; the need to score the test as you administer it in order to determine the starting point for the next subtest; and the lack of formal error analysis procedures.

CLINICAL APPLICATIONS OF THE PIAT-R/NU

Since the original publication of the PIAT, numerous studies have compared performances on the PIAT with those on other measures of achievement, including the K-TEA, WRAT-R, WRAT 3, WIAT, and others. Rapid Reference 3.27 provides references for some of these studies, the majority of which have examined its relationship with other achievement tests and its interrater reliability in scoring the Written Expression subtest. In addition, studies have examined use of the test with students referred for possible special education services, primarily due to learning disabilities.

The PIAT-R/NU and Achievement Measures

The majority of studies with the PIAT-R and PIAT-R/NU have examined its relationship with other achievement tests. For example, Slate (1996) compared

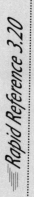

Rapid Reference 3.20

Strengths and Weaknesses of the PIAT-R/NU:
Effective Range of Subtest and Composite Scores, by Age (based on raw score of 0)

Age	General Information	Reading Recognition	Reading Comprehension	Total Reading	Mathematics	Spelling	Total Test
5/0–5/2	68	76	76	76	55	75	75
5/3–5/5	67	73	73	73	55	71	55
5/6–5/8	65	70	70	70	55	67	55
5/9–5/11	64	66	66	66	55	60	55
6/0–6/2	63	62	62	62	55	55	55
6/3–6/5	61	58	58	58	55	55	55
6/6–6/8	60	55	55	55	55	55	55
6/9–6/11	56	55	55	55	55	55	55
7/0–22/11	55	55	55	55	55	55	55

Rapid Reference 3.21

Strengths and Weaknesses of the PIAT-R/ NU: Effective Range of Subtest Scores, by Age
(based on maximum raw score)

Age	General Information	Reading Recognition	Reading Comprehension	Total Reading	Mathematics	Spelling	Total Test
5/0–14/8	145	145	145	145	145	145	145
14/9–14/11	144	145	145	145	145	145	145
15/0–15/2	142	145	145	145	145	145	145
15/3–15/5	141	145	144	145	144	145	145
15/6–15/8	141	145	143	145	143	145	145
15/9–15/11	140	145	141	145	142	145	145
16/0–16/2	140	145	139	145	141	144	145
16/3–16/5	140	145	138	145	141	143	145
16/6–16/8	140	145	137	145	140	142	145
16/9–16/11	139	145	137	145	140	142	145
17/0–17/2	139	145	137	145	140	141	145
17/3–17/5	138	145	137	145	139	141	145
17/6–17/8	138	145	137	145	139	140	145

(continued)

Age	General Information	Reading Recognition	Reading Comprehension	Total Reading	Mathematics	Spelling	Total Test
17/9–17/11	137	145	136	145	139	139	145
18/0–18/2	136	145	136	144	139	139	145
18/3–18/5	136	145	136	144	139	138	145
18/6–18/8	135	145	136	144	138	137	144
18/9–18/11	135	145	135	144	138	137	144
19/0–19/11	134	145	135	144	137	136	144
20/0–20/11	132	145	134	143	136	136	143
21/0–21/11	130	145	132	143	134	135	143
22/0–22/11	129	145	130	142	132	135	142

≡Rapid Reference 3.22

References Comparing Performance on the PIAT-R with Other Achievement Measures

Kaufman Test of Educational Achievement

Bookman & Peach (1988)

Hultquist & Metzke (1993)

Prewett & Giannuli (1991)

Shapiro & Derr (1987)

Webster & Braswell (1991)

Wide Range Achievement Test–Revised
Wide Range Achievement Test 3

Lassiter, D'Amato, Raggio, & Whitten (1994)

Prewett & Giannuli (1991)

Webster & Braswell (1991)

Wechsler Individual Achievement Test

Muenz, Ouchi, & Cole (1999)

Slate (1996)

the performance of 202 students with learning disabilities on the PIAT-R and other tests, including the WIAT, and found moderate to strong correlations among similar constructs (reading, spelling, arithmetic). Prewett and Giannuli (1991) administered the reading subtests of the PIAT-R, K-TEA, WRAT-R, and Woodcock Johnson Psychoeducational Battery–Revised to a sample of elementary-age students referred for academic difficulties. Factor analysis indicated that the subtests loaded on one factor and that reading scores on the PIAT-R and WRAT-R were significantly lower than the scores on the K-TEA and Woodcock-Johnson–Revised.

Much research has focused on the Written Expression subtest of the PIAT-R and PIAT-R/NU. As noted earlier, the interrater reliability coefficients reported in the test manual are moderate at best. Ouchi, Cole, Muenz, and Kaufman (1996) examined this issue with a sample of individuals aged 13 to 46, and found values similar to those reported in the test manual.

AN ILLUSTRATIVE CASE REPORT

In this section, our focus turns to a psychoeducational report for a student referred by his parents to determine eligibility for gifted and talented programming. We will be interpreting Barry's PIAT-R/NU results along with additional test data.

Reason for Referral

Barry was referred for evaluation by his parents. They state that he is doing 4th-grade math and excelling in reading. The purposes of the evaluation are to determine Barry's eligibility for gifted and talented programming and to develop specific recommendations for programming that can be used by his classroom teacher.

Background Information

Barry is currently enrolled in the 1st grade in a rural school district. He lives with his parents, two brothers, and one sister. He has an older brother, 10 years of age, and a younger brother and sister. None of these siblings has exhibited learning or behavior concerns.

Barry's mother is a licensed nurse and his father is a controller for a hotel chain. The family spends much time together and engages in one-on-one time with books, puzzles, and games each evening. Barry's parents report that he takes pleasure in solitary time, working on the computer, reading books, and engaging in fantasy play. Barry's physical growth has been within normal limits and there have been no medical or developmental concerns. He is not taking any medication at the present time. His vision and hearing are normal as are his communication skills.

Barry has expressed mixed feelings about school. Although he reports that he enjoys participating in the academics, particularly math and reading, he has also had to cope with some bullying that takes place at school. Barry's parents report that he cries easily while at school and has few friends. His mother, especially, is concerned about his level of self-esteem. She feels that he is not challenged academically and is experiencing boredom while at school. Barry is currently receiving physical therapy at school for poor muscle tone and mild sensory deficits.

Behavioral Observations

During the evaluation, Barry was cooperative and highly motivated; rapport was easily established and maintained. He was very confident about his abilities, but frequently asked for positive feedback. Barry displayed appropriate on-task behavior, and overall test results are believed to reflect his current level of intellectual and academic functioning. Throughout the testing sessions, Barry remained calm and relaxed and displayed a mature disposition.

On tests that required handwriting or printing, Barry used his right hand and wrote laboriously with legible manuscript. Letter reversals were occasional, but he noticed each and told me what letter it was supposed to be before moving on. Upper- and lowercase letters were mixed indiscriminately, which is common for his age.

Throughout the testing, Barry was very verbal. He told the examiner on numerous occasions that he was very smart. He constantly asked if his answers were correct. When he knew his answer was not correct he requested an explanation of what the correct answer was. On the math portions of the ability and achievement tests, he described aloud how he was solving the problem. He also commented on his confidence in math while solving the problems mentally. The only subtest that Barry did not seem to enjoy was the Reading Comprehension subtest. He commented on several occasions that he was ready to stop.

On the basis of these observations, it appears that the test results obtained are a valid estimate of his level of cognitive and academic performance.

Evaluation Procedures and Instruments

Interview with parents
Behavioral observations
Differential Ability Scales (DAS)
Peabody Individual Achievement Test–Revised Normative Update
   (PIAT-R/NU)

Test Results

DAS Results

Cluster	Standard Score	95% Confidence Interval	Percentile
Verbal	135	123–143	99
Nonverbal Reasoning	152	140–159	99
Spatial	122	113–130	93
General Conceptual Ability	145	137–150	99

Core Subtests	T-Score	Diagnostic Subtests	T-Score
Word Definitions	77	Recall of Digits	60W
Similarities	65	Recall of Objects	58W
Matrices	80	Speed of Information Processing	61W
Sequential and Quantitative Reasoning	80	Pattern Construction	53W
Recall of Designs	74		

Achievement Subtest	Standard Score	Percentile
Basic Number Skills	145	99.9
Spelling	98	61.0
Word Reading	125	97.0

Note. "W" represents a significant relative weakness, $p < .05$.

PIAT-R/NU

Subtests and Composites	Standard Score	95% Confidence Interval	Percentile
General Information	139	132–146	99
Reading Recognition	128	124–132	97
Reading Comprehension	132	124–140	98
Mathematics	145	137–153	99
Spelling	118	111–125	88
Written Language	106	99–113	99
Total Reading	133	128–138	99
Total Test	140	136–144	66

Analysis of Results

The DAS is an individually administered cognitive abilities battery for students from preschool through high school. The battery consists of core subtests, which are the best measure of overall ability, diagnostic subtests, which measure specific cognitive skills such as memory, and achievement subtests measuring reading decoding, spelling, and arithmetic. The core subtests are divided into three scales: Verbal, Nonverbal Reasoning, and Spatial. The General Conceptual Ability (GCA) score represents the overall performance on the six core subtests.

On this administration of the DAS, Barry achieved an overall GCA score of 145. The chances are 95 out of 100 that if Barry were tested again on the DAS, his score would fall within the range of 137–150, which is at the 99th percentile. His GCA places him in the superior range of intellectual ability.

It should be noted that all of Barry's subtest scores and composite scores are average or above, with most of them in the high average to superior range. However, an examination of Barry's scores shows some variability among his levels of performance. His highest scores are on the GCA, the best measure of overall intellectual functioning, and the Nonverbal Reasoning cluster. The Nonverbal Reasoning cluster is a measure of fluid intelligence and emphasizes problem solving that is not dependent on previous learning. His scores on the two subtests comprising this cluster were 3 SD above the mean, suggesting exceptional skill in this area. He displayed excellent perception of spatial orientation and perceptual motor skills. His Verbal and Spatial cluster scores were lower, but still well above average. Barry was able to define words and use verbal reasoning to solve problems on a level exceeding that of 93% of students at his chronological age. The Spatial cluster is a measure of visual intelligence and the ability to interpret and organize information presented visually and spatially. Within this cluster, Barry excelled in his ability to reproduce from memory geometric designs after he viewed them for 5 seconds. His lowest score (in the average range) was on a task requiring him to reproduce a geometric design with plastic blocks. He approached this task in a methodical manner but was physically slow. This slowness penalized his level of performance, because the score is based in part on the speed with which each task is solved. Consequently, the overall Spatial cluster score probably underestimates Barry's true level of performance on such tasks.

Barry's performance on subtests measuring more specific skills and skills that are cognitively less complex was somewhat lower, although still above average. These skills include short-term auditory memory, short-term visual memory, and speed in solving simple tasks. It seems that Barry performs at a higher level on more complex activities and on tasks that are conceptual in nature and require reasoning skills (verbal and nonverbal).

The achievement subtests of the DAS are best used as a screening device and show that Barry's word recognition or reading decoding skills and arithmetic skills are very well developed. They compare favorably with the GCA, indicating that Barry is functioning at a level consistent with his ability in these two areas. His performance in spelling, while in the average range, is considerably lower than in the other two areas. His level of academic achievement is examined in considerably more detail on the PIAT-R/NU.

The PIAT-R/NU is an individually administered achievement test providing assessment in six content areas: General Information, Reading Recognition, Reading Comprehension, Mathematics, Spelling, and Written Language. Once again, all of Barry's subtest scores are in the average range or higher, with the majority of them in the superior range and exceeding the performance of 90% of his peers, with the exception of Written Language. His level of performance in reading, mathematics, and general information is at a level typical of the average student in 3rd or 4th grade.

Barry's Total Reading score places him at the 99th percentile. Reading Recognition and Reading Comprehension skills show uniform development, with standard scores of 128 and 132, respectively. His Reading Recognition score of 128 compares favorably with the Word Reading score of 125 on the DAS. Barry's performance suggests that he has mastered a phonetic approach to word recognition and is able to apply those skills successfully to unfamiliar words. Similarly, he demonstrates an understanding of material that he reads, which is partly attributable to his well-developed vocabulary as shown on the DAS.

Barry's performance on the spelling subtests of the two instruments varied to some degree. His overall score on the PIAT-R/NU was about 1 SD higher than his performance on the DAS; this is most likely due to the different formats of the two tests. On the PIAT-R/NU the student chooses the correct spelling of the word from four choices rather than writing the dictated word, which eliminates the impact of handwriting or paper-and-pencil skills on spelling. As noted previously in the Behavioral Observations section, Barry had some difficulty with such tasks. Traditional spelling tests, therefore, may produce scores that underestimate his skills in spelling.

Barry was administered Level I of the Written Expression subtest. This subtest examines early writing skills such as copying letters, words, and sentences. Results on Written Expression are reported in scores called "stanines," which range from 1 to 9. A stanine of 9 is considered high; 7 and 8 are above average; 4 to 6 are average; 2 and 3 are below average; and 1 is low. Barry received a stanine of 2, which is considered below average in relation to the scores of other students in the 1st grade. Since this subtest and the Spelling subtest comprise the Written Language composite, it is not surprising that this was his lowest composite score and was due to his difficulty on Written Expression, not on Spelling.

In Mathematics Barry received identical scores of 145 on the Basic Number Skills subtest of the DAS and the Mathematics subtest of the PIAT-R/NU. He was able to solve problems involving addition and subtraction, including regrouping, as well as problems in multiplication and division. All problems were solved mentally and Barry simply wrote down the answer for the DAS and chose the correct answer for the PIAT-R/NU.

Summary

Barry is a 6-year-old boy who is currently functioning in the high average to superior range of cognitive functioning as measured by the DAS. Academically, he is functioning at a similar level in reading and mathematics. Barry excels in tasks that require verbal or nonverbal reasoning, solving novel problems, and completing tasks that involve verbal concepts and an understanding of language. He does less well on memory tasks and tasks that place a premium on speed. Tasks requiring paper-and-pencil skills are also more difficult for Barry. His achievement scores are more typical of a student in 3rd or 4th grade than of one in 1st grade.

Recommendations

1. Since Barry is performing cognitively and academically at the 99th percentile, consideration should be given to providing him with gifted and talented programming, particularly in the areas of reading and arithmetic.

2. Barry seemed to encounter some difficulty with written tasks primarily due to awkwardness in manipulating a pencil. If this difficulty persists, a referral to the physical therapist or occupational therapist is in order.

3. While Barry is a very verbal youngster with well-developed language skills, his profile does show a variable pattern of abilities. Written tasks, rote memory activities, and tasks requiring little reasoning are types of activities on which Barry's level of performance may be somewhat lower as compared to verbal and reasoning activities. The current evaluation suggests that the reason for this is less-developed skills (although they are average to above-average compared to those of his peers), rather than motivational problems. His unique pattern of strengths and weaknesses should be considered in such circumstances.

Douglas K. Smith, PhD, NCSP
Director, School of Psychology Training

Amy Rother, MSE
Examiner

TEST YOURSELF

1. **The starting point for administering the General Information subtest is**
   (a) the student's age level.
   (b) the student's grade level.
   (c) the raw score from Reading Decoding.
   (d) the raw score from Reading Comprehension.

2. **The discontinue rule for subtests is**
   (a) five consecutive errors.
   (b) seven consecutive errors.
   (c) 10 consecutive errors.
   (d) five errors in seven consecutive responses.

3. **The basal level is**
   (a) five consecutive correct answers.
   (b) seven consecutive correct answers.
   (c) 10 consecutive correct answers.
   (d) five correct answers in seven consecutive responses.

4. **Test item responses should be scored as you administer them.** True or False?

5. **If more than one basal is determined, use**
   (a) the lowest basal.
   (b) the highest basal.

6. **If more than one ceiling is determined, use**
   (a) the lowest ceiling.
   (b) the highest ceiling.

7. **Scores from the Written Expression subtest are included in the Total Test score.** True or False?

8. **Fall, winter, and spring norms are provided for**
   (a) grade-based standard scores.
   (b) age-based standard scores.
   (c) neither.
   (d) both.

9. **The Written Language composite is based on scores on _____ and _____.**

10. **If comparing the PIAT-R/NU scores to scores from an ability test, you should use**
   (a) age-based standard scores.
   (b) grade-based standard scores.
   (c) age equivalents.
   (d) grade equivalents.

Answers: 1. b; 2. d; 3. a; 4. True; 5. b; 6. a; 7. False; 8. a; 9. Spelling, Written Expression; 10. a

Four

WECHSLER INDIVIDUAL ACHIEVEMENT TEST I/II

OVERVIEW

The Wechsler Individual Achievement Test (WIAT; The Psychological Corporation, 1992) consists of two forms: the Comprehensive Battery and the WIAT Screener. The Comprehensive Battery, consisting of eight subtests and requiring 30 to 60 minutes to administer, is the emphasis of this chapter; the WIAT Screener consists of three subtests and requires 10 to 15 minutes to administer, and is discussed following the Comprehensive Battery. The WIAT-II, scheduled for release in 2001, is discussed at the end of the chapter.

Description of the WIAT

The WIAT covers the age range 5 years 0 months through 19 years 11 months. Administration time varies from 30 to 60 minutes. The Comprehensive Battery is composed of the following subtests: Basic Reading, Mathematics Reasoning, Spelling, Reading Comprehension, Numerical Operations, Listening Comprehension, Oral Expression, and Written Expression. The subtests produce four composite scores—Reading, Mathematics, Language, and Writing—along with a Total Composite. Standard scores with a mean of 100 and SD of 15 are provided for subtests and composites. Grade equivalents, age equivalents, percentile ranks, and normal curve equivalents are also available.

Each of the composite scores is based on the two subtests comprising the composite. The composition of the composites is found in Rapid Reference 4.1. Subtests are described in Rapid Reference 4.2.

I would like to thank Dr. Donna Smith, WIAT-II Project Director, and Dr. Denise Hildebrand for their assistance in sharing materials for the WIAT-II section of this chapter.

Standardization of the WIAT

The WIAT was standardized on 4,252 students in 13 age groups enrolled in kindergarten through grade 12. The sample was designed to match data from the U.S. Bureau of the Census for March 1988 and was stratified on the basis of age, grade, gender, race/ethnicity, geographic region, and parent educational level. Students enrolled in both public and private schools were included. Since students with disabilities receiving "mainstream special services" (p. 130) were included in the sample, 6% of the standardization sample consisted of students with learning disabilities, speech/language impairments, emotional disturbances, and physical impairments. An additional 1.4% were classified as borderline or mildly mentally retarded.

≡Rapid Reference 4.1

Subtests Comprising the WIAT Composite Scores

Composites	Subtests
Reading	Basic Reading, Reading Comprehension
Mathematics	Mathematics Reasoning, Numerical Operations
Language	Listening Comprehension, Oral Expression
Writing	Spelling, Written Expression

The match between the sample and the U.S. population is generally close. The greatest disparity is on the geographic region variable, with the South overrepresented and the Northeast underrepresented. It should be noted that statistical weighting was used on the race/ethnicity variable, with five to seven White children and five minority children at each age being statistically weighted. Detailed standardization data are presented in the manual.

A linking sample of 1,284 students, aged 5 through 19 years, was created and was administered either the Wechsler Preschool and Primary Scale of Intelligence–Revised (WPPSI-R), the Wechsler Intelligence Scale for Children–Third Edition (WISC-III), or the Wechsler Adult Intelligence Scale–Revised (WAIS-R). As noted by Ferrara (1998), there is "no information on percentages of learning disabled students in the linking sample" (p. 1130). Rapid Reference 4.3 compares the linking sample with the overall standardization sample.

Within the linking sample, the WIAT and WISC-III were administered to

≡Rapid Reference 4.2

Description of the WIAT Subtests

Subtest	Description
Basic Reading	Measures decoding and word-reading ability using a series of pictures and printed words
Mathematics Reasoning	Measures the ability to reason mathematically using visual stimuli for many items with the text being presented both orally and in print (for most items) and the student responding in a variety of ways
Spelling	Measures encoding and spelling abilities using a series of dictated letters, sound, and words with the student writing responses
Reading Comprehension	Measures skills such as recognizing stated detail and making inferences, using a series of both printed passages and orally presented questions with the student responding orally
Numerical Operations	Measures the ability to write dictated numerals and solve calculation problems and equations using paper and pencil
Listening Comprehension	Measures listening comprehension such as listening for detail with items requiring the picture that corresponds to an orally presented word and on the student's comprehension of orally presented passages accompanied by pictures (early items require the student to respond by pointing, while later items require a verbal response)
Oral Expression	Measures the ability to verbally express words, describe scenes, give directions, and explain steps using items consisting of pictures accompanied by orally presented instructions
Written Expression	Measures writing skills such as development and organization of ideas, capitalization, and punctuation using one of two writing prompts

Note. Adapted from The Psychological Corporation (1992).

about 100 students at ages 6–16. The WIAT/WPPSI-R combination was administered to 84 5-year-olds and the WIAT/WAIS-R was administered to 82 adolescents aged 17–19. In order to equate the linking sample for the WISC-III with the standardization sample on FSIQ, case-weighting techniques were used. Following the weighting procedures, the ability-achievement discrepancy statistics were calculated.

≡Rapid Reference 4.3

Comparison of the Linking Sample and Overall Standardization Sample

Variable	Linking Sample	Standardization Sample	Census Data Estimate
Race/ethnicity			
White	75.6	70.8	70.1
Black	12.4	15.0	15.4
Hispanic	9.9	10.5	10.7
Other	2.0	3.6	3.8
Geographic region			
Northeast	19.1	16.4	19.2
North Central	23.4	24.4	25.1
South	40.9	38.9	34.5
West	16.6	20.3	21.0
Parent educational level			
8th grade or less	5.0	4.6	6.6
Grade 9–11	10.1	11.3	12.2
High school	34.4	37.3	36.8
1 to 3 years college	27.0	26.5	20.4
4 or more years college	23.4	25.8	18.5

Psychometric Characteristics

Detailed reliability and validity data are presented in the test manual. The reader is encouraged to study these data before using the test. In the meantime, I have summarized some of the more important features of these data.

Reliability

Split-half reliability coefficient procedures, as used with the Wechsler scales, were used for the WIAT as a measure of internal consistency. Mean split-half reliability coefficients for the subtests range from .81 (Written Expression) to .92 (Basic Reading) and for the composites from .90 (Language, Writing) to .95 (Reading). The Total Composite mean coefficient was .97. Mean test-retest correlations for the composites range from .78 (Language) to .96 (Total) for a

Rapid Reference 4.4

Mean WIAT Reliabilities

Composites	Split-Half Reliabilities	Test-Retest Reliabilities
Reading	.95	.93
Mathematics	.92	.91
Language	.90	.78
Writing	.90	.94
Total	.97	.96
Subtests		
Basic Reading	.92	.94
Mathematics Reasoning	.89	.89
Spelling	.90	.94
Reading Comprehension	.88	.85
Numerical Operations	.85	.86
Listening Comprehension	.83	.76
Oral Expression	.91	.68
Written Expression	.81	.77

sample of 367 students in grades 1–10, tested 17 days apart (on average; actual range 12–52 days). These data demonstrate that the WIAT is a stable measure of achievement. See Rapid Reference 4.4 for specific test-retest reliabilities.

Four of the WIAT subtests, Reading Comprehension, Listening Comprehension, Oral Expression, and Written Expression, are somewhat subjective to score; Oral Expression and Written Expression are the most subjective. Thus, interrater reliability studies were conducted and showed high levels of agreement in scoring responses to these subtests.

Validity

A multistage process was used to establish WIAT validity. Initially, experts in assessment (both ability and curriculum areas) were consulted, along with curriculum experts and national organizations representing their respective curriculum areas. It was then decided to develop subtests to cover the areas of academic achievement specified in the Individuals with Disabilities Education Act (IDEA;

PL 94-142). Following designation of the domains (reading, arithmetic, language, oral expression, and written expression), specific subtests were developed.

Within each subtest, specific curriculum objectives were developed from which subtest items would be written. These objectives were based on the results of previous research studies, curriculum guides (from representative school districts, state educational agencies, and textbooks), and consultations with national curriculum organizations. Detailed descriptions of the types of items for each subtest are found on pages 122–127 of the manual.

Tryout testing of the instrument took place in 1989 and included 2,238 students. Item analysis procedures were then used to eliminate biased items, determine item difficulty, and order the items for the standardization edition. Similar procedures were used following standardization to develop the final revision of the instrument.

The procedures previously discussed in this section provide considerable evidence of content validity. Construct validity was evaluated primarily by examining the intercorrelations of the subtests and by correlations with the Wechsler scales. Criterion validity was addressed in more detail with studies relating WIAT scores to those on the K-TEA (Kaufman & Kaufman, 1985), WRAT-R (Jastak & Wilkinson, 1984), WJ-R (Woodcock & Johnson, 1989), DAS (Elliott, 1990), and PPVT-R (Dunn & Dunn, 1981). Results of these studies are presented in the WIAT test manual. Tables are presented showing the correlations between similar subtests but not between total test composites. In addition, validity studies were completed with group-administered tests and with various groups of students with disabilities. The studies presented indicate the WIAT is a valid measure of achievement. Rapid Reference 4.5 provides basic information on the test and its publisher.

HOW TO ADMINISTER THE WIAT

As with any other standardized test, the WIAT examiner should follow closely the test administration instructions contained in the test manual. Although the test is quite easy to administer, it is imperative that the examiner become very familiar with the test directions and practice administration of the test before it is used in the clinical setting. Chapter 2 of the test manual describes a number of testing considerations, including suitability of the test, testing time, and materials needed. There is also an extensive discussion of standard procedures to follow in test administration, including the necessary physical conditions for

===Rapid Reference 4.5

Wechsler Individual Achievement Test

Author: The Psychological Corporation

Publication Date: 1992

What the Test Measures: Reading decoding, reading comprehension, spelling, mathematics reasoning, mathematics computation, listening comprehension, oral expression, written expression

Age Range: 5 years 0 months through 19 years 11 months

Administration Time: 30 to 60 minutes, depending on the age of the student

Qualification of Examiners: Training in educational or psychological testing with graduate-level training in assessment

Publisher: The Psychological Corporation
555 Academic Court
San Antonio, TX 78204-2498
(800) 872-1726
www.PsychCorp.com

Prices: Complete test kit $307.00 (2001 catalog price)
Computer scoring program: $155.00 (2001 catalog price)

DON'T FORGET

Order of Subtest Administration

1. Basic Reading
2. Mathematics Reasoning
3. Spelling
4. Reading Comprehension
5. Numerical Operations
6. Listening Comprehension
7. Oral Expression
8. Written Expression

---

testing and the importance of rapport in the testing process, as well as a section on testing students with physical impairments. The examiner should read these sections before administering the test.

The WIAT utilizes the easel format, in which the subtest items are presented on the student's side of the easel. Subtests are administered in the order of their presentation in the easels. Test materials consist of two test easels, the Comprehensive Battery Record Form, and the Response Booklet for the Numerical

Operations and Written Expression subtests. In addition, the examiner must supply blank white paper (for the Mathematics Reasoning subtest) and a pencil with eraser (for the Mathematics Reasoning, Spelling, Numerical Operations, and Written Expression subtests).

For each subtest, the first page of the easel outlines the general administration procedures. On the left side of the page, starting points are indicated and explanations of the reverse rule and the discontinue rule are given; these features make testing more efficient (see Rapid Reference 4.6). Verbatim instruc-

≡Rapid Reference 4.6

Starting Points, Reverse Rule, and Discontinue Rule

Starting Points	Based on the grade level of the student. The examiner is allowed to use the starting point for the next-lowest or next-highest grade if he or she suspects that the student is functioning below or above grade placement, respectively.
Reverse Rule	Designed to assure a minimum number of consecutive correct responses for all subtests except Oral Expression and Written Expression. If the student scores 0 on any one of the first *five* items administered, administer the preceding items *in reverse order* until the student makes five consecutive correct responses. For Numerical Operations, item sets are used and the student must score 1 on every item in one set.
Discontinue Rule	Specifies the criteria for discontinuing subtest administration. These rules vary by subtest and are listed below.

Basic Reading:	0 on 6 consecutive items
Mathematics Reasoning:	0 on 4 consecutive items
Spelling:	0 on 6 consecutive items
Reading Comprehension:	0 on 4 consecutive items
Numerical Operations:	0 on every item in *one* set
Listening Comprehension:	0 on 4 consecutive items
Oral Expression:	Administer items 1–10 and sample item preceding items 11–16. For items 11–16: no response for 2 consecutive items
Written Expression:	Discontinue after 15 minutes of writing.

tions for the examiner to use both to introduce the individual subtest and to present test items are presented in blue. Stimulus Book 1 (easel one) consists of the Basic Reading, Mathematics Reasoning, and Spelling subtests, which are also the subtests comprising the WIAT Screener. The remaining subtests are presented in Stimulus Book 2 (easel two).

Before administering the WIAT you should address several details. First, complete the biographical information on the front page of the Record Form. This includes the student's name, gender, school, grade, teacher, examiner's name, referral source, and reason for referral. (Record behavioral observations in the space indicated after testing is complete.) Next, calculate the chronological age for the student. Always double-check your calculations, which will be the most likely source of error. When you have to borrow from the Months column to the Days column, always borrow 30 days. As a third check, I usually ask the student his or her age or birthday, because sometimes discrepancies occur and school records can be incorrect. Test administration pointers are presented in Rapid Reference 4.7.

Subtest-by-Subtest Notes on Administration

Basic Reading

This subtest is among the easiest to administer. The student's side of the easel contains the visual stimulus, and the examiner provides instructions. In the initial items the student points to words with beginning or ending sounds identical to the stimulus picture. The next items require the child to point to the word that names the picture. For these first seven items, you must be able to see where the student is pointing.

From item 8 on, the student reads words that are printed on the stimulus page. Allow the student about 10 seconds per word. On the record form, the words are divided into syllables. You should record the student's response to each item and use whatever notations are necessary to capture the student's pronunciation of the word. When the student encounters an unfamiliar word, consult the section titled "Child's Behavior When Presented with Unfamiliar Words" in the Record Form to describe the student's behavior (this will be useful when you analyze the student's reading decoding skills). Item responses are scored correct (1) or incorrect (0).

≡Rapid Reference 4.7

Test Administration Pointers

1. **Record the student's response** in the response column of the Record Form. For some subtests this involves circling the student's response and for others it involves writing the student's response.

2. **Only the Written Expression subtest has a fixed time limit (15 minutes).** For other subtests, general time guidelines are provided and are indicated on the Record Form by the clock symbol. These are suggestions only, because the subtests are basically untimed.

3. **Teaching items** are provided for some subtests. What you are to say in this procedure is outlined on your side of the Stimulus Book.

4. Items and instructions **may be repeated once on most subtests** if the student misunderstands them or asks you to repeat them. **Each Spelling item can be presented only once,** while **Listening Comprehension passages cannot be repeated.**

5. **Verbal probing** of a response is usually not needed. The only exception to this is **item 32 of Listening Comprehension,** which contains specific instructions for querying. If a student's response is vague, probe for clarification with such phrases as "Tell me more" or "Explain what you mean."

6. Some students are hesitant during the testing process and may need **prompting.** If this is the case, use encouraging phrases such as "Just try it once more," "Try it just a little longer," "I think you can do it," or "Let's go on."

7. **If the student gives more than one response to a test item, you must determine which response is the one to score.** The WIAT assumes that the final response is the one to be scored. In the case of multiple responses you must determine which is the final response. In some cases you may need to ask the student which is the final response.

8. **Spoiled responses** are responses that may contain some correct information but are spoiled by comments from the student that indicate a misconception of the item.

Starting Point   Grades K–2: Item 1
                   Grades 3–4: Item 8
                   Grades 5–12: Item 16

Discontinue Rule   Score of 0 on each of 6 consecutive items

Mathematics Reasoning

For each item on this subtest, the student is allowed about one minute to respond. Paper and pencil should be provided. The first four items require the student to point to the stimulus page so you need to be able to see the student's side of the Stimulus Book. The remainder of the items require a verbal response from the student. Be sure to complete the "Child's Behavior When Presented with Difficult Items" section. All items are scored correct (1) or incorrect (0).

Starting Point   Grades K–3: Item 1
                       Grades 4–7: Item 10
                       Grades 8–12: Item 20

Discontinue Rule   Score of 0 on each of 4 consecutive items

Spelling

For this subtest, you need Stimulus Book 1, a pencil with an eraser, and the record form. Items 1–4 require the student to write selected letters of the alphabet. Items 5 and 6 require the student to "write the letter that spells a sound." The remaining items resemble a traditional spelling test, in which you pronounce a word, read it in a sentence, and pronounce the word again, and the student writes the word on the spelling page that you have removed from the Record Form. *Do not repeat any items.* Responses are scored correct (1) or incorrect (0).

Starting Point   Grades K–1: Item 1
                       Grades 2–4: Item 7
                       Grades 5–7: Item 16
                       Grades 8–12: Item 21

Discontinue Rule   Score of 0 on each of 6 consecutive items

Reading Comprehension

This subtest should not be administered if the student's raw score for Basic Reading is 8 or less. Also, standard scores are not provided for students aged 5 years 0 months through 5 years 11 months. This subtest is somewhat different from other measures of reading comprehension, in that pictorial stimuli are used for the initial items. For these items (1–8) the student silently reads a sentence on his or her side of the Stimulus Book and answers questions posed by the examiner. Accompanying each sentence is a picture that illustrates all or part of the sentence. For the remaining items (9–38), the student reads a sentence or paragraph and answers questions posed by the examiner.

Students should be allowed about 15 seconds to respond to each item. If there is no response after one minute, proceed to the next item. The student's response should be recorded *verbatim* in the space provided on the Record Form. Responses are scored correct (1) or incorrect (0). Examples of correct and incorrect responses are provided on the examiner's side of the Stimulus Book. Required criteria for correct responses are also indicated.

Starting Point	Grades K–3:	Item 1
	Grades 4–5:	Item 9
	Grades 6–12:	Item 12
Discontinue Rule	Score of 0 on each of 4 consecutive items	

Numerical Operations

This subtest consists of 10 sets of four items each. The first set of items requires the student to write numbers dictated by the examiner while the remaining sets involve arithmetic computation. All responses are written in the separate Response Booklet. The student should be given about 5 minutes to complete each set for items 5–28 and 7 minutes for each set for items 29–40. Responses are scored correct (1) or incorrect (0).

Starting Point	Grades K–3:	Item 1
	Grades 4–5:	Item 5
	Grades 6–7:	Item 13
	Grades 8–12:	Item 17
Discontinue Rule	Score of 0 for every item in one set	

Listening Comprehension

This subtest assesses two types of skills: understanding of orally presented words (items 1–9) and understanding of orally presented passages (items 10–36). For the first set of items, the student points to the correct response on the Stimulus Book, so you need to be able to see the student's side of the easel. The student has about 10 seconds to respond. Item 1 is a teaching item, and detailed instructions are included on your side of the Stimulus Book. Items 2–9 are not teaching items, but may be repeated. Circle the letter corresponding to the student's response.

The student has about 15 seconds to respond to items 10–36. You read a passage for each item and the student responds verbally. *Passages cannot be re-*

CAUTION

Types of Incorrect Responses for Listening Comprehension

- Responses with details from the passage but not the requested information
- Responses with information that is not contained in the passage (even if the information is in the accompanying picture)
- Responses with the correct information that are spoiled by additional information not contained in the passage
- Responses that require two different elements or pieces of information, for which the student states the same element twice

peated. Record the student's responses *verbatim* in the space provided on the Record Form.

All items are scored correct (1) or incorrect (0). Items 10–36 are more difficult to score than items 1–9. Correct responses are listed on your side of the Stimulus Book, and Table 3.1 of the test manual contains extensive examples of both correct and incorrect responses to items 10–36.

Starting Point   Grades K–3: Item 1

                        Grades 4–12: Item 5

Discontinue Rule   Score of 0 on each of 5 consecutive items

Oral Expression

This subtest is divided into two sets of items. The first set of items (1–10) assess the student's ability to express a target word verbally. You show a picture illustrating the word and then define it. The student responds verbally with the word. The second set of items (11–16) assesses the student's ability to describe scenes, give directions, and explain steps. For each item, you present pictures or maps, and the student describes the picture, gives directions, or explains the steps in a process.

The student has about 10 seconds for each response to items 1–10. Item 1 is a teaching item; teaching and prompting are not allowed for items 2–10. A sample item is presented after item 10; item 11 is another teaching item, with complete instructions on the examiner's side of the Stimulus Book. Items 12 and 13, while not teaching items, do allow the examiner to provide some prompts if needed. All responses should be recorded *verbatim* for accurate scoring.

The scoring for items 1–10 is dichotomous: either correct (1) or incorrect (0). The scoring for items 11–16, however, is more complex. There are five criteria for each item and each criterion is scored independently. The criteria vary by item type with separate criteria for items 11–12, 13–14, and 15–16. For each criterion, the score is either correct (1) or incorrect (0); thus, each item can produce a score ranging from 0 to 5. Detailed examples of correct and incorrect responses are presented on pages 61–69 of the test manual.

> # CAUTION
>
> ## Types of Incorrect Responses for Oral Expression Items 1–10
>
> - Responses focusing on either the picture or the definition, but not both
> - Responses that simply restate the definition
> - Responses that are "invented words" or words that do not exist

Starting Point   Grades K–12: Item 1

Discontinue Rule   All students receive items 1–10 and the sample item following item 10. For items 11–16, discontinue if there is no response for two consecutive items.

Written Expression

This is the only formally timed subtest on the WIAT. The student has 15 minutes to write on the topic presented in the prompt. The prompt is presented both verbally and in print and the student writes his or her response in the separate Response Booklet. This subtest is administered only to students in grade 3 and above. If a student receives a raw score of 15 or less on Spelling, the examiner should use his or her professional judgment in deciding whether to administer the Written Expression subtest. Prompt 1 is suggested for initial WIAT administrations and Prompt 2 for subsequent administrations.

This subtest can be scored two ways: the analytic method or the holistic method. The analytic method emphasizes the parts or elements of the response, whereas the holistic method emphasizes the response as a whole. Standard scores are provided for the analytic scoring method only. Advantages and disadvantages of the two methods are presented in Rapid References 4.8 and 4.9.

Regardless of the method you use for scoring the Written Expression sub-

═Rapid Reference 4.8

Advantages and Disadvantages of Holistic Scoring of the Written Expression Subtest

Advantages	Disadvantages
• Quickly scored	• Does not lend itself to determining strengths and weaknesses
• Reliabilities higher than for analytic scoring	• Does not focus on the parts or elements of writing, such as vocabulary and development of ideas
• High interrater reliabilities	• Does not produce a standard score

═Rapid Reference 4.9

Advantages and Disadvantages of Analytic Scoring of the Written Expression Subtest

Advantages	Disadvantages
• Produces a standard score	• Takes more time to complete than holistic scoring
• Provides differentiated information about the writing sample	
• Scoring data can be used to determine strengths and weaknesses	
• Emphasis is on the elements of writing, including vocabulary, sentence structure and variety, and grammar and usage	
• Some studies suggest it produces higher reliabilities than holistic scoring	

test, subjectivity is involved. You are encouraged to read and study the section on scoring this subtest in the test manual (pages 72–75) and the analytic scoring approach and scoring examples provided (pages 76–105). The holistic method is discussed on page 106 of the test manual with examples on pages 107–116. The scoring elements for the analytic method are presented in Rapid Reference 4.10.

The choice of scoring method to use is a difficult one. I usually use the analytic method so that I can derive standard scores. Then, if weaknesses are noted, I go back and rescore the subtest using the holistic method.

Starting Point — Administered only to students in grades 3 and above

Discontinue Rule — Discontinue after 15 minutes of writing

<table>
<tr><td>≡Rapid Reference 4.10</td></tr>
<tr><td>Scoring Elements for the Analytic Method
• Ideas and development
• Organization, unity, and coherence
• Vocabulary
• Sentence structure and variety
• Grammar and usage
• Capitalization and punctuation</td></tr>
</table>

HOW TO SCORE THE TEST RECORD FORM

The WIAT yields two types of scores: raw scores and standard scores. Raw scores reflect the number of points earned by the student on each subtest. These scores by themselves are meaningless because they are not norm-based scores. They are converted to standard scores, which *are* norm-based and allow us to compare the student's performance with that of peers. The WIAT standard scores have a mean of 100 and SD of 15. The range of standard scores for the subtests and composites is 40 to 160. We assume that achievement test performance is distributed on a normal curve with the majority of students scoring within ±1 SD of the mean. Thus, about two-thirds (66%) of students score in the range of 85 to 115. Less than 3% of students score above 130 or below 70.

Step-by-Step Scoring of the WIAT

Scoring the WIAT subtest items is facilitated by the dichotomous nature of the items, with the exception of the Written Expression subtest. Each item is scored as correct (1) or incorrect (0). For Oral Expression, this system applies to each of the criteria listed for each item. You should enter the correct score for each item in the score column of the record form. Always double-check your scoring.

Raw Scores

All subtest raw scores are computed in the same way. Add the raw scores for each subtest and enter the number in the box labeled "Raw Score."

Transfer the subtest raw scores to their respective blue boxes on the front page of the Record Form. Then add the raw scores in each column (Reading, Mathematics, Language, and Writing) and record the total in the blue oval. Next, add these column totals in the blue ovals together and place the sum in the pink oval under "Total Composite."

Standard Scores

The conversion of raw scores to standard scores requires a decision: whether to use age-based or grade-based norms, the answer to which depends on whether you want to compare the student's test performance with that of same-age peers or same-grade peers. In most cases the resulting standard scores will be similar. However, important differences can occur if the student has been retained or has received an accelerated grade placement, or if he or she began school earlier or later than is typical. In these cases, the age-based norms are probably more relevant. If you are comparing the student's performance on the WIAT with performance on an ability measure, almost *always* use age-based norms, which are the basis for standard scores on ability measures. Indicate your choice of scores by checking the appropriate box (Age or Grade) on the front page of the Record Form.

Standard scores are obtained by entering the appropriate table in the test manual (A.1 for age and A.2, A.3, and A.4 for grade) with the student's raw score and age or grade (depending on type of norm). If you use grade-based norms you should use the fall norms if testing occurred in August, September, October, or November; winter norms for testing in December, January, or February; and spring norms for testing in March, April, May, June, or July. The tables for both age and grade norms are arranged in the same way: Subtests (in order of administration and listing on the Record Form) are listed across the top of the page on the left side; composites are listed similarly on the right. Enter the table by subtest and locate the student's raw score. Then read across the table to the Standard Score column (located on the extreme left and extreme right of the page), and record this score in the appropriate box on the Record Form.

Since all scores have error associated with them, it is standard practice to create bands of error or confidence intervals around individual scores. The WIAT allows you to choose from 90% and 95% confidence intervals by using Tables B.1 through B.4 in the test manual. (If you wish to use other confidence intervals [68%, 85%, or 99%], you will need to calculate them based on the subtest and composite SEMs provided in Table 5.2 in the test manual.) My recommendation is to use the 95% confidence level. To use these tables, enter the one you choose with either the student's chronological age (in years) or grade placement, select the confidence level, and read across the table for subtests or composites for the confidence level. This number is then added to and subtracted from the obtained standard score to form the range of scores comprising the confidence interval. The procedure for subtest conversions and composite conversions is the same. Rapid Reference 4.11 provides a summary of the tables to use for standard score and confidence interval determination.

Percentiles, Age and Grade Equivalents, and Normal Curve Equivalents
Percentile rank equivalents are obtained from Table B.5 in the test manual. Enter this table with the student's standard scores on the subtests and composites; then read across the table for the percentile rank equivalent, the normal curve equivalent, and stanine (if needed).

≡Rapid Reference 4.11

Tables for Standard Score and Confidence Interval Determination

Standard Score/Confidence Interval	Table
Age-based standard scores (subtests and composites)	A.1
Age-based confidence intervals (subtests)	B.1
Age-based confidence intervals (composites)	B.2
Grade-based standard scores—fall (subtests and composites)	A.2
Grade-based standard scores—winter (subtests and composites)	A.3
Grade-based standard scores—spring (subtests and composites)	A.4
Grade-based confidence intervals (subtests)	B.3
Grade-based confidence intervals (composites)	B.4

The column labeled "Other" may be used to record the normal curve equivalent, stanine, or age/grade equivalent. Although age and grade equivalents are frequently used to explain test performance, they are also frequently misunderstood. They lack the precision of standard scores and percentiles and often suggest large differences in performance when, in fact, the differences are insignificant. For example, a raw score of 44 on Basic Reading yields an age equivalent score of 12 years 3 months, and a raw score of 48 on the same subtest yields an age equivalent of 14 years 6 months. For a student at 12 years 3 months of age, the respective standard scores are 104 and 112. Thus, age and grade equivalents should be used very cautiously. Figure 4.1 shows the completed Record Form Summary for Laura.

Ability-Achievement Discrepancy Analysis

The next step in scoring the test record is to compare the student's performance on the WIAT with his or her performance on a Wechsler measure of ability (WPPSI-R, WISC-III, or WAIS-R). This involves completing the back page of the Record Form Summary. *This analysis requires the use of age-based standard scores on the WIAT.*

The first step is to record the Ability standard score in the column with that label for each ability-achievement discrepancy you want to calculate. The *WIAT Manual* requires you to use the FSIQ from the WPPSI-R, WISC-III, or WAIS-R, while the computer scoring program will allow you to use the VIQ or the PIQ. Flanagan and Alfonso (1993a, b) constructed tables for the VIQ and PIQ to determine ability-achievement discrepancies in the diagnosis of learning disabilities.

The second step is to indicate whether you are using the predicted-achievement method or the simple-difference method. The predicted-achievement method is based on a comparison of the obtained achievement score with the achievement score that is predicted based on the ability score. This procedure is more fair for students at all levels of ability and is the preferred method to use. Indicate the method you plan to use by checking the appropriate box (Predicted or Simple).

The next step is to record the achievement score in the appropriate column for the ability-achievement discrepancies you want to calculate. You will find the predicted achievement score from Tables C.1 (WISC-III FSIQ), C.2

Record Form

Summary

Child's Name __LAURA__   Sex __F__

School _____ Grade __6__

Teacher _____ Examiner __Douglas K. Smith__

Referral Source __SPECIAL EDUCATION TEACHER__

Reason for Referral __RE-EVALUATION__

	Year	Month	Day
Date Tested	00	11	06
Date of Birth	89	3	02
Age	11	8	04

Behavioral Observations _____

WIAT Subtests

☒ Age ☐ Grade

	Raw Scores			Standard Score	Confidence Interval 95 %	Percentile	Other ☐ Equivalent ☐ NCE
Basic Reading	17			68	60 – 76	2	
Mathematics Reasoning		26		85	96 – 94	16	
Spelling			13	64	56 – 72	1	
Reading Comprehension	4			54	45 – 63	<1	
Numerical Operations		17		69	59 – 79	2	
Listening Comprehension		20		85	74 – 96	16	
Oral Expression		15		84	76 – 92	14	
Written Expression			7	68	54 – 82	2	

Composites

☒ Age ☐ Grade

	Reading	Mathematics	Language	Writing	Total Composite
Sum of Raw Scores	21 +	43 +	35 +	20 =	119
Standard Score	58	73	81	59	62
Confidence Interval 95 %	51 – 65	67 – 80	73 – 89	50 – 68	58 – 66
Percentile	<1	4	10	<1	1
Other ☐ Equivalent ☐ NCE					

THE PSYCHOLOGICAL CORPORATION®
Harcourt Brace & Company
SAN ANTONIO
Orlando • Boston • New York • Chicago • San Francisco • Atlanta • Dallas
San Diego • Philadelphia • Austin • Fort Worth • Toronto • London

Figure 4.1 Completed Record Form Summary for Laura

(WPPSI-R FSIQ), and C.3 (WAIS-R FSIQ) in the test manual. Enter the table using the FSIQ and read across for the predicted achievement score for the subtests and composites. Then enter these scores in the first shaded column under "Predicted." Record the *actual WIAT* scores in the *second* shaded column under "Predicted." If you are using the simple-difference method, enter the WIAT achievement test scores for the subtests and composites under the "Simple" heading.

Step four involves (1) for the predicted method, subtracting the actual achievement score from the predicted achievement score and entering the difference in the Difference column; or (2) for the simple method, subtracting the actual WIAT score from the ability score and entering the difference in the Difference column.

Step five involves determining whether the differences are statistically significant. You should decide which level of significance you want to use (.05 or .01) and then enter the level in the pink box under "Significance." I routinely use the .05 level. Then refer to Table C.4 in the test manual for the predicted-achievement method or Table C.8 for the simple-difference method. Both tables are designed similarly, with age listed across the top and subtests and composites listed in order in the first column. Find the level of significance (.05 or .01) for each subtest and composite, read across the table to the appropriate age, and transfer the value indicated to the Significance column on the Record Form. If the value in the Difference column exceeds the tabled value, the difference is significant and should be indicated with an *S*. Otherwise indicate *NS* (not significant) next to the value in the Significance column.

The final step involves determining how frequently the discrepancy occurs in the population. We may have a significant difference between the predicted and actual achievement scores, but it may be at a level that occurs frequently. Clinicians disagree as to how frequently a discrepancy must occur before it is considered unusual. Some clinicians prefer to label discrepancies as unusual if they occur in less than 10% of the standardization sample, while others are less stringent and regard differences occurring in 15% of the standardization sample as unusual. Some states (e.g., Wisconsin) have criteria for learning-disabilities diagnosis that indicate the discrepancy must occur in 4% or less of the standardization sample before it is considered significant for placement purposes. The frequencies are presented in Tables C.5, C.6, and C.7 in the test manual for the WISC-III, WPPSI-R, and WAIS-R, respectively, for the pre-

≡Rapid Reference 4.12

Average Correlations between WIAT Subtests and Composites and the WISC-III Full Scale IQ

WIAT	WISC-III FSIQ
Subtests	
Basic Reading	.60
Mathematics Reasoning	.72
Spelling	.52
Reading Comprehension	.67
Numerical Operations	.58
Listening Comprehension	.61
Oral Expression	.42
Written Expression	.46
Composites	
Reading	.68
Mathematics	.71
Language	.58
Writing	.53

dicted method, and in Tables C.9, C.10, and C.11 for the WISC-III, WPPSI-R, and WAIS-R, respectively, for the simple method.

The predicted achievement scores are based in part on the correlations between the WIAT and the Wechsler scales. Rapid Reference 4.12 presents the correlations between the WIAT subtests and composites and the WISC-III FSIQ.

Completing the Profile

Results of the testing can be presented graphically by completing the profile at the bottom of the Ability-Achievement Discrepancy Analysis page. Record the ability standard score and the WIAT subtest and composite standard scores in the spaces provided; then mark their positions on the graph and connect the values for the WIAT scores. I find this presentation of the data to be very useful in explaining a student's performance. Figure 4.2 presents the completed Ability-Achievement Discrepancy Analysis and Profile for Laura.

Ability-Achievement Discrepancy Analysis

USE AGE NORMS	Ability Standard Score	Achievement Score ☒ Predicted	☐ Simple	Difference	Significance .01	Frequency of Difference in Norm. Sample
WIAT Subtests						
Basic Reading	93	96	68	−28	18.49	<1%
Mathematics Reasoning	93	95	85	−10	16.50	15%
Spelling	93	96	64	−32	22.10	<1%
Reading Comprehension	93	95	54	−41	16.50	<1%
Numerical Operations	93	96	69	−27	18.29	<1%
Listening Comprehension	93	96	85	−11	18.39	15%
Oral Expression	93	97	84	−13	25.29	20%
Written Expression	93	97	68	−29	16.66	2%
Composites						
Reading	93	95	58	−37	17.67	<1%
Mathematics	93	95	73	−22	17.89	2%
Language	93	96	81	−15	20.95	10%
Writing	93	96	59	−37	19.58	<1%

Ability Measure __WISC-III__   Date of Ability Testing __11/06/00__

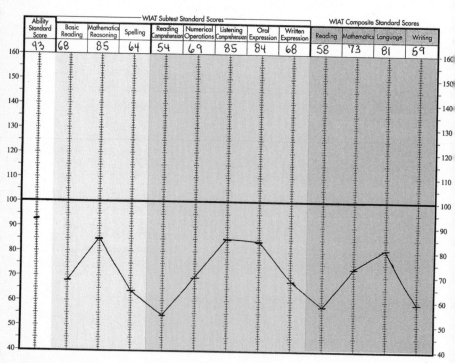

Figure 4.2 Completed Ability-Achievement Discrepancy Analysis

Note: Wechsler Individual Achievement Test. Copyright © 1992 by The Psychological Corporation, a Harcourt Assessment Company. Reproduced by permission. All rights reserved.

"Wechsler Individual Achievement Test," "WIAT," and "W" logo are trademarks of The Psychological Corporation registered in the United States of America and/or other jurisdictions.

HOW TO INTERPRET THE WIAT

Interpretation of the WIAT test results is a multilevel process. Initially, we focus on composite comparisons and comparisons with peers. Since the purpose of many academic assessments is to compare achievement level with cognitive level, we also focus on such comparisons. The final level of interpretation is to examine the student's relative strengths and weaknesses through subtest comparisons and skills analysis.

The goal of interpretation is twofold. The first goal is to provide a comparison with peers; the second is to provide information on the individual student's academic strengths and weaknesses. In the latter process, emphasis is placed on examining the skills measured by the individual subtests and generating hypotheses to explain the student's pattern of scores. These hypotheses can then be explored further through other test data, classroom products, teacher observations, and classroom observations.

Composite Score Comparisons

We begin the interpretive process with the Total composite. This score is the most reliable and valid measure of the student's overall achievement level in reading, spelling, mathematics, listening comprehension, oral expression, and written expression. It provides information on how the student's performance compares to that of peers. Is the student functioning at an average level? an above average level? a below average level?

Next, we compare the composite scores with each other to determine whether the student's academic skills are evenly or unevenly developed. We are interested only in statistically significant differences—those that are large enough that they are not likely to have occurred by chance. WIAT tables use the .15 and .05 levels of significance. I *strongly recommend* that you use the *.05 level* of significance. If a significant difference occurs, we can then say with 95% confidence that the scores represent true differences in level of skill development. Rapid Reference 4.13 presents the range of difference scores that are significant at the .05 levels for the possible comparisons. If a difference score falls in the ranges indicated, then Table D.1 of the manual should be consulted for the exact value. The values vary by age of student. Table D.2 presents the frequencies of such discrepancies in the standardization sample.

≋Rapid Reference 4.13

Range of Differences Required for Comparing Composite Scores at the .05 Level of Significance

Comparison	Standard Score Range	Average for All Ages
Reading/Mathematics	8.81–12.48	11.05
Reading/Language	9.75–13.79	11.62
Reading/Writing	10.60–13.13	11.62
Mathematics/Language	10.18–15.26	12.44
Mathematics/Language	10.59–12.81	12.44
Language/Writing	11.38–13.79	12.94

Note. Actual standard score difference required for significance at the .05 level varies by age; Table D.1 of the test manual should be consulted for the exact value

Let's consider an example. Laura was administered the WIAT on November 6, 1999, and her Record Form Summary is presented in Figure 4.1. Her overall Total Composite score of 62 is in the lower extreme range. Composite scores range from 58 in Reading to 81 in Language, with all scores being below average. The pattern of composite scores is quite variable and four of the possible six comparisons are statistically significant. Her scores for Reading and for Writing are each significantly lower than her Mathematics and Language scores. The mean of her individual subtest scores is 72.13, with a range from 54 to 85. However, only Reading Comprehension differs significantly from her overall mean and indicates a relative weakness; her score of 54 also represents a weakness in comparison to peers, as do her scores on Basic Reading, Spelling, Numerical Operations, and Written Expression.

Finding that a significant discrepancy exists among composite scores and subtests, as Laura exhibits, provides us with useful (but limited) information. If we are considering a possible learning disability, this information helps us to pinpoint the general area of academic deficiency. This area can then be compared with overall ability to determine whether there is a significant difference between academic achievement and ability.

Laura was administered the WISC-III as part of the assessment process. She obtained a Verbal Scale IQ (VIQ) of 88, a Performance IQ (PIQ) of 104, and a Full Scale IQ (FSIQ) of 95. The ability-achievement discrepancy analysis (Figure 4.2) reveals significant differences between the predicted scores (based on her WISC-III FSIQ) and the actual achievement scores. The discrepancies for the Reading, Mathematics, and Writing composites were all significant at the .01 level and likely to occur in 2% or less of the population. Thus, Laura would qualify on this criterion for learning disabilities services in most (if not all) states requiring a severe discrepancy between ability and achievement. However, we need more specific information to pinpoint deficit skills.

The next level of interpretation is to compare subtest scores within each composite. In the reading area, we compare Basic Reading with Reading Comprehension. In Laura's case, the difference between the two subtest scores is 14 points. By referring to Table D.4 in the test manual, we find that this difference is significant at the .05 level. Thus, Laura's understanding of what she reads is less well developed than her ability to decode words. However, both scores are significantly low as compared to those of her peers. By referring to the behavior checklist for the Basic Reading subtest we note that Laura gave up easily on this subtest and did not display any strategy for decoding words. These observations suggest that she lacks basic reading decoding skills.

In the arithmetic area, a comparison of subtest scores on Mathematics Reasoning (85) and Numerical Operations (69) reveals a 15-point difference between the two scores. By referring to Table D.4 in the manual we find that this difference in scores is not statistically significant at the .05 level; both sets of skills do show below-average development, however. Additional information can be gained by examining the behavior checklist for Mathematics Reasoning and analyzing her errors on the two subtests. Both subtests provide the specific skills measured by each subtest item. By analyzing the items Laura answered incorrectly, we can gain valuable information on the skills she has yet to master.

In the writing area, a comparison of subtest scores on Spelling (64) and Written Expression (68) reveals a 4-point difference between the two scores. Table D.4 in the manual indicates that this difference is not significant, although both subtest scores are considerably below average. The skills analysis procedure for the Spelling subtest indicates that Laura had difficulty with all three types of words (those with regular spellings, irregular spellings, and homonyms).

Skills Analysis

The purpose of skills analysis is to determine the skills in each subtest area that the student has or has not mastered. Following an overview of this approach, we will apply it to Laura's test results.

The Basic Reading subtest can be interpreted on the basis of the typical grade level at which subtest items are usually presented, and by focusing on the elements of word reading that the subtest items measure. Rapid Reference 4.14 compares the typical grade level of items from both the Basic Reading and Spelling subtests. Rapid Reference 4.15 summarizes the elements of word reading drawn from the subtest items. Both Rapid References are adapted from the WIAT *Manual.*

In the arithmetic area, two different approaches to skills analysis are applied. Items are classified by curriculum objectives in the case of Mathematics Reasoning, while they are classified by type of operation in the case of Numerical Operations. These classifications, as adapted from the *WIAT Manual,* are summarized in Rapid References 4.16 and 4.17.

The Reading Comprehension and Listening Comprehension subtests utilize the same skills analysis curriculum objectives. Items on these two subtests are classified by the curriculum objectives in Rapid Reference 4.18; these in-

≡Rapid Reference 4.14

Typical Grade Level of Items on Basic Reading and Spelling Subtests

Typical Grade Level	Basic Reading Items	Spelling Items
Preprimer and Primer	8–16	1–6
Grade 1	17–19	7–14
Grade 2	20–24	15–23
Grades 3–4	25–31, 33, 36	24–29
Grades 5–6	32, 34, 35, 37–42	30–39
Grades 7–8	43–50	40–47
Grades 9 and above	51–55	48–50

Note. Adapted from the WIAT Manual (The Psychological Corporation, 1992).

Rapid Reference 4.15

Elements of Word Reading on Basic Reading Subtest

Element	Grade Level	Subtest Item
Sight vocabulary words	1	8–10, 13, 16, 18, 19
Initial or final consonant	1–2	12, 15, 16, 20, 24
Consonant digraphs (th, sh, ph, ch)	1–2+	8, 13, 24, 32, 36
Consonant blends (ls, fr, pl, cl)	1–2+	15, 20, 25, 41
Consonant-vowel-vowel-consonant pattern	1–3+	12, 17, 20, 21, 29, 35, 37
Syllabication	3+	2, 11, 14, 17, 18, 22, 25–55
Prefixes, suffixes, and roots	4+	25, 27, 30, 33, 37
Understanding pronunciation and accent	5+	32–55

Note. Adapted from the WIAT Manual (The Psychological Corporation, 1992).

Rapid Reference 4.16

Curriculum Objectives by Item for Mathematics Reasoning

Curriculum Objective	Items	Total Number of Items
Problem Solving		
Word Problems	3, 7, 13, 17, 19, 20, 29, 32, 35, 38, 43, 45, 48, 50	14
Consumer Math	9, 11, 14–16, 21–24, 30, 44	11
Numeration/Number Concepts	1, 5, 8, 10, 25, 27, 31, 34, 36, 40, 41, 49	12
Graphs and Statistics	18, 33, 37, 47	4
Geometry	4, 12, 26, 46	4
Measurement	2, 6, 28, 39, 42	5
Total		50

Note. Adapted from the WIAT Manual (The Psychological Corporation, 1992).

Rapid Reference 4.17

Numerical Operations Items Classified by Operation and Number Type

Number Type	Addition	Subtraction	Operation Multiplication	Division	Total Number of Items
Whole Numbers					
One-digit	5, 6, 8, 10–11	7, 9	15, 20		9
Two-digit	13	12, 14	24	18	5
Renaming	16	19			2
Three-digit				23, 27	2
Renaming	17	21	22, 28		4
Fractions	25	26		35	3
Renaming	29				1
Reducing	36		32		2
Decimals					
Renaming	31	30	33		3
Total number of items	12	8	7	4	31

Note. Adapted from the WIAT Manual (The Psychological Corporation, 1992).

≡Rapid Reference 4.18

Reading Comprehension and Listening Comprehension Items Classified by Curriculum Objectives

Curriculum Objectives	Reading Comprehension	Listening Comprehension
Using picture clues	1–8	1–9
Recognizing stated detail	14, 20, 27, 33, 35	10, 14, 15, 19, 24, 26, 30, 32–34
Sequencing	9, 28, 31	11, 12, 20
Recognizing stated cause and effect	16, 21, 23, 24, 34	16, 17, 18, 28
Recognizing implied cause and effect	12, 15, 32, 37	23, 35
Making inferences		
Predicting events and outcomes	17, 19, 26, 29	13, 31
Drawing conclusions	10, 13, 22, 25, 36	22, 27, 36
Comparing and contrasting	11, 18, 30, 38	21, 25, 29

Note. Adapted from the *WIAT Manual* (The Psychological Corporation, 1992).

terpretive principles are illustrated in more detail in the psychoeducational report presented later in this chapter.

STRENGTHS AND WEAKNESSES OF THE WIAT

Although the WIAT has been in use for less than 10 years, its linking with the Wechsler scales, the most popular measures of ability, has led to many reviews of the test and to numerous research studies. (Rapid Reference 4.19

≡Rapid Reference 4.19

Reviews of the WIAT

Ackerman (1998)
Cohen (1993)
Ferrara (1998)
Flanagan (1997)
Salvia & Ysseldyke (1998, 2001)
Taylor (1998–1999)

Strengths and Weaknesses of the WIAT

Strengths	Weaknesses
Test Development	
Rationale for item selection using curriculum consultants and school-district curriculum guides to shape item selection	Inadequate floor at lower age and ability levels
Extensive tryout testing using samples with representation by sex and race/ethnicity approximately equal to U.S. census estimates	Inadequate ceiling at higher age and ability levels
Easel format for presenting subtest items	
Use of colorful, attractive materials	
Use of extensive item analysis procedures to eliminate biased items and items with poor psychometric properties	
Use of a panel of reviewers to review items for final selection	
Development of subtests covering major achievement areas outlined in IDEA	
Linkage with Wechsler scales for ability-achievement discrepancy analysis	
Standardization	
Inclusion of students receiving special education services	Use of case-weighting procedures to adjust the race/ethnicity properties to census data
Size of the standardization sample (approximately 300–350 students per age level except for ages 5 and 17–19)	Use of case-weighting procedures for linking sample to adjust the linking sample's mean FSIQ to match that of standardization sample
	Lack of details on demographic characteristics of linking sample
	Limited number of students in the linking sample

Strengths	Weaknesses
Administration and Scoring	
User-friendly layout of test protocol	Correct responses provided on test plates but not protocol for Mathematics Reasoning, Spelling, Reading Comprehension, Numerical Operations, Listening Comprehension
Clearly marked starting points based on grade	
Consistent reverse rule on most subtests	
Easel format	Complex scoring procedure for Written Expression
Appropriate administration time (about 60–75 minutes)	Standard scores not provided for the holistic scoring of Written Expression
Dichotomous scoring of most subtests	
Both age and grade norms provided	
Reliability	
High mean split-half reliabilities for subtests and composites (.77 and higher)	Relatively low interrater reliability for Written Expression
Test-retest reliabilities exceed .85 for composites (except Language composite for grades 5 and 8)	Limited number of students in test-retest reliability study
	Practice effects may be significant on Listening Comprehension and Written Expression
Test-retest reliabilities exceed .80 for subtests (except Numerical Operations, Oral Expression at grade 3; Listening Comprehension, Oral Expression, Written Expression at grades 5 and 8)	
Validity	
Strong face validity based on use of curriculum guides and skill development in reading and mathematics	Some constructs are not measured in sufficient depth on Numerical Operations and Mathematics Reasoning
Positive but limited construct validity, as demonstrated by correlations with measures of ability, group achievement tests, and intercorrelations of subtests	Small sample sizes for validity studies
Validity studies with other individually administered achievement tests (including K-TEA, WRAT-R, WJ-R) provide strong correlation coefficients (> .70)	

(continued)

Strengths	Weaknesses
Interpretation	
Both subtests and composites sufficiently reliable for interpretation	Insufficient floor for younger students with below average skills
Skills analysis procedures and behavior checklists that facilitate interpretation	Insufficient ceiling for older students with above average skills
	Lack of skills analysis norms
Linking with Wechsler scales allows ability-achievement discrepancy analysis	Early items in Listening Comprehension and Oral Expression seem to measure different skills than later items do
Can use successive-levels approach to interpretation	

presents a list of reviews of the WIAT.) In this section I summarize my views of the major strengths and weaknesses of the test. In so doing I focus on the specific areas of test development, standardization, administration and scoring, reliability, validity, and interpretation. This information is summarized in Rapid References 4.20–4.24.

Summary of the WIAT Strengths and Weaknesses

This summary of the strengths and weaknesses of the WIAT is drawn from the formal reviews listed in Rapid Reference 4.19 as well as from my own experience with the instrument as a practitioner and university trainer. Feedback from practitioners in a variety of areas has also contributed to my analysis of the instrument.

There are many strengths with the WIAT: the theoretical base of the test and the subsequent validity data, measurement of the achievement areas specified in IDEA, the inclusion of students with disabilities in the standardization sample, the reliabilities of the subtests and composites, and the linking of the test with the Wechsler scales. As with any test there are also weaknesses, which include the limited floor and ceiling of the test, with the standard score range of 40–160 not occurring at many age levels; the necessity to use case weighting procedures for the standardization sample, as well as for the linking sample; lack of norms for the skills analysis procedures; and relatively weak interrater reliability data for scoring Written Expression.

Rapid Reference 4.21

Strengths and Weaknesses of the WIAT: Effective Range of Subtest Scores, by Age
(based on raw score of 0)

Age	Basic Reading	Mathematics Reasoning	Spelling	Reading Comp	Numerical Operations	Listening Comp	Oral Expression	Written Expression[a]
5/0–5/3	93	74	77	—	72	71	79	—
5/4–5/7	92	73	76	—	70	77	77	—
5/8–5/11	91	72	75	—	68	75	75	—
6/0–6/3	89	70	75	87	66	72	72	—
6/4–6/7	88	69	74	84	64	71	70	—
6/8–6/11	84	68	72	81	63	69	67	—
7/0–7/3	80	66	70	79	63	68	65	—
7/4–7/7	76	65	68	76	62	66	62	—
7/8–7/11	72	64	66	72	61	64	60	—
8/0–8/3	69	62	64	68	59	61	57	79
8/4–8/7	65	61	62	64	58	59	55	78
8/8–8/11	63	60	61	62	57	57	54	77
9/0–9/3	61	58	60	61	56	56	54	75
9/4–9/7	59	57	59	59	55	54	53	74
9/8–9/11	58	56	58	57	54	53	52	72

(continued)

Age	Basic Reading	Mathematics Reasoning	Spelling	Reading Comp	Numerical Operations	Listening Comp	Oral Expression	Written Expression[a]
10/0–10/3	57	55	57	56	52	51	50	71
10/4–10/7	56	54	56	54	51	50	49	69
10/8–10/11	54	53	55	52	48	48	47	68
11/0–11/3	52	52	53	49	45	47	46	66
11/4–11/7	50	51	52	47	42	45	44	65
11/8–11/11	49	50	51	46	41	43	43	64
12/0–12/3	47	49	49	45	40	42	43	64
12/4–12/7	46	48	48	44	40	40	42	63
12/8–12/11	45	47	47	43	40	40	41	62
13/0–13/3	44	46	46	41	40	40	41	61
13/4–13/7	43	45	45	40	40	40	40	60
13/8–13/11	42	44	44	40	40	40	40	59
14/0–14/11	40	43	42	40	40	40	40	57
15/0–15/11	40	40	40	40	40	40	40	54
16/0–16/11	40	40	40	40	40	40	40	52
17/0–19/11	40	40	40	40	40	40	40	48

Note. Comp = Comprehension. Long dashes indicate scores not available at this age.

[a]Based on minimum raw score of 6.

⟲Rapid Reference 4.22

Strengths and Weaknesses of the WIAT: Effective Range of Composite Scores, by Age (based on raw score of 0)

Age	Reading	Mathematics	Language	Writing	Total
5/0–5/3	—	68	76	—	72
5/4–5/7	—	66	73	—	69
5/8–5/11	—	64	70	—	66
6/0–6/3	93	62	67	—	64
6/4–6/7	88	60	64	—	61
6/8–6/11	83	59	62	—	59
7/0–7/3	77	58	60	—	56
7/4–7/7	72	57	58	—	54
7/8–7/11	69	55	55	—	53
8/0–8/3	66	54	53	47	47
8/4–8/7	63	52	50	47	47
8/8–8/11	60	51	48	47	47
9/0–9/3	57	49	45	47	47
9/4–9/7	54	48	43	47	47
9/8–9/11	53	47	42	47	45
10/0–10/3	51	46	41	47	44
10/4–10/7	50	45	40	47	42
10/8–10/11	47	43	40	45	41
11/0–11/3	45	42	40	44	41
11/4–11/7	42	40	40	42	40
11/8–11/11	41	40	40	41	40
12/0–12/3	41	40	40	41	40
12/4–19/11	40	40	40	40	40

Note. Long dashes indicate scores not available at this age.

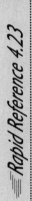

Rapid Reference 4.23

Strengths and Weaknesses of the WIAT: Effective Range of Subtest Scores, by Age (based on maximum raw score)

Age	Basic Reading	Mathematics Reasoning	Spelling	Reading Comp	Numerical Operations	Listening Comp	Oral Expression	Written Expression
5/0–5/11	160	160	160		160	160	160	—
6/0–6/11	160	160	160	160	160	160	160	—
7/0–7/7	160	160	160	160	160	160	159	—
7/8–7/11	158	160	160	160	160	160	157	—
8/0–8/3	155	160	160	160	160	160	154	160
8/4–8/7	153	160	160	160	160	160	152	160
8/8–8/11	151	160	160	160	160	160	151	160
9/0–9/3	148	160	160	160	160	160	149	160
9/4–9/7	146	160	160	160	160	160	148	160
9/8–9/11	143	160	158	158	156	159	146	158
10/0–10/3	140	160	155	157	152	159	144	156
10/4–10/7	137	160	153	155	148	158	142	154

Age	Basic Reading	Mathematics Reasoning	Spelling	Reading Comp	Numerical Operations	Listening Comp	Oral Expression	Written Expression
10/8–10/11	135	157	151	153	146	156	141	152
11/0–11/3	133	154	149	152	144	155	141	151
11/4–11/7	131	151	147	150	142	153	140	149
11/8–11/11	130	149	146	149	140	152	139	148
12/0–12/3	129	147	145	147	137	152	139	147
12/4–12/7	128	145	144	146	135	151	138	146
12/8–12/11	127	142	143	145	132	150	137	142
13/0–13/3	126	138	143	143	130	148	137	142
13/4–13/7	125	135	142	142	127	147	136	140
13/8–13/11	124	134	141	142	126	146	135	139
14/0–14/11	123	132	140	141	123	145	134	136
15/0–15/11	121	130	138	140	120	143	133	132
16/0–16/11	117	127	134	136	119	138	132	129
17/0–19/11	114	123	128	134	118	135	128	126

Note. Comp = Comprehension. Long dashes indicate scores not available at this age.

≡ *Rapid Reference 4.24*

Strengths and Weaknesses of the WIAT: Effective Range of Composite Scores, by Age (based on maximum raw score)

Age	Reading	Mathematics	Language	Writing	Total
5/0–5/11	—	160	160	—	160
6/0–7/11	160	160	160	—	160
8/0–8/7	160	160	160	160	160
8/8–8/11	158	160	160	160	160
9/0–9/3	156	160	160	160	160
9/4–9/7	154	160	160	160	160
9/8–9/11	151	160	159	160	160
10/0–10/3	147	160	159	160	160
10/4–10/7	144	160	158	160	160
10/8–10/11	144	157	156	158	158
11/0–11/3	144	155	155	157	155
11/4–11/7	144	152	153	155	153
11/8–11/11	143	150	153	154	152
12/0–12/3	141	147	152	154	152
12/4–12/7	140	145	152	153	151
12/8–12/11	138	142	151	152	150
13/0–13/3	137	138	150	150	149
13/4–13/7	135	135	149	149	148
13/8–13/11	136	134	149	148	147
14/0–14/11	139	131	148	145	146
15/0–15/11	146	127	147	141	146
16/0–16/11	140	125	144	138	137
17/0–19/11	131	122	139	131	136

Note. Long dashes indicate scores not available at this age.

As with most tests, the WIAT is not as precise in measuring its constructs at the youngest and oldest age ranges, particularly with individuals considerably below average or above average in achievement. Rapid References 4.21–4.24 document this. Although the standard score range is designed to be from 40 to 160 at all ages, a perusal of Rapid Reference 4.21 shows that this occurs at rather limited age ranges. The subtest ceilings are somewhat better, with subtest scores of 160 (based on maximum raw score points) occurring for Mathematics Reasoning, Spelling, Numerical Operations, and Listening Comprehension at ages 5 years zero months through 9 years 7 months. For adolescents, maximum raw score points can yield subtest standard scores as low as 114. Basic Reading and Numerical Operations are the worst offenders in this respect.

A similar pattern emerges with the composite scores. Standard scores of 40 on all composites (based on raw scores of 0) occur only at ages 12 years 4 months through 19 years 11 months. The Reading Composite is the most troublesome of the composites. At the other end of the continuum, standard scores of 160 (based on maximum raw scores) occur on all composites at ages 5 years zero months through 8 years 7 months only. Once again, the Reading Composite is the most troublesome. Thus, use caution in interpreting both subtest and composite scores with very low raw scores or very high raw scores, especially at the extremes of the age range.

CLINICAL APPLICATIONS OF THE WIAT

Many of the studies with the WIAT have focused on its relationships with other measures of achievement, including the PIAT-R, K-TEA, WRAT-R/WRAT3 and WJ-R. Rapid Reference 4.25 provides references for some of these studies. Other studies have examined performance patterns of students with certain types of disabilities. A final area of research has focused on some of the challenges and difficulties in measuring written language skills.

The WIAT and Achievement Measures

Many of the studies with the WIAT have examined its relationship with other achievement tests. For example, Martelle and Smith (1994) found significant

≡Rapid Reference 4.25

Studies Comparing Performance on the WIAT with That on Other Achievement Measures

Kaufman Test of Educational Achievement
Gentry, Sapp, & Daw (1995)

Peabody Individual Achievement Test–Revised
Muenz, Ouchi, & Cole (1999)
Riccio, Boan, Staniszewski, & Hynd (1997)
Slate (1996)

Wide Range Achievement Test–Revised
Wide Range Achievement Test 3
Smith & Smith (1998)

Woodcock-Johnson Psycho-Educational Battery–Revised Tests of Achievement
Martelle & Smith (1994)
Mason, Seese, & Teska (2000)

Wechsler Intelligence Scale for Children–Third Edition
Albers (1998)
Flanagan & Alfonso (1993a,b)
Glutting, McDermott, Prifitera, & McGrath (1994)
Glutting, Oakland, & Konold (1994)
Glutting, Oh, Ward, & Ward (2000)
Glutting, Robins, & de Lancey (1997)
Glutting, Youngstrom, Ward, Ward, & Hale (1997)
Konold (1999)
Konold, Glutting, Oakland, & O'Donnell (1995)
Saklofske, Schwean, & O'Donnell (1996)
Sapp & Emens (2000)
Slate (1994)
Weiss & Prifitera (1995)

correlations between the Reading and Mathematics composites of the WIAT and related cluster scores on the WJ-R, using a sample of 48 students referred for possible learning disabilities. WIAT scores were significantly lower than WJ-R scores. Meanwhile, Slate (1996) found moderate to strong correlations between the WIAT and PIAT-R on similar constructs, using a sample of 202 students with learning disabilities. These studies, as well as the ones cited in Rapid Reference 4.25, suggest moderate to strong relationships between the WIAT and other measures of achievement.

Another line of research with the WIAT has focused on the Written Expression subtest. For example, Mason, Seese, and Teska (2000) found no significant correlations between the WIAT Written Expression subtest and the WJ-R Writing Samples subtest in a sample of college students. They concluded that the two subtests measure different skills, at least with college students. On the other hand, Muenz, Ouchi, and Cole (1999) examined the reliability and validity of the Written Expression subtests of the WIAT and the PIAT-R and concluded that the WIAT had more items that were both reliable and valid. Riccio, Boan, Staniszewski, and Hynd (1997) found moderate correlations between the WIAT and PIAT-R Written Expression subtests using a sample of 120 school-aged students. These studies and the lesser reliability of these subtests when compared to the other subtests in each battery suggest that we should be cautious in our interpretation of these scores.

The WIAT and the WISC-III

Perhaps the greatest number of research studies has compared performance on the WIAT with that on the WISC-III. Many of the studies have compared the correlations of the two tests reported in the test manual with correlations produced from studies of various groups of students. Slate (1994), for example, used a sample of students with learning disabilities, mental retardation, and students referred for (but not placed in) special education and found many differences from the correlations reported in the WIAT manual. Most of the correlations he obtained were higher than those reported in the manual.

The ability-achievement discrepancy analysis has also been a subject of research. Flanagan and Alfonso (1993a, b) developed tables for use in determining ability-achievement discrepancies with the predicted-achievement method and either VIQ or PIQ, rather than the FSIQ only, as contained in the WIAT manual. Weiss and Prifitera (1995) examined the predictive bias of discrepancy analysis in White, Black, and Hispanic students and found a lack of bias in using the IQ score to predict achievement. Konold (1999), using a sample of 300 students, found that the WISC-III index scores provided a better prediction of the WIAT achievement composites than did the WISC-III FSIQ. It is likely that the ability-achievement discrepancy analysis will continue to be a subject of considerable interest to researchers and practitioners.

AN ILLUSTRATIVE CASE REPORT

In this section our focus turns to a psychoeducational report for a student referred for possible special education placement. We will be interpreting Debbie's WIAT results along with additional test data.

Reason for Referral

Debbie was referred for evaluation as part of the three-year reassessment process to determine her educational programming. She is currently in the 5th grade and is 10 years 4 months of age.

Debbie's mother reported that she has no major concerns regarding Debbie's academic performance. She indicated that the school year has been going well for Debbie. Debbie supported this by explaining to me that school is going "okay." She stated that she enjoys working on the computer but dislikes social studies because "it is too boring."

Background Information

Debbie was originally evaluated in March 1995. She qualified for special education services under Other Health Impaired (OHI). She was evaluated again in December of 1996 resulting in a classification in the area of Emotional and Behavioral Disability (E/BD) as her primary disability (her secondary disability at that time was OHI). She was also evaluated in November, 1997. Concerns throughout previous evaluations were difficulties with academics, verbalizing feelings, and following directions, and a lack of positive interactions with adults and peers.

Debbie lives at home with her biological parents, a 16-year-old brother, and a 7-year-old brother. Her mother reported that there were no complications during her pregnancy and childbirth with Debbie. Debbie's developmental milestones, such as walking and talking, were reached within normal age ranges. There is no history of health problems. Debbie's health at the time of testing was fine. She is taking Ritalin for Attention-Deficit Hyperactivity Disorder (ADHD).

Both Debbie and her mother reported that Debbie enjoys playing with her brothers and watching television. Debbie reported that her brothers, especially the 7-year-old, are the people she plays with the most. She also reported that she enjoys spending time at her grandmother's, where she often helps her grandmother cook. Debbie has chores around the home for which she is responsible. Her mother reported that she must often remind Debbie to complete her chores. When they are not completed, she is usually grounded. Her mother reported that she and her husband usually agree regarding discipline issues.

Debbie's cognitive ability and achievement levels were last assessed in November, 1997. At that time she was administered the Kaufman Assessment Battery for Children (K-ABC) and the Woodcock-Johnson Psycho-Educational Battery–Revised Tests of Achievement (WJ-R TA). The results were as follows.

K-ABC

	IQ score	Percentile	Classification
Mental Processing Composite	83	13	Low Average
Sequential Processing Composite	80	9	Low Average
Simultaneous Processing Composite	89	23	Low Average

WJ-R TA

	Standard score	Percentile	Classification
Broad Reading	86	18	Low Average
Broad Mathematics	92	30	Average
Written Language	87	19	Low Average

Behavioral Observations

Debbie was observed in the classroom on two occasions. The first observation occurred during Social Studies. During this observation, Debbie was in a large-group, cooperative setting with approximately 25 students working with the teacher to review various world explorers. Students were asked to complete a study guide by copying notes from the chalkboard. Debbie displayed frustration during this task by explaining to the teacher that she was going too fast. At the same time, Debbie slouched and put her head in her hands. When given extra time to complete her study guide, she attempted the task and worked quietly. Debbie was on task 85 percent of the time as compared to her peers, who were on task 100 percent of the time. Off-task behaviors included playing with her pencil and a pencil sharpener.

The second classroom observation took place in Music class. During this observation, Debbie was in a class with about 25 students. The group performed some warm-up activities and then practiced different pieces of music. Debbie appeared interested in the activities. She listened closely to classroom announcements, performed the warm-up exercises, and sang along to the different songs that were performed. She also volunteered to answer a question regarding what kind of sound should be made for a certain word. Though she was incorrect, she appeared motivated and willing to participate. Debbie was on task 90 percent of the time as compared to her peers, who were on task 95 percent of the time.

During the testing Debbie was very pleasant and cooperative. Her dress and health appeared fine. She followed instructions well and remained attentive throughout the session. She was also talkative during testing, indicating a good level of rapport with me. She appeared at ease, calmly answering questions throughout the testing.

She reacted appropriately to both success and failure and attempted to complete all tasks that were presented. This effort was supported by the various strategies that she displayed during testing. She used finger-counting strategies during arithmetic; checked over her work when on several nonverbal tasks; and verbalized her strategies on other tasks.

Debbie appeared much more restless during the achievement testing. She moved around more in her chair and needed to be reminded to focus on the task at hand. Although she appeared restless, she did seem to be trying her best. She listened well and was interested in most of the tasks presented to her. On the basis of these observations, the current evaluation is a valid and reliable estimate of Debbie's cognitive and achievement skills.

Evaluation Procedures/Instruments

Review of school records
Interviews with parents
Classroom observations
Wechsler Intelligence Scale for Children–Third Edition (WISC-III)
Wechsler Individual Achievement Test (WIAT)
Behavior Assessment System for Children (BASC)

Test Results

WISC-III Results

Scale/Index	IQ	95% Confidence Interval	Percentile Rank
Verbal Scale	79	77–93	8
Performance Scale	84	77–93	14
Full Scale	80	75–86	9
Verbal Comprehension	77	72–85	8
Perceptual Organization	90	83–99	25
Freedom from Distractibility	87	79–98	19
Processing Speed	80	73–93	9

Verbal Subtests	Scaled Score	Performance Subtests	Scaled Score
Information	6	Picture Completion	8
Similarities	5	Coding	5
Arithmetic	8	Picture Arrangement	5
Vocabulary	5	Block Design	10
Comprehension	7	Object Assembly	10
Digit Span	7	Symbol Search	7

WIAT Results

Subtests/Composites	Standard Score	95% Confidence Interval	Percentile Rank
Basic Reading	81	74–88	10
Mathematics Reasoning	85	77–93	16
Spelling	84	76–92	14
Reading Comprehension	84	75–93	14
Numerical Operations	79	70–88	8
Listening Comprehension	76	66–86	5
Oral Expression	92	84–100	30
Written Expression	69	56–82	2
Reading	80	74–86	9
Mathematics	79	72–86	8
Language	83	75–91	13
Writing	75	67–83	5
Total Composite	79	75–83	8

Analysis of Results

The WISC-III is an individually administered test of cognitive abilities covering the age range of 6 to 16 years. It consists of six subtests emphasizing verbal content and six subtests emphasizing nonverbal content. The Full Scale IQ combines both sets of subtests and produces the most valid overall score. Debbie's performance on the WISC-III falls solidly in the below average range of intellectual functioning. Her overall score of 80 ±5.5 places her at the 9th percentile, indicating that she is functioning at a level equal to or greater than that of 9 percent of students of her age. Furthermore, the Verbal, Performance, and Index scores are quite consistent, ranging from 77 to 90. Thus, Debbie's verbal/language skills as well as her nonverbal reasoning skills and ability to organize visual information are uniformly developed. All subtest scores were consistent with no relative strengths or weaknesses.

Debbie's performance on the WIAT was consistent with her performance on the WISC-III. Her Total composite score on the WIAT was 79 and places her at the 8th percentile, indicating that she is functioning academically at a level equal to or greater than that of 8 percent of the other students her age. Her academic performance across composites and individual subtests is on a 3rd-grade level and shows uniform development across curriculum areas.

Within the reading area, her ability to decode words and to remember what she has read are uniformly developed within the low average range. When encountering unfamiliar words, Debbie attempted to use decoding skills but had difficulty with multisyllable words and quickly gave up on them. Word endings were a particular area of difficulty. She also mispronounced several basic sight-vocabulary words and exhibited difficulties with basic syllabication. In Spelling, Debbie experienced the most difficulty in trying to spell homonyms. Most of her errors were confined to multisyllable words, homonyms, and word endings. In Reading Comprehension, Debbie made good use of picture cues but had difficulty inferring cause-and-effect relationships and drawing inferences from what she read.

Debbie was successful with the arithmetic problems involving addition and subtraction, including those requiring regrouping. However, she was unsuccessful with problems involving multiplication, division, and fractions. There was no difference between her ability to solve orally presented problems and her ability to solve those presented in a worksheet format. Her scores on the two WIAT subtests involving math and the WISC-III Arithmetic subtest were quite consistent.

Within the language area, there was a significant difference between Debbie's levels of performance on the two subtests that make up the composite. Her ability to express herself verbally is significantly better developed (in the average range) than her skills in listening comprehension (in the borderline range). Thus, Debbie appears to be more proficient in using words to express herself than she is at understanding what is said to her or presented verbally. In Listening Comprehension, as in Reading Comprehension, she experienced difficulty in recognizing cause-and-effect relationships and making inferences from what she heard. Her use of picture clues was very strong. These results, in combination with her performance on the Perceptual Organization factor of the WISC-III, suggest that Debbie may function more efficiently with the visual presentation of material.

The final area measured by the WIAT was Debbie's writing skills. She had considerable difficulty with such skills as the development of ideas, vocabulary, and appropriate grammar usage. Her response to the writing prompt was lacking in detail, with little elaboration of the detail that was presented. In addition, the vocabulary she used was simplistic and lacked variety. Since her response was quite brief it was not possible to analyze sentence structure and variety. Spelling skills were also below average. A comparison of Debbie's scores on Written Expression and Oral Expression shows that she is much more adept at expressing herself verbally than in writing. In completing written tasks, Debbie is physically slow and somewhat awkward, often leading to frustration in completing such tasks. Her deficit in Written Expression qualifies as an area of severe discrepancy when compared to her overall ability.

It should be noted that the results of the current evaluation (cognitive and achievement) are consistent with her K-ABC and WJ-R TA results from November, 1997. Her overall WISC-III FSIQ is within 3 points of her K-ABC Mental Processing Composite. In the achievement area, her reading scores are similar, while her arithmetic and written language scores are somewhat lower (but not significantly lower).

The Behavior Assessment System for Children (BASC) was completed by Debbie's mother, Debbie's classroom teacher, and Debbie herself. The BASC is a rating scale of both problem behaviors and adaptive behaviors. Similar items are contained on the parent and teacher versions of the BASC. Debbie's mother reported problem behaviors at a clinically significant level in hyperactivity, aggression, conduct problems, anxiety, depression, and attention problems. She also indicated that Debbie had difficulty adapting to changes in the environment and was lacking in social skills. Meanwhile, Debbie's classroom teacher reported difficulties in the academic area and in Debbie's tendency to avoid social contact. Some concern was noted for depression and for Debbie's difficulty in adapting to changes in the environment. Her study skills were also described as very weak.

Summary

Debbie, a 10-year-old 5th-grader, was assessed as part of the 3-year reevaluation process for special education services in the area of Emotional/Behavioral Disability. Debbie displayed a good amount of effort during testing. She worked hard at solving all problems, regardless of their difficulty levels. At times during both classroom observations and testing, Debbie appeared frustrated. She displayed this behavior with verbal statements or by placing her hands on her head. Though she appeared frustrated, Debbie still attempted to complete the required task. The current evaluation suggests that Debbie's overall level of intellectual and academic functioning is in the below average range. Overall, Debbie's cognitive and academic skills are evenly developed with the exception of written expression skills. In this area she is achieving at a level significantly below her overall level of intellectual functioning. This area of difficulty was verified by her regular and special education teachers. There were several concerns reported in the area of emotional and behavioral development. Consistent themes that were reported by her mother and teacher were concerns regarding hyperactivity, aggression, and depression. In addition, Debbie was described as having difficulty adapting to change and interacting with peers. A lack of study skills was also indicated.

Recommendations

1. It is suggested that the Individual Educational Plan team recommend continuation of special education services to Debbie in the area of Emotional/Behavioral Disability. She continues to exhibit difficulties in this area both at home and at school, as indicated by the parent/teacher interviews and the results of the BASC. Particular attention should be focused on the continued development of social and interpersonal skills. As noted earlier in this report, Debbie exhibited quite a bit of frustration during assessment and classroom observation. This should also be an area of intervention.

2. Consultation with the learning disabilities staff is also suggested regarding Debbie's deficit in written expression and written language skills. Her performance on the WIAT indicates much difficulty in spelling and grammar usage, a limited vocabulary, and limitations in the written expression of ideas.

3. Although Debbie was off task to a greater degree than her peers were during the classroom observations, this does not seem to be a major concern. Her ability to remain on task and complete classroom assignments is not greatly impaired at this time. On occasion, however, she may require additional time for assignments. This is particularly true for written assignments. Debbie responds favorably to attention from the teacher and this should be utilized when possible.

4. Debbie should be taught keyboarding skills if at all possible. Written work is especially difficult for Debbie and causes considerable

frustration. Being able to type rather than write assignments may lead to greater productivity and lessen the frustration that she encounters.

Douglas K. Smith, PhD, NCSP
Director, School Psychology Training

Robert Griffith, EdS
Examiner

THE WIAT SCREENER

The WIAT Screener is an individually administered measure of academic achievement for students aged 5 years 0 months through 19 years 11 months. It is best used as a screening test and provides global scores for Reading, Mathematics, and Spelling, as well as a Screener Composite.

The subtests comprising the WIAT Screener are Basic Reading, Mathematics Reasoning, and Spelling; these are presented in Stimulus Book 1. Each subtest is administered, scored, and interpreted in the same way as it is with the WIAT itself. The tables used to convert raw scores to derived scores are the same as for the WIAT, as are the interpretive principles.

The WIAT Screener can be used in ability-achievement discrepancy analysis in the same way as the WIAT. This represents an advantage over other screening instruments, such as the K-TEA/NU Brief Form.

Reliability and validity data are the same for both the WIAT Screener and the WIAT, with the exception of the Screener Composite; Rapid Reference 4.26 presents a comparison of the WIAT Screener Composite and the WIAT Composite. A major advantage of the WIAT Screener, as compared to the K-TEA/NU Brief Form and the WRAT3, is that the Screener can be administered initially and the remainder of the Comprehensive Battery can be administered at a later date. Thus, we can use the WIAT Screener as a screening test, and if academic difficulties or a significant discrepancy between ability and achievement is indicated, a more comprehensive evaluation can be undertaken using the remainder of the WIAT subtests. In this way our testing time may be used more efficiently. Rapid Reference 4.27 provides basic information on the test and its publisher.

≡Rapid Reference 4.26

Comparison of WIAT Screener and WIAT on Selected Reliability Measures

	Screener Composite	WIAT Total Composite
Average split-half reliability coefficient[a]	.96	.97
Corrected stability coefficients		
Grade 1	.95	.94
Grade 3	.93	.95
Grade 5	.97	.97
Grade 8	.96	.95
Grade 10	.95	.96
Average standard error of measurement[a]	3.14	2.56

[a]Age-based scores

≡Rapid Reference 4.27

WIAT Screener

Author: The Psychological Corporation

Publication Date: 1992

What the Test Measures: reading, spelling, and mathematics skills

Age Range: 5 years 0 months through 19 years 11 months

Administration Time: 10 to 15 minutes, depending on the age of the student

Qualification of Examiners: Training in educational or psychological testing with graduate-level training in assessment

Publisher: The Psychological Corporation
555 Academic Court
San Antonio, TX 78204-2498
(800) 872-1726
www.PsychCorp.com

Price: Complete test kit $127.00 (2001 catalog price)

A PREVIEW OF THE WIAT-II

Overview

The Wechsler Individual Achievement Test–Second Edition (WIAT-II), scheduled for publication in 2001, incorporates some important changes from the original edition. New subtests have been added and others have been revised. In addition, the age range has been extended at both ends and now covers the range of 4 years through adults, with norms for college students. It is also conormed with the Process Assessment of the Learner (PAL): Test Battery for Reading and Writing.

Description of the WIAT-II

As practitioners, we often fail to recognize the substantial time investment in the development of a new assessment instrument or the revision of an existing test. In the case of the WIAT-II, the development process has been underway since 1995; Rapid Reference 4.28 shows the phases in its development.

Two major purposes in revising the WIAT were to correct two problems with the original WIAT: inflated scores on the Written Expression subtest and the ceiling/floor problems discussed earlier. In addition, the WIAT-II was designed to update the normative base, provide a more thorough assessment of the achievement areas specified in IDEA 1997, and to establish links with the WISC-III, WAIS-III, and WPPSI-R for ability-achievement discrepancy analysis. Rapid Reference 4.29 shows the IDEA achievement areas and the corre-

≡Rapid Reference 4.28

Stages of Development for the WIAT-II

Stage	Activity	Time Period
1	Blueprint development of subtests	1995–1996
2	Pilot testing of subtests and items	Spring 1997
3	National tryout testing	Fall 1997–1998
4	National standardization	1999–2000
5	Development of norms and final test components	2000–2001

≡Rapid Reference 4.29

IDEA Achievement Areas and WIAT Subtests

IDEA Areas	WIAT-II Subtests
Basic reading skills	Pseudoword Decoding[a]
	Word Reading
Reading comprehension	Reading Comprehension
Written expression	Written Expression
	Spelling
Oral expression	Oral Language[a]
Listening comprehension	Listening Comprehension
Mathematics reasoning	Math Reasoning
Mathematics calculation	Numerical Operations

[a]New subtest

sponding WIAT-II subtests, while Rapid Reference 4.30 describes each of the subtests. The nine WIAT-II subtests together compose the overall test composite score. Rapid Reference 4.31 shows the subtest composition of the other composites: Reading, Math, Written Expression, and Oral Expression.

Standardization of the WIAT-II

Standardization data are currently being analyzed; thus, only limited information is currently available. The standardization sample, however, was designed to be representative of the U.S. population (1999 census estimates) and the standardization took place in 1999–2000. Demographic variables used in standardization included age, sex, geographic region, race/ethnicity, and parent educational level. Students with disabilities were included in the standardization sample and came from the following areas: ADHD, mental retardation, learning disabilities, E/BD, hearing impairments, and language impairments. Standardization data for a gifted and talented group were also collected. A unique feature of the standardization process was the inclusion of English-speaking Canadian students. Separate norms are planned for this group be-

≡ Rapid Reference 4.30

Description of WIAT-II Subtests

Word Reading	Assesses the student's ability to read familiar words aloud from a list. Both accuracy and automaticity are measured.
Pseudoword Decoding	Assesses the student's ability to apply phonetic de- coding skills. The student is presented a list of pseudo- words designed to mimic the phonetic structure of words in the English language. The student is asked to read them aloud.
Reading Comprehension	Reflects the type of reading conducted in general ed- ucation classrooms. Initial items include matching a written word with its representative picture. Students also read different types of passages and respond to questions involving comprehension of content, such as identifying main ideas, making inferences, interpret- ing content, and defining vocabulary by using context cues. Students are also asked to read short sentences aloud and respond to comprehension questions. Stu- dents are evaluated on their ability to accurately read grade-level target words aloud using content cues.
Numerical Operations	Evaluates the student's ability to identify and write dic- tated numerals and solve written calculation problems and equations involving all basic operations (addition, subtraction, multiplication, and division).
Math Reasoning	Presents a series of problems both verbally and visu- ally to assess the student's ability to reason mathemat- ically. Students demonstrate their ability to count using one-to-one correspondence; to identify geometric shapes; to solve single-step and multistep problems related to time, money, and measurement, using both whole numbers and fractions or decimals; to interpret graphs; to identify mathematical patterns; and to solve problems related to probability.
Spelling	Evaluates the student's ability to spell by writing dic- tated letters, letter blends, and words. The inclusion of homonyms requires the student to use context cues from the dictated sentence to select the appropriate spelling of the word.

Written Expression	Evaluates the student's writing skills at the letter, word, sentence and text levels by asking him or her to write the alphabet from memory within a time limit, to demonstrate written word fluency, to combine sentences, to generate sentences from visual cues, and to produce a well-constructed paragraph (grades 3–6) or persuasive essay (grades 7 and up). Performance is measured using a rubric scoring system that evaluates organization, vocabulary, theme development, and writing mechanics.
Listening Comprehension	Measures the student's ability to listen for details.
Oral Language	Measures receptive and expressive vocabulary, verbal fluency at the word level, and the ability to generate descriptions and stories from verbal cues. Performance is measured using a rubric scoring system that evaluates the student's ability to use language effectively to communicate ideas.

≡Rapid Reference 4.31

Subtest Composition of WIAT-II Composites

Reading Composite	Math Composite	Written Expression Composite	Oral Expression Composite
Word Reading	Numerical Operations	Spelling	Listening Comprehension
Pseudoword Decoding	Math Reasoning	Written Language	Oral Language
Reading Comprehension			

cause some test items were changed for this part of standardization. At the present time, separate prekindergarten (ages 4 and 5 years) through high school norms, college norms, and adult norms are planned. Prekindergarten through middle school norms will be based on 300 cases per grade, while high school norms will be based on 200 cases per grade.

The WIAT-II raw scores will be converted to standard scores (mean = 100, SD = 15), percentile ranks, grade equivalents, age equivalents, normal curve equivalents, and stanines.

Psychometric Characteristics

Reliability and validity data for the WIAT-II are currently being analyzed. Validity studies comparing performance on the WIAT-II with that on the WIAT, WRMT-R/NU, PPVT-III, WJ-R, DAS, WPPSI-R, WISC-III, and WAIS-III are underway.

How to Administer the WIAT-II

Like the WIAT, the WIAT-II utilizes an easel format. The Standardization Edition consisted of two easels with Word Reading, Numerical Operations, Reading Comprehension, and Spelling in Stimulus Booklet 1. Stimulus Booklet 2 consisted of Math Reasoning, Written Expression, and Oral Language. As with the WIAT, the materials are colorful and attractive.

Reverse rules, starting points based on grade level, and discontinue rules are utilized. Actual discontinue and reverse rules varied from subtest to subtest on the Standardization Edition. Estimated administration times are 30–50 minutes for prekindergarten through elementary-age students and 55–75 minutes for older students.

Most subtest items are dichotomously scored, with the exception of Written Expression and Oral Language. The scoring system for Written Expression is being revised from the WIAT and will have both objective (word count, spelling errors, punctuation) and subjective scoring measures. The subjective measures in the Standardization Edition (organization, theme development, and vocabulary) had specific criteria or rubrics associated with them; these rubrics were then scored on a scale ranging from 0 to 4. Numerous examples of scoring and practice exercises were provided. It is anticipated that in the fi-

Rapid Reference 4.32

WIAT and WIAT-II Content Differences

WIAT Subtest	Measures	WIAT-II Subtest	Measures
Basic Reading	Word recognition	Word Reading	Phonological awareness Alphabet principle (letter-sound awareness) Automaticity of word recognition Word recognition
		Pseudoword Decoding	Phonological decoding Automaticity of word decoding Accuracy of word decoding
Reading Comprehension	Literal comprehension Inferential comprehension	Reading Comprehension	Oral reading accuracy Oral reading fluency Oral reading comprehension Word recognition in context Literal comprehension Inferential comprehension Lexical comprehension Reading rate

(continued)

WIAT Subtest	Measures	WIAT-II Subtest	Measures
Numerical Operations	Numerical writing Calculation (addition, subtraction, multiplication, division) Fractions, decimals, algebra	Numerical Operations	Counting One-to-one correspondence Numeral identification and writing Calculation (addition, subtraction, multiplication, division) Fractions, decimals, algebra
Mathematics Reasoning	Quantitative concepts Problem solving Money, time, and management Geometry Reading and interpreting charts and graphs Statistics	Mathematics Reasoning	Quantitative concepts Multistep problem solving Money, time, and measurement Geometry Reading and interpreting charts and graphs Statistics and probability Estimation Patterns
Spelling	Alphabet principle (sound-letter awareness) Written spelling of regular and irregular words Written spelling of homonyms (integration of spelling and lexical comprehension)	Spelling	Same as WIAT

WIAT Subtest	Measures	WIAT-II Subtest	Measures
Written Expression	Descriptive writing (evaluated on extension and elaboration, grammar and usage, ideas and development, organization, unity, and coherence, and sentence structure and variety) Narrative writing (evaluated on the same criteria as descriptive)	Written Expression	Alphabet writing Word fluency (written) Sentence combining Sentence generation Written responses to verbal and visual cues Descriptive writing (evaluated on theme, organization, and mechanics) Persuasive writing (evaluated on theme, organization, and mechanics)
Listening Comprehension	Receptive vocabulary Listening (literal comprehension) Listening (inferential comprehension)	Listening Comprehension	Receptive vocabulary Expressive vocabulary Word fluency (oral) Auditory short-term recall for contextual information
Oral Expression	Expressive vocabulary Giving directions Explaining steps in sequential tasks	Oral Language	Story generation Giving directions Explaining steps in sequential tasks Listening (inferential comprehension)

Note. From prepublication materials for the WIAT-II. Copyright © 2000 The Psychological Corporation. Adapted and reproduced by permission. All rights reserved.

≡ *Rapid Reference 4.33*

Wechsler Individual Achievement Test II

Author: The Psychological Corporation

Publication Date: 2001

What the Test Measures: Reading decoding, reading comprehension, spelling, mathematics reasoning, mathematics calculation, oral expression, written expression, and listening comprehension

Age Range: 4 years 0 months through adulthood

Administration Time: 30 to 75 minutes depending on age of student

Qualifications of Examiners: Graduate-level training in educational or psychoeducational testing

Publisher: The Psychological Corporation
555 Academic Court
San Antonio, TX 78204-2498
(800) 211-8378
www.PsychCorp.com

Prices: Complete test kit $300.00 (2001 catalog price); $350.00 for Combo Kit with scoring software for educators; $399.00 for Combo Kit with SAWS or SAWS-A for clinicians
Computer scoring program: $125.00 for Score Plus Software (2001 catalog price); $150.00 for SAWS or SAWS-A (2001 catalog price)

nal edition the scoring system for this subtest will be much improved from that for the original WIAT.

The Oral Language subtest, during standardization, consisted of seven sections that were scored separately. They included One-Word Receptive Vocabulary, Verbal Fluency, One-Word Expressive Vocabulary, Sentence Repetition, Sentence Comprehension, Visual Passage Recall, and Giving Directions. Although many of these components were dichotomously scored, some were not; however, detailed scoring criteria were provided. While this subtest provides a wealth of data, scoring may be somewhat complex.

An expanded skills analysis procedure is to be included when the WIAT-II is published. There will also be a variety of computer scoring programs. The basic program, WIAT-II Score Plus, will create a detailed skills analysis of the students results as well as converting raw scores to derived scores. Separate WISC-III/WIAT-II and WAIS-III/WIAT-II Scoring Assistants for the

Wechsler scales will also be available in both diskette and CD-ROM versions. Also in the planning/development stages are a WISC-III/WIAT-II Writer and a WAIS-III/WIAT-II Writer.

WIAT/WIAT-II Content Differences

Because the WIAT-II reflects a major emphasis on skills analysis, there have been changes in the content measured by the subtests that originally composed the WIAT. In some cases an existing subtest has been reorganized into two subtests. Rapid Reference 4.32 outlines these content differences. Basic information on the test and its publisher is presented in Rapid Reference 4.33.

 TEST YOURSELF

1. **The WIAT subtests measure all of the achievement areas described in IDEA (1997) for learning disabilities.** True or False?

2. **Subtests can be administered in any order.** True or False?

3. **Subtest starting points are based on**
   (a) grade level.
   (b) age level.
   (c) raw score on Basic Reading.
   (d) raw score on Spelling.

4. **The discontinue rule is the same for all subtests except Written Expression.** True or False?

5. **When the reverse rule is invoked, preceding items are administered**
   (a) beginning with item 1.
   (b) in reverse order.
   (c) in sets of two.
   (d) beginning with the next-earliest starting point.

6. **The Language composite is made up of the scores on the Oral Expression and Written Expression subtests.** True or False?

7. **The WIAT Screener consists of the subtests** _____, _____, and _____.

(continued)

8. **Standard scores for the Written Expression subtest are derived from which of the following scoring methods?**

   (a) holistic

   (b) analytic

   (c) synthetic

   (d) free-form

9. **The ability-achievement discrepancy analysis procedure requires the use of**

   (a) grade-based standard scores.

   (b) age-based standard scores.

   (c) either age-based or grade-based standard scores.

   (d) raw scores.

10. **To facilitate ability-achievement discrepancy analysis, the WIAT is linked with the following Wechsler scales:** _____, _____, and _____.

Answers: 1. True; 2. False; 3. a; 4. False; 5. b; 6. False; 7. Basic Reading, Mathematics Reasoning, Spelling; 8. b; 9. b; 10. WISC-III, WPPSI-R, WAIS-R

Five

WIDE RANGE ACHIEVEMENT TEST 3

OVERVIEW

The Wide Range Achievement Test 3 (WRAT3; Wilkinson, 1993) and its predecessors trace their history to the 1930s, when the original version of the instrument was developed by Joseph Jastak as a supplement to the Wechsler Bellevue scales. The original instrument consisted of measures of word recognition, spelling, and arithmetic computation (Wilkinson, 1993). The WRAT3 is a revision of the Wide Range Achievement Test–Revised (WRAT-R; Jastak & Wilkinson, 1984) and is designed to measure basic academic skills in individuals 5–75 years of age. A single-level format is used rather than the dual-level format of the WRAT-R. Unlike the other achievement tests we have discussed, the WRAT3 has two forms. While the scores produced on these forms are similar, they are not identical. For example, the Tan Form yields slightly higher standard scores for the same raw score at certain ages. Mabry (1995) has also noted that in the arithmetic area the two forms do not measure the same skills. For example, "the Blue Form includes an algebra problem with two unknown quantities and a fraction problem; only the Tan Form includes a compound interest and a logarithm problem" (Mabry, 1995, p. 1108).

Description of the WRAT3

The WRAT3 is an individually administered, normative test of academic achievement, designed to be a screening test of academic achievement similar to the K-TEA Brief Form and the WIAT Screener. Age-based standard scores (mean = 100, SD = 15) are provided for each form as well as a combined form. In addition, percentiles, grade equivalent scores, and absolute scores are pro-

≡≡Rapid Reference 5.1

Description of the WRAT3 Subtests

Reading   Measures the abilities to recognize and name letters (upper case only) and pronounce words

Spelling   Measures the abilities to write one's name, write letters, and to spell words read aloud by the examiner and used in sentences (oral spelling of words is not allowed)

Arithmetic   Measures the abilities to count, read numbers aloud, solve orally presented arithmetic problems, and to complete a series of written computation problems (the written arithmetic section has a time limit of 15 minutes)

Note. Adapted from Wilkinson (1993)

vided. Subtests included on the WRAT3 are Reading, Spelling, and Arithmetic. Rapid Reference 5.1 describes each of the subtests.

Standardization of the WRAT3

Standardization of the WRAT3 took place in 1992 and 1993, using 4,433 individuals ranging in age from 5 years 0 months through 74 years 11 months. This national stratified sample controlled for age, geographic region, gender, ethnicity, and socioeconomic level designed to match 1990 U.S. census data. Tables showing a breakdown by age and gender; within region by age, gender, and ethnicity; and by occupational group are provided in the test manual. The test manual does not indicate whether students or adults with disabilities were included in the standardization sample. Unlike with other achievement tests, socioeconomic level is measured by occupational status of the individual or of the student's parent rather than by educational level. Insufficient data are provided in the test manual to determine the closeness of the match with U.S. Bureau of the Census data.

Individuals were administered both forms of the test in counterbalanced order during the testing session. Standardization examiners were allowed to administer the Spelling and Arithmetic subtests in small groups. Group size was limited to three for students 7 years of age or younger and to five for students 8 years of age through high school. Larger groups were allowed for adults.

Psychometric Characteristics

Reliability and validity data are presented in the test manual. You are encouraged to study these data before using the test; in the meantime, I have attempted to summarize some of the more important features of those data.

Reliability

Internal consistency for the WRAT3 was established through coefficient alphas. Median coefficient alphas ranged from .85 to .95 for the WRAT3 subtests and from .92 to .95 for the combined tests. Median coefficient alphas and the range by age group are summarized in Rapid Reference 5.2. Median alternate form reliabilities (for raw scores) range from .89 to .93 for the subtests; Rapid Reference 5.3 provides more detailed information.

Test-retest reliability was established by administering the WRAT3 to a

≡Rapid Reference 5.2

Range of WRAT3 Coefficient Alphas, by Age

Subtests	Range of Coefficient Alphas	Median Coefficient
Reading Combined	.91–.97	.95
Reading (Blue Form)	.88–.95	.91
Reading (Tan Form)	.88–.94	.90
Spelling Combined	.89–.97	.95
Spelling (Blue Form)	.83–.95	.91
Spelling (Tan Form)	.83–.94	.89
Arithmetic Combined	.72–.96	.92
Arithmetic (Blue Form)	.69–.92	.86
Arithmetic (Tan Form)	.70–.92	.85

Rapid Reference 5.3

Range of WRAT3 Alternate Form Correlations

Subtest	Range of Correlations	Median Correlation	Sample Correlation
Reading	.87–.99	.92	.98
Spelling	.86–.99	.93	.98
Arithmetic	.82–.99	.89	.98

sample of 142 individuals from the standardization sample and ranging in age from 6 to 16 years. These coefficients range from .91 to .98 and are presented in more detail in Rapid Reference 5.4.

Validity

WRAT3 validity is demonstrated in a number of ways. Content validity is demonstrated through the use of the Rasch statistic of item separation. As reported by the test author (Wilkinson, 1993, p. 176), "the highest item separation score possible, 1.00 is found" for each of the WRAT3 subtests. Detailed information on how specific test items were selected is not provided and there were no studies relating test content to commonly used curricula in school districts. Data are provided to show that there is a positive correlation between scores on each test with age, indicating that the skills measured by the WRAT3 are developmental in nature.

Validity studies were conducted comparing WRAT3 scores with scores on the WISC-III and the WAIS-R. Correlations between the WRAT3 combined tests and the

Rapid Reference 5.4

Average WRAT3 Test-Retest Reliability

Subtest	Test-Retest Reliability
Reading Combined	.98
Reading (Blue Form)	.98
Reading (Tan Form)	.96
Spelling Combined	.96
Spelling (Blue Form)	.93
Spelling (Tan Form)	.96
Arithmetic Combined	.93
Arithmetic (Blue Form)	.94
Arithmetic (Tan Form)	.91

═Rapid Reference 5.5

Wide Range Achievement Test 3

Author: Gary Wilkinson

Publication Date: 1993

What the Test Measures: Reading decoding, spelling, mathematics computation

Age Range: 5 years 0 months through 74 years 11 months

Administration Time: 15 to 30 minutes, depending on the age of the individual

Qualification of Examiners: Training in educational testing

Publisher: Wide Range, Inc.
P.O. Box 3410
Wilmington, DE 19804-0250
(800) 221-9728
www.widerange.com

Prices: Complete test kit, $125.00 (2000 catalog price)
Computer scoring program, $99.00 (2000 catalog price)

WISC-III Full Scale score ranged from .66 to .73, and from .49 to .60 with the WAIS-R. In a study of 77 children given the WRAT3 followed 82 days later (on average) by the WRAT-R, the correlations ranged from .66 to .92. Additional studies are reported comparing WRAT3 scores with group standardized achievement tests and yielding modest to high correlations. These data are reported in detail in the WRAT3 *Manual for Administration and Scoring*. Rapid Reference 5.5 provides basic information on the test and its publisher.

HOW TO ADMINISTER THE WRAT3

As with any standardized test, the WRAT3 examiner should closely follow the test administration instructions contained in the test manual. While the test is very easy to administer, it is important that the examiner become very familiar with the test directions and practice administration of the test before it is used in the clinical setting. Examiners should be familiar with testing procedures in general and have experience working with individuals similar in age to those being evaluated. General testing procedures are reviewed on pages 11–25 of the test manual.

The WRAT3 consists of two alternate forms, a Blue Form and a Tan Form. An individual may be administered either one, or both. Norms are provided for each form of the test as well as for a Combined Form. The test is a four-page form that contains demographic information as well as test items (Arithmetic), spaces for the examinee to write in responses (Spelling), and a page for the examiner to record examinee responses on the Reading subtest.

Subtests can be administered in any order. The Reading subtest must be administered individually, while the Spelling and Arithmetic subtests can be administered individually or in a small-group setting.

Before beginning formal administration of the test, complete the personal data section of page 1, which includes the examinee's name and gender, the date of test administration, the examinee's birthdate and current age, school, and grade (if applicable), the referral source, and the examiner's name. Calculate the examinee's chronological age and double-check this calculation.

Subtest-by-Subtest Notes on Administration

Reading

Although subtests can be administered in any order, my preference is to begin with Reading, followed by Spelling and then Arithmetic. The Reading subtest has two parts: Letter Reading and Word Reading. Letter Reading is administered to students aged 5–7 years, and to older examinees *only if they have fewer than five correct responses on Word Reading*. Verbatim instructions for each part of the subtest are highlighted in red on page 12 of the test manual.

Reading cards are used for this subtest. The examinee is asked to read the 15 letters at the top of the card (if beginning with Letter Reading) and then to pronounce the words that are printed on the subsequent lines. For examinees 8 years of age and older, you should complete the Word Reading section first, then give Letter Reading if the score on Word Reading is less than 5. A pronunciation guide is provided on page 4 of the record form. Cross through the first letter of each word that is incorrect and circle the number of the item if it is correct. A checklist of administration pointers for the Reading subtest is provided in Rapid Reference 5.6.

Spelling

The Spelling subtest consists of two parts, Name/Letter Writing and Word Spelling. Examinees 7 years of age or younger begin with the Name/Letter

≡Rapid Reference 5.6

Administration Pointers for the Reading Subtest

1. Be sure to use the reading cards provided with the test.

2. If the examinee is 8 years of age or older, begin with the Word Reading items.

3. If the examinee is less than 8 years of age, begin with the Letter Reading items.

4. Discontinue testing after *10 consecutive items are missed.*

5. If the examinee is 8 years of age or older and scores *less than 5* on the Word Reading section, return to the Letter Reading items and administer them.

6. *5/10 Rules:* Administer the Letter Reading items if there are fewer than *5* correct responses on Word Reading, and discontinue the subtest after *10* consecutive errors.

7. Record incorrect responses by drawing a line through the first letter of the word.

8. Record correct responses by circling the item number.

9. After the first error, ask the examinee to repeat the word that was missed; if the word is pronounced correctly, score as correct.

10. After this first error, do not ask the examinee to repeat a response unless you did not hear the word clearly.

Writing items. Older examinees begin with the Word Spelling items. For this subtest, the examinee writes on the test record form. Verbatim instructions for each part of the subtest are highlighted in red on pages 17–19 of the test manual. This subtest also follows the 5/10 Rules described in Rapid Reference 5.6 for the Reading subtest. The items for this subtest may be administered from the plastic cards or from pages 18–19 of the test manual. For the Name/Letter Writing items, the examinee has 5 seconds to write the letter. For the spelling items, pronounce each word, read the sentence provided, and pronounce the word again. You may repeat words if necessary. The examinee has 15 seconds to spell each word. Discontinue testing after 10 consecutive failures. A checklist of test administration pointers is presented in Rapid Reference 5.7.

Arithmetic

The Arithmetic subtest consists of two parts: Oral Arithmetic and Written Arithmetic. Examinees aged 7 years or younger begin with the Oral Arithmetic

≋Rapid Reference 5.7

Administration Pointers for the Spelling Subtest

1. Be sure to use the plastic spelling card, because the examinee writes his or her responses on the test record form.
2. If the examinee is 7 years of age or younger, begin with the Name/Letter Writing items.
3. If the examinee is 8 years of age or older, begin with the Spelling items.
4. Discontinue testing after *10 consecutive items are missed.*
5. If the examinee is 8 years of age or older and scores *less than 5* on the Spelling items, return to the Name/Letter Writing items and administer them.
6. *5/10 Rules:* Administer the Name/Letter Writing items if there are fewer than 5 correct responses on Spelling. Discontinue the subtest after 10 consecutive errors.
7. Examinees have 5 seconds for each Letter Writing item and 15 seconds for each Spelling item.

items, while examinees aged 8 years or older begin with the Written Arithmetic items. For this subtest, the examinee writes on the test record form. Verbatim instructions for each part of the subtest are highlighted in red on pages 20–21 of the test manual. This subtest also follows the 5/10 Rules previously described for the Reading and Spelling subtests. The examinee has 15 minutes to complete the Written Arithmetic items. The testing can be discontinued in less than 15 minutes if it is clear that examinee has completed all the items he or she is able to complete. A checklist of administration pointers for the Arithmetic subtest is provided in Rapid Reference 5.8.

SCORING THE INDIVIDUAL TEST RECORD FORM

The WRAT3 yields six types of scores: raw scores, absolute scores, standard scores, grade scores, percentiles, and normal curve equivalents (NCEs). Raw scores reflect the number of points earned by the examinee on each subtest; these scores by themselves are meaningless because they are not norm-based. Absolute scores are based on Rasch analysis of the difficulty level of each item on an interval scale with a mean of 500. These scores are usually used in statistical studies, pre- and posttesting, and in local norming. The WRAT3 standard scores have a mean of 100 and SD of 15. The range of standard scores is 45–155, depending on age range. It is assumed that achievement test performance is distributed on a normal curve, with the majority of examinees scoring within ±1 SD of the mean. Thus, about 66 percent of examinees score in the range of 85–115. Less than 3 percent of students score above 130 or below 70. Grade scores are ordinal scores and should be interpreted very cautiously. They simply indicate the average grade level of individuals receiving a specific raw score. Percentile scores and NCEs range from 0 to 100 and are norm-based scores.

Step-by-Step Scoring of the WRAT3

Scoring the WRAT3 test items is facilitated by the dichotomous nature of the items—each item is either correct or incorrect. One point is given for each correct response. The raw scores are recorded in the appropriate boxes for each subtest. For example, in the Reading subtest, the examiner records separately the score for Letter Reading and Word Reading, then combines the two scores. This procedure is identical for each subtest. If the initial items of a subtest (Letter Reading, Name/Letter Writing, Oral Arithmetic) are not administered, the examinee is given full credit for those items.

Raw Scores

All subtest raw scores are completed in the same way. Record the raw score for each section of the subtest and then add them together. Once this is done, transfer the total score for each subtest to the shaded box in the upper right corner of

---

≡ Rapid Reference 5.8

Administration Pointers for the Arithmetic Subtest

1. If the examinee is 8 years of age or older, begin with the Written Arithmetic items.

2. If the examinee is less than 8 years of age, begin with the Oral Arithmetic items.

3. Discontinue the Written Arithmetic section after 15 minutes.

4. If the examinee is 8 years of age or older and scores *less than 5* on the Written Arithmetic items, return to the Oral Arithmetic items.

DON'T FORGET

Types of Scores on the WRAT3

Raw scores
Absolute scores
Standard scores
Grade scores
Percentile scores
Normal curve equivalents

page 1 of the test record form. Then convert the raw scores to standard scores, percentiles, grade scores, and absolute scores using the appropriate tables.

Score Conversion

Tables for converting raw scores to the various derived scores are found on pages 35–99 of the test manual for the Blue and Tan forms of the test, and on pages 100–163 for the Combined Form. Both tables are arranged by the chronological age of the examinee. On each page there are three boxes (one for each subtest) and within each box there are four columns: Raw Score, Absolute Score, Standard Score, and Grade Score. *Note that the order of scores in the tables is not the same as on the Test Score box on page 1 of the test record form.*

The Blue norms are presented on the even-numbered pages in the manual and the Tan norms are presented on the odd-numbered pages. For each subtest, locate the correct age table and form. Enter the table with the raw score and read across the table for the appropriate scores, then record them on the test record form.

≡ Rapid Reference 5.9

Constructing Confidence Intervals

1. Confidence intervals for test scores are constructed by taking the obtained score and adding/subtracting a value based on the standard error of measurement (SEM).
2. The value to be added and subtracted is based on the product of the z-score (for the specific confidence interval) and the SEM.
3. The formula for confidence intervals (CIs) is CI = obtained score ± (z-score × SEM).
4. An example follows:

   John, a student of 9 years 5 months, receives a standard score of 95 on the Reading subtest of the WRAT3 (Blue Form). In order to construct a 95 percent CI, we need to determine the SEM for his age and test score and the z-value for that CI. Table 12, page 174 in the test manual reveals that the SEM on Reading for his age and the Blue Form is 4.8. The z-value for a 95 percent CI is 1.96.

   Thus, the formula becomes

   95% CI = 95 ± (1.96 × 4.8)

   95% CI = 95 ± 9.4

   95% CI = 85.6 – 104.4.

≡ Rapid Reference 5.10

Sample Score Summary for Sarah

Name: Sarah   **Gender:** Female
Date: 10/16/00   **Birthdate:** 10/15/88   **Age:** 12 years 0 months
School: Johnson Middle School   **Grade:** 6
Referred by: Ms. Stinson   **Examiner:** Douglas K. Smith

Test Scores (Blue Form)

	Raw Score	Standard Score	Percentile	Grade Score
		(95% CI)		
Reading	31	82	12	3
		73–91		
Spelling	23	75	5	2
		66–84		
Arithmetic	30	83	13	4
		73–93		

It should be noted that unlike those for the other achievement tests we have discussed, confidence intervals for the derived scores are not provided in the norm tables. Rather, they are found in Table 13 (p. 175 of the test manual) for standard scores. Two choices are provided: 68 percent or 95 percent. For more precise calculations by age, use Table 12 (p. 174 of the test manual), which presents standard errors of measurement for standard scores by subtest and age. Using these data, you can construct a more precise confidence level. Standard scores should always be reported with the confidence interval. This procedure is illustrated in Rapid Reference 5.9; Rapid Reference 5.10 shows the completed Blue Form score-summary for Sarah.

DON'T FORGET

Z-Values for Common Confidence Intervals

Confidence Interval	Z-Value
68%	1.00
90%	1.68
95%	1.96
99%	2.53

HOW TO INTERPRET THE WRAT3

Since the WRAT3 is basically a screening test of academic achievement, interpretation is relatively simple. Within the test itself, scores can be compared among the Reading, Spelling, and Arithmetic subtests. As a rule of thumb, standard scores that differ from each other by 1 SD (15 points) represent a statistically significant difference.

In the case of Sarah (Rapid Reference 5.10), the three achievement scores are relatively consistent, all falling within the low average range. Thus, there is little variation in skill development among reading decoding, spelling, and basic arithmetic skills.

The next level of interpretation is an informal analysis of skill development within each achievement area. This involves examining Sarah's errors and generating possible explanations for her performance. These explanations or hypotheses should then be confirmed or disconfirmed by looking at classroom products, examining previous achievement test results, and discussing Sarah's classroom performance with her teachers. In Sarah's case, an analysis of her responses to the Reading and Spelling subtests indicated that she tried to use a phonetic approach to both subtests but was unsuccessful, especially in Spelling. In addition, she made many careless errors, suggesting a lack of attention to detail. She had particular difficulty with prefixes and suffixes. Sarah was also very reluctant to guess on items that were difficult for her. In Arithmetic, she solved problems of addition, subtraction, and multiplication, including addition and subtraction problems that involved regrouping. She did not attempt any problems requiring division or fractions.

The final step in interpretation is to compare the achievement scores with any available ability scores. At the time Sarah was given the WRAT3 she was also given the WISC-III. Subtest scores ranged from 3 to 9; global scale IQ scores included a

DON'T FORGET

Steps in Interpreting the WRAT3

1. Compare standard scores across the three subtests (Reading, Spelling, Arithmetic).

2. Examine the errors made on the three subtests and generate hypotheses about the student's level of skill development.

3. Compare scores on the WRAT3 with a measure of ability (if available) to determine possible discrepancies.

VIQ of 79, a PIQ of 77, and an FSIQ of 76. The 95 percent confidence interval for her FSIQ is 71 to 83. Thus, the achievement and ability scores are very similar and do not differ significantly from each other. Sarah's level of academic performance is similar to her level of intellectual ability.

STRENGTHS AND WEAKNESSES OF THE WRAT3

The WRAT3 and its predecessors have been in use for more than 60 years. Consequently, there have been many reviews of the test and many studies of its use. Rapid Reference 5.11 presents a list of reviews of the WRAT3. Some of these reviews present conflicting views of the WRAT3; thus it is worthwhile to read each of them to obtain a comprehensive picture of the diversity of opinions about this instrument.

In this section I summarize my views of the major strengths and weaknesses of the test based on my experience with the test as well as on formal reviews of the test. In so doing, I focus on these specific areas: test development, standardization, administration and scoring, reliability, validity, and interpretation. This information is summarized in Rapid References 5.12–5.14.

Summary of WRAT3 Strengths and Weaknesses

From a practitioner's viewpoint, the ease of administration and scoring of the WRAT3 is among its strengths. Likewise, the short period of time required for testing is an advantage. Within the school setting I have found that the similarity of the tasks on the WRAT3 and classroom assignments is a positive. This is particularly true for spelling and arithmetic.

Users of the WRAT3 should be aware that many of the reviews of the test have been negative and also contradictory. For example, Mabry (1995) stated that "Suspicions of inadequacy here are confirmed by test content, item formats, obsolescence, underlying philosophy, potential for bias, and insufficient evidence of validity or reliability" (pp. 1109–1110). And Ward (1995)

≡Rapid Reference 5.11

Reviews of the WRAT3

Clark (1994)
Harrison (1994)
Mabry (1995)
Salvia & Ysseldyke (1998, 2001)
Ward (1995)

≡Rapid Reference 5.12

Strengths and Weaknesses of the WRAT3

Strengths	Weaknesses
Test Development	
Builds on foundation of previous editions (WRAT/WRAT-R)	Insufficient information on procedure for test-item selection
Test format resembles the way constructs are measured in the classroom	Lack of bias studies
Development of alternate forms allowing for test-retest	
Combined form allows for a larger sample of behavior	
Standardization	
Size of standardization sample	Lack of information about individuals with disabilities in standardization sample
	Lack of detail regarding exact nature of standardization sample
	Not using individual or parent educational level as measure of socioeconomic status
Administration and Scoring	
Easy to administer and score	Ten consecutive errors for discontinue rule is excessively negative
Clear and consistent starting and stopping points	Lack of calculated confidence intervals for standard scores
Use of one level, not two	
Dichotomous scored items	
Reliability	
Test-retest reliability is adequate	Large SEMs as compared to other achievement tests

Strengths	Weaknesses
Validity	
Face validity of items is strong	No evidence of construct validity
	No evidence that test content relates to classroom curriculum
	No evidence relating performance on WRAT3 to other individual achievement tests
Interpretation	
Subtests measure specific skills that are easy to interpret.	Insufficient ceiling at age 14 years 0 months and up
Format of subtests mimic class-room activities and facilitate gener-alization to classroom performance.	Insufficient floor at age 5 years

discussed the lack of an operational definition of achievement. While describ-ing the validity of the test as questionable, Salvia and Ysseldyke (1998) indi-cated that the reliability of the test was adequate and that it was well standardized. Yet Harrison (1994) criticized the WRAT3 for not using socioe-conomic status as a stratification variable, stating that "research clearly shows that socioeconomic status has a stronger relationship with achievement than does race or many other variables" (p. 67).

As with most tests, the WRAT3 is not as precise in measuring its major construct (achievement) at the youngest and oldest age ranges, particularly with individuals considerably below average or above average in achieve-ment (Rapid References 5.13 and 5.14 document this). For the individual considerably below average in achievement, the floor of the test is insuffi-cient at ages 5 years 0 months through 6 years 5 months. In the most extreme case, for example, a 5-year-old receiving a raw score of 0 in Reading would receive a standard score of 76. At the other end of the continuum—the in-dividual considerably above average in achievement—the ceiling of the test is insufficient at ages 13 years 0 months through 74 years 11 months. The ef-fect is to underestimate the level of achievement. For example, as shown in Rapid Reference 5.14, an individual 17 years of age with a maximum raw

≡Rapid Reference 5.13

Strengths and Weaknesses of the WRAT3: Effective Range of Subtest Scores, by Age (based on raw score of 0)

Age	Reading		Spelling		Arithmetic	
	Blue	Tan	Blue	Tan	Blue	Tan
5/0–5/2	76	76	69	69	58	58
5/3–5/5	71	71	64	64	54	54
5/6–5/8	66	66	59	59	48	48
5/9–5/11	62	62	53	53	<49	<49
6/0–6/2	58	58	48	48	<45	<45
6/3–6/5	53	53	<47	<48	<45	<45
6/6–6/8	48	48	<46	<46	<46	<46
6/9–6/11	<45	<45	<46	<46	<45	<45
7/0–7/2	<45	<47	<48	<48	<48	<45
7/3–7/5	<45	<45	<47	<47	<48	<48
7/6–7/8	<47	<47	<48	<48	<48	<48
7/9–7/11	<45	<45	<46	<46	<46	<46
8/0–8/5	<47	<47	<45	<45	<45	<45
8/6–8/11	<45	<45	<45	<45	<45	<45
9/0–9/5	<45	<45	<46	<46	<45	<45
9/6–9/11	<45	<45	<45	<45	<45	<45
10/0–10/5	<45	<45	<47	<47	<45	<45
10/6–10/11	<45	<45	<45	<45	<45	<45
11/0–11/5	<45	<45	<46	<46	<45	<45
11/6–64/11	<45	<45	<45	<45	<45	<45
65/0–74/11	<45	<45	<46	<46	<45	<46

≡Rapid Reference 5.14

Strengths and Weaknesses of the WRAT3: Effective Range of Subtest Scores, by Age (based on maximum raw score)

Age	Reading		Spelling		Arithmetic	
	Blue	Tan	Blue	Tan	Blue	Tan
5/0–7/11	>155	>155	>155	>155	>155	>155
8/0–8/5	153	154	>155	>155	>155	>155
8/6–8/11	153	155	>155	>155	>155	>155
9/0–9/5	155	155	>155	>155	>155	>155
9/6–9/11	155	155	155	155	>155	>155
10/0–10/5	154	154	153	154	154	152
10/6–10/11	155	154	155	155	155	153
11/0–11/5	153	153	155	154	153	154
11/6–11/11	149	152	154	153	154	153
12/0–12/11	147	147	154	153	153	153
13/0–13/11	139	142	146	151	144	152
14/0–14/11	134	137	140	146	140	147
15/0–15/11	131	133	136	143	135	142
16/0–16/11	127	129	133	138	133	138
17/0–19/11	125	128	131	135	130	135
20/0–24/11	122	124	129	133	130	134
25/0–34/11	120	123	127	132	129	134
35/0–44/11	117	120	124	129	129	131
45/0–54/11	118	121	126	129	130	132
55/0–64/11	119	121	123	126	128	130
65/0–74/11	120	122	125	128	137	138

score on Reading would receive a standard score of 125 (Blue Form) or 128 (Tan Form).

CLINICAL APPLICATIONS OF THE WRAT3

As indicated in chapter 1, all of the achievement tests discussed in this book are used on a frequent basis. Those in the WRAT series, however, are cited as the most frequently used achievement tests whether in studies of American Psychological Association members (Harrison et al., 1998) or National Association of School Psychologists members (Hutton, Dubes, & Muir, 1992), with adolescents (Archer, Marnish, Imhof, & Piotrowski, 1991), or in neuropsychological assessments (Sellers & Medler, 1992). The WRAT3, however, is not without critics. For example, Flanagan and colleagues (1997) noted that "the brevity of the WRAT is at the expense of valid domain coverage" (p. 100).

A major concern with the WRAT3 is its lack of a measure of reading comprehension. Nevertheless, the author of the WRAT3 describes this as a strength. "The WRAT3 was intentionally designed to eliminate, as totally as possible, the effects of comprehension" (Wilkinson, 1993, p. 10). As an informed user of the test, however, you should be aware of this controversy.

The WRAT3 and Achievement Measures

While limited validity data are found in the test manual, the validity of the WRAT3 and its predecessors has been assessed by independent researchers. Flanagan and colleagues (1997), for example, used a sample of adults and compared performance on the WRAT3 with performance on the Mini-Battery of Achievement (MBA; Woodcock, McGrew, & Werder, 1994) and the Kaufman Functional Academic Skills Test (K-FAST; Kaufman & Kaufman, 1994). Similar mean scores for reading and mathematics were obtained across the three tests. (Spelling was not measured in a separate subtest by the MBA and K-FAST.) Correlations among the reading and mathematics scores of the WRAT3, the MBA, and the K-FAST were moderate for both reading (r) = .31 to .48) and mathematics (r) = .52 to .54.

Use of the WRAT3 has also been examined in several special populations. Smith and Smith (1998) found correlations that were moderate to high between the WRAT3 subtests and the WIAT Basic Reading, Spelling, and Mathematics Reasoning subtests for a sample of students with learning disabilities. Mean scores were similar between the two tests.

The WRAT3 and the WISC-III

Many studies have also examined the relationship between the WRAT3 and the WISC-III. Since this combination of tests is frequently used in the school setting, their relationship assumes even greater importance. In addition, eligibility for learning disabilities services are often determined through the use of discrepancy tables that require the user to enter the table with the correlation between the ability and achievement measures. Vance and Fuller (1995), using a sample of students referred for possible special education services, found significant correlations between the two tests and concluded that the study contributed to the concurrent validity of the WRAT3. Likewise, Smith, Smith, and Smithson (1995) found correlations between .45 and .66 between the WRAT3 and the WISC-III FSIQ in a sample of students referred for academic difficulties.

As mentioned earlier, tests in the WRAT series are among the most frequently used achievement tests. In addition to the functions we have discussed so far, they are often used to establish achievement levels for individuals in research studies. For examples, researchers have often used the WRAT-R and WRAT3 in conjunction with the WISC-III for samples of students with hearing disabilities (Slate & Fawcett, 1995); with students at school entry who had extremely low birth weight (Saigal, Szatmari, & Rosenbaum, 1992); in studying recidivism in male juvenile offenders (Duncan, Kennedy, & Patrick, 1995); in looking at heritability across groups (Determan, Thompson, & Plomin, 1990); with school drop-outs subsequently incarcerated (Ahrens, Evans, & Barnett, 1990); with adults with mild cognitive impairment (Peterson et al., 1999); to rate spellers for subsequent studies (Lennox & Siegel, 1996); and in comparing memory in young girls with Turner syndrome (Ross, Roeltgen, Feuillan, Kushner, & Cutler, 2000).

Cautions with the WRAT3

Although the WRAT3, like the WRAT-R and the WRAT, is easy to administer and score, it is always wise to double-check your administration procedures

> # CAUTION
> ....
> In contrast to the PIAT-R/NU, K-TEA/NU, and WIAT, the WRAT3 is a screening test for reading decoding, spelling, and arithmetic skills. It is not a comprehensive measure of achievement and should not be used that way. It is best compared to the K-TEA/NU Brief Form and the WIAT Screener.

and actual scoring of protocols. For example, a study in 1991 addressing examiner errors on the WRAT-R found errors occurring in 95 percent of the examiner protocols, with an average of three errors per protocol. The sample size was small, but the results are important. The most common errors were in failure to establish basals and ceilings (Peterson, Stege, Slate, & Jones, 1991).

Unlike the other achievement tests we have examined, the WRAT3 requires a relatively long series of errors before discontinue criteria are met. For both the Spelling and Reading subtests, *10 consecutive errors* are required before the subtests are discontinued. Many examiners regard this number as excessive and sometimes discontinue after 7 or 8 consecutive errors. This is not appropriate because it varies from the standardization procedures. Also, it can result in a subtle form of bias, in which examinees who are scoring in the below average range and exhibiting a slower, more reflective response style are given fewer test items.

AN ILLUSTRATIVE CASE REPORT

In this section our focus turns to a psychoeducational report for a student referred for a triennial evaluation to determine whether special education services (for learning disabilities) continue to be needed. We will be interpreting Greg's WRAT3 results along with additional test data.

Reason for Referral

Greg was referred for his triennial evaluation. The purposes of the evaluation are to provide current information as to his ability and achievement levels, to confirm his need for special education services, and to provide information for updating his individual education plan.

Background Information

Greg is currently enrolled in the 8th grade and is receiving special education services from the learning disabilities resource teacher. Greg was first referred for special education services 3 years ago. Testing at that time placed Greg at the 2nd- to 3rd-grade levels in reading, spelling, and mathematics skills. His level of intelligence, as measured by the Wechsler Intelligence Scale for Children–Third Edition (WISC-III), was within the average range with a Full Scale IQ Score of 99. Greg was subsequently placed in the program for students with learning disabilities.

Behavioral Observations

Greg was observed during his second-hour English class, which is co-taught by Mr. Spears and Ms. Drake. Since Greg had not yet met the examiner, he was unaware of being observed. After receiving teacher directions, the class was asked to work independently on an assignment. During that time, Greg worked quietly on the assignment. He was attentive to the teachers when they were talking and remained focused on the task at hand. Greg was called on in class and also volunteered an answer during the observational period. In each instance, Greg provided the correct answer to the question. Later in the class period, Greg worked cooperatively with another student. Throughout the observational period of 45 minutes, Greg's behavior was appropriate and on task.

During the testing session, Greg was somewhat shy but very pleasant. He appeared comfortable with the testing situation and seemed to put forth his best effort. He was quite cooperative throughout the session and was a student with whom it was easy to work. Rapport was quickly established and maintained throughout the testing session. The scores obtained from this evaluation are a valid estimate of Greg's current level of intellectual and academic performance.

Evaluation Procedures and Instruments

Review of school records
Interviews with teachers
Classroom observation
Wechsler Intelligence Scale for Children–Third Edition (WISC-III)
Wide Range Achievement Test 3 (WRAT3)

Test Results

WISC-III Results

Scale or Index	IQ	95% Confidence Interval	Percentile Rank
Verbal Scale	93	87–100	32
Performance Scale	98	90–106	45
Full Scale	95	90–101	37
Verbal Comprehension	99	92–106	47
Perceptual Organization	104	95–112	61
Freedom from Distractibility	72	66–85	3
Processing Speed	83	76–95	13

Verbal Subtests	Scaled Score	Performance Subtests	Scaled Score
Information	10	Picture Competion	11
Similarities	11	Coding	6
Arithmetic	5	Picture Arrangement	11
Vocabulary	9	Block Design	10
Comprehension	9	Object Assembly	10
Digit Span	5W	Symbol Search	7

Note. "W" represents a significant relative weakness, $p < .05$.

WRAT3

Subtests	Standard Score	95% Confidence Interval	Percentile Rank
Reading	79	70–88	8
Spelling	73	64–82	4
Arithmetic	85	74–96	16

Analysis of Results

The WISC-III is an individually administered test of cognitive abilities covering the age range of 6 to 16 years. It consists of six subtests emphasizing verbal content and six subtests emphasizing nonverbal content. The Full Scale IQ combines both sets of subtests and produces the most valid overall score. Greg's performance on the WISC-III falls within the lower end of the average range of intellectual functioning. His overall score of 95 ±5.5 places him at the 37th percentile, indicating that he is functioning at a level equal to or greater than that of 37 percent of students his age. Furthermore, his Verbal and Performance scores range from 93 to 98 and are both in the lower end of the average range. His index scores, however, show more variability and range from 72 to 104. Both his verbal/language skills and his nonverbal reasoning skills are within the average range. However, his skills in completing written tasks quickly and solving tasks requiring attention were less well developed.

A closer examination of Greg's results shows a relative weakness on the Digit Span subtest, along with low scores (as compared to those of peers) on Arithmetic, Coding, and Symbol Search. These four subtests comprise the Freedom from Distractibility factor (Arithmetic, Digit Span) and Processing Speed factor (Coding, Symbol Search). In addition to requiring attention, the Digit Span and Arithmetic subtests require short-term auditory memory, which may also be an area of weakness for Greg. Both Coding and Symbol Search place a premium on speed and require the student to use a pencil. His performance suggests that he may require a somewhat longer time in which to complete classroom assignments than other students, especially if the assignments are of a written nature. Timed tests and assignments could be particularly problematic for Greg.

Greg's performance on subtests measuring verbal/language skills, including vocabulary development, verbal reasoning, verbal expression, and the use of verbal concepts, are all in the average range. Likewise, his abilities to interpret visually presented material and to organize information spatially are in the average range.

Greg's performance on the WRAT3 was consistent in the below average to low average range. His scores in Reading, Spelling, and Arithmetic do not differ significantly from each other and are at a level 10 to 16 points below his WISC-III Full Scale IQ. On the Reading subtest, Greg broke the words into sections by covering parts of each word with his finger. It appeared that he was using a phonetic approach to pronouncing the words but was having considerable difficulty implementing this strategy effectively. Likewise, he used a similar approach on the Spelling subtest. Overall, these scores show little improvement from his initial evaluation 3 years ago. In Arithmetic, Greg was able to solve problems in addition, subtraction, multiplication, and division. His overall performance on the WRAT3 Arithmetic subtest was significantly higher than his performance on the WISC-III Arithmetic subtest. It should be noted that the two subtests differ in format, with the WRAT3 using a visual/written format and the WISC-III using a verbal format.

Behavioral observations in the classroom and during the testing session were consistent. Off-task behavior and distractibility were not indicated. Thus, the score on the Freedom from Distractibility index of the WISC-III more likely represents a weakness in short-term auditory memory. Interviews with Greg's teachers confirmed that classroom behavior is not an issue. In addition, they indicated that the achievement test results were consistent with their estimates of his classroom performance. They also indicated that most new material is presented verbally in the classroom.

Summary

Greg is a 14-year-old male who is currently functioning in the lower end of the average range of cognitive functioning, as measured by the WISC-III. Academically, he is functioning at a significantly lower level, with specific weaknesses in reading and spelling. His cognitive strengths, relative to his own average, include verbal comprehension and visual-perceptual skills, while his relative weaknesses include auditory short-term memory and processing speed. On the basis of this part of the reevaluation, Greg continues to meet the criteria for a learning disability.

Recommendations

1. Greg continues to meet the criteria for a learning disability; therefore, the child study team should consider the continuation of these services because Greg's level of academic performance in reading and spelling is significantly below his level of cognitive ability.
2. It is recommended that a comprehensive diagnostic reading evaluation be conducted to determine Greg's specific level of skill development in reading and spelling.
3. Due to Greg's relative weakness in short-term auditory memory, it is

recommended that information and instructions be provided both verbally and visually. The use of visual presentation formats, whenever possible, is encouraged.

4. Written assignments may take Greg more time to complete than his peers. Consideration should be given to shortening assignments or providing additional time (such as 20 percent more) as needed. When appropriate, Greg could also be allowed to provide verbal answers rather than written answers.

Douglas K. Smith, PhD, NCSP
Director, School Psychology Training

Amy Jones, EdS
Examiner

 TEST YOURSELF

1. **The Reading subtest of the WRAT3 measures**
   (a) reading comprehension.
   (b) reading decoding.
2. **Name the two forms of the WRAT3.**
3. **The scores produced on the two forms of the WRAT3 are identical.** True or False?
4. **On the WRAT3, the socioeconomic variable in standardization is measured by educational level.** True or False?
5. **Which subtests can be administered in a small-group setting?**
6. **The WRAT3 subtests must be administered in the following order: Reading, Spelling, and Arithmetic.** True or False?
7. **The discontinue rule on subtests is**
   (a) 5 consecutive errors.
   (b) 7 consecutive errors.
   (c) 10 consecutive errors.
   (d) 12 consecutive errors.
8. **The WRAT3 consists of two levels.** True or False?
9. **The WRAT3 is most appropriately compared with the** (continued)

(a) WIAT Screener.

(b) K-TEA/NU Comprehensive Form.

(c) PIAT-R/NU.

10. Overall test-retest reliabilities are highest for the

(a) Blue Form.

(b) Tan Form.

(c) Combined Form.

Answers: 1. b; 2. Blue Form, Tan Form; 3. False; 4. False; 5. Spelling, Arithmetic; 6. False; 7. c; 8. False; 9. a; 10. c.

Six

DEVELOPING TESTING ACCOMMODATIONS FOR THE K-TEA/NU, PIAT-R/NU, WRAT3, AND WIAT/WIAT-II

OVERVIEW

Providing testing accommodations for individuals with disabilities is not a new concept. Within the educational setting, accommodations have been required since the passage of Public Law 94-142 (the Education for All Handicapped Children Act of 1975) and its subsequent reauthorizations (Individuals with Disabilities Education Act [PL 94-142] and Individuals with Disabilities Education Act Amendments of 1997 [PL 105-17]). Testing accommodations may not be needed by all individuals with disabilities, nor for all assessments. Thus, the need for such accommodations must be determined on a case-by-case basis, considering the individual involved and the specific nature and purpose of the assessment.

TESTING ACCOMMODATIONS

Accommodations reflect changes in the standard or usual way in which a test is administered so that an individual with a disability is not penalized by the disability. Testing accommodations may involve changes in the setting, timing, scheduling, presentation, or response (Thurlow, Elliott, & Ysseldyke, 1998). With individual achievement testing, accommodations in timing may include providing the individual with additional time to respond to test items, allowing additional exposure time for test stimuli, or providing frequent breaks. Scheduling accommodations may include changing the order of subtest administration or administering the test in more than one sitting. Changes in presentation mode may involve the use of sign language, gesture, pantomime, large print, or braille, or the repetition of directions. Response accommodations may involve having the examinee write responses rather than respond verbally, use a word processor rather than write, or respond in sign language or a language other than English.

These accommodations may have a substantial impact on examinee scores and may affect the validity of those scores. As testing professionals we are guided by the ethical standards of our professional organizations as well as by relevant state and federal laws. The most influential of these is the *Standards for Educational and Psychological Testing* (American Educational Research Association, American Psychological Association, & National Council for Measurement in Education, 1999), which devotes an entire chapter to the assessment of individuals with disabilities. The chapter addresses some of the more common types of accommodations, situations in which accommodations may or may not be appropriate, and possible effects of accommodations on test scores. Before testing individuals with disabilities, it is recommended that the 1999 *Standards* be consulted as well as such other resources as *Assessing People with Disabilities in Educational, Employment, and Clinical Settings* (Ekstrom & Smith, in press). A checklist for developing testing accommodations is presented in Rapid Reference 6.1.

The achievement tests reviewed in this chapter (K-TEA/NU, PIAT-R/NU, WRAT3, and WIAT) measure academic skills in a number of areas. As indicated in the individual chapters on each test, presentation and response formats vary among the tests as well as accommodations and modifications that are appropriate. To facilitate the selection of the most appropriate measures for individuals with disabilities, the subtests of each battery have been classified into seven achievement domains: reading decoding, reading comprehension, spelling, written expression, oral expression, mathematics computation, and mathematics applications. These domains are reasonably consistent with the achievement areas described in IDEA (1997) with regard to the diagnosis of learning disabilities. While scores across subtests are not equivalent (except for the subtests of the K-TEA/NU and PIAT-R/NU, which were renormed in 1997 using linking samples), they do provide information on the level of performance in each area even though the formats of the subtests differ. This classification is presented Rapid Reference 6.2, which shows that all of the batteries provide measures of reading decoding skills and spelling. Oral expression, however, is measured by only one battery (the WIAT), while reading comprehension is measured by three batteries (PIAT-R/NU, K-TEA/NU, and WIAT). Written expression is measured by two bat-

≡Rapid Reference 6.1

Checklist for Developing Testing Accommodations

1. List any limitations in the examinee's receptive (auditory, visual) skills.
2. List any limitations in the examinee's expressive (verbal, motoric) skills.
3. Check off each skill to be assessed.

_____ Word recognition	_____ Oral expression
_____ Reading comprehension	_____ Written expression
_____ Spelling	_____ Listening comprehension
_____ Mathematics reasoning	_____ Other (please specify)
_____ Mathematics computation	_____

4. Check the purpose of the assessment.

_____ Normative comparison	_____ Determine presence or absence of specific skills
_____ Develop academic interventions	

5. List the test(s) you plan to use.
6. List the receptive skills required by the test(s).
7. List the expressive skills required by the test(s).
8. Does the examinee have the receptive skills required by the test(s)? Yes_____ No _____
9. Does the examinee have the expressive skills required by the test(s)? Yes_____ No_____
10. Are testing accommodations needed? Yes_____ No_____ (If yes, describe the accommodations.)
11. Will the proposed accommodations compromise the test results and restrict the use of the test norms? Yes_____ No_____ (If yes, describe.)

Note. Based on material contained in Smith (in press).

teries (PIAT-R/NU and WIAT). Arithmetic skills are measured by all four batteries.

All of the tests covered in this chapter are norm-based measures and indicate levels of skill development in various academic areas. The use of accommodations or modifications to the standardized testing format must be carefully considered when using the normative information and comparing the student's performance with that of students of similar age or grade level.

══Rapid Reference 6.2

Achievement Domains and Subtest Composition: K-TEA/NU, PIAT-R/NU, WIAT, and WRAT3

Achievement Domain	Achievement Battery			
	K-TEA/NU	PIAT-R/NU	WIAT	WRAT3
Reading decoding	Reading Decoding	Reading Recognition	Basic Reading	Reading
Reading comprehension	Reading Comprehension	Reading Comprehension	Reading Comprehension	
Spelling	Spelling	Spelling	Spelling	Spelling
Written expression		Written Expression	Written Expression	
Oral expression			Oral Expression	
Mathematics computation	Mathematics Computation		Numerical Operations	Arithmetic
Mathematics reasoning	Mathematics Applications	Mathematics	Mathematics Reasoning	

Such changes may have a significant impact on the appropriateness of the test norms in interpreting the student's test performance.

AN ANALYSIS OF THE K-TEA/NU, PIAT-R/NU, WIAT, AND WRAT3

The remainder of this chapter is devoted to presenting relevant information on these tests. You are encouraged to consult the test manuals for more detailed information. A variety of information is presented for each test: suggestions from the test author(s) regarding accommodations and modifications; an analysis of the presentation and response formats of each test; and my recommended use of each test with students with disabilities, based on my analysis of the subtests.

Kaufman Test of Educational Achievement/Normative Update

Accommodations and Modifications
Students with disabilities were included in the standardization sample in proportions approximate to those that occur in the U.S. school-age population. The test authors emphasize that the test "must be administered in accordance with set procedures" (Kaufman & Kaufman, 1997, p. 20). A deviation from these procedures "represents a violation of the ground rules, thereby rendering the norms of limited (and sometimes no) value" (20). Whenever a verbal response is required (except for the Reading Decoding subtest), the student may respond in English, sign language, or any other language. There is no provision for translating subtest directions into other languages, however. Students are allowed to spell words orally on the Spelling subtest if they cannot write adequately.

Recommended Use of the K-TEA/NU with Students with Disabilities
The presentation and response formats and the recommendations for use of each subtest with students who have hearing, speech, vision, or physical disabilities are presented in Rapid Reference 6.3. All K-TEA/NU subtests involve verbal stimuli and verbal directions; four of the five subtests also utilize visual stimuli. Verbal responses are required for three of the subtests and paper-and-pencil skills are required for two.

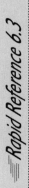

Rapid Reference 6.3

K-TEA/NU Subtests: Appropriateness of Presentation and Response Formats for Students with Disabilities

Subtest	Presentation Format	Response Format	Use with Students with Disabilities?			
			Hearing	Speech	Vision	Physical
Mathematics Applications	Visual/verbal	Verbal/writes responses[a]	No[b]	Yes	No	—
Reading Decoding	Visual/verbal	Verbal responses	Yes	—	No	Yes
Spelling	Verbal	Writes words or spells orally	No[b]	Yes	Yes	Yes
Reading Comprehension	Visual (verbal directions)	Uses gestures (items 1–8); verbal responses (items 9–45); acts out commands (items 46–50)	No[b]	—	No	—
Mathematics Computation	Visual (verbal directions)	Writes responses	Yes	Yes	No	—

Note. Long dash means use depends on severity of disability.

[a]Use of paper and pencil to solve problems is optional.

[b]Responses may be given in English, sign language, or another language, but there are no provisions to alter standard format either when giving directions or for subtest items.

For students with hearing disabilities or auditory receptive difficulties, the Mathematics Applications, Spelling, and Reading Comprehension subtests are problematic for norm-based assessment. Although responses may be in English, sign language, or any other language, instructions cannot be provided in alternative ways. If instructions are provided in sign language, for example, normative comparisons should not be made.

For students with visual disabilities, the Mathematics Applications, Reading Decoding, Reading Comprehension, and Mathematics Computation subtests are not appropriate. No provisions are made for translating test materials into braille. If normative comparisons are not being made, the use of braille translations could be used for Reading Decoding, Reading Comprehension, and Mathematics Computation. Spelling could be given in the standardized manner with the student orally spelling the words. Large-print versions of Reading Decoding and Reading Comprehension could also be used for students whose visual disabilities are not severe and for students who receive this type of accommodation in the classroom. Normative comparisons would not be seriously compromised in such cases.

For students with physical disabilities, Spelling could be administered in the standardized format with the student orally spelling the words. The appropriateness of the Reading Comprehension subtest depends on the severity of the impairment because the first eight items involve a gestural response. Likewise, Mathematics Computation involves written responses, and thus may pose a problem depending on the severity of the motor impairment. Having the student respond verbally impacts the normative comparisons but provides information on the level of skill development.

Students with expressive language disabilities and speech disabilities may have a problem with the Reading Comprehension subtest because items 9–45 require a verbal response. Similarly, Reading Decoding could be a problem depending on the severity of the disability. Mathematics Applications, Spelling, and Mathematics Computation are appropriate in their standardized format.

Peabody Individual Achievement Test–Revised/NU

Accommodations and Modifications

Students with disabilities were included in the standardization sample in proportions approximate to those of the 1995 U.S. population estimates. The test author indicates that interpretation of test results "is meaningful only if the examiner has followed the test instructions precisely and has read the wording of the items as given" (Markwardt, 1998, p. 5). At the same time, the examiner is encouraged to adapt test administration to the student's situation, and specific suggestions are provided for several subtests.

In testing students with disabilities who cannot point to or say the number of the multiple-choice items, the examiner may point to each response in consecutive order and elicit some indication (e.g., nodding or blinking) of the student's response. Likewise, an appropriate accommodation for General Information is ask students to write their responses if they cannot respond orally. The test author adds that "there is no effective way to adapt either Written Expression or Items 17–100 of Reading Recognition if the subject is unable to respond" (p. 7).

Recommended Use of the PIAT-R/NU with Students with Disabilities

The format of the PIAT-R/NU (multiple-choice for most subtests) varies considerably from that of most traditional achievement tests, making it an appropriate choice for many students with disabilities because expressive language skills and motoric responses are minimized. While some practitioners have expressed concern that the multiple-choice format of the test is easier for students than the open-ended format of other tests, the conorming of the test with the K-TEA/NU, WRMT-R/NU, and KeyMath-R/NU provides an equivalency of scores for subtests measuring the same domain (regardless of test format).

The presentation and response formats and recommendations for the use of each subtest with students who have hearing, speech, vision, and physical disabilities are presented in Rapid Reference 6.4. Five of the six subtests utilize visual stimuli along with verbal directions. Pointing to responses is used with five of the six subtests, and written responses are required for one subtest.

For students with hearing disabilities, the General Information subtest is not appropriate. The other subtests all rely on visual stimuli with verbal directions that could be presented by gesture or pantomime. If this accommodation is implemented, norms should be used cautiously and interpreted as a conservative estimate of the student's performance. Useful information regarding skill development in academic areas, however, would be generated.

For students with visual disabilities, all subtests are *inappropriate*. For stu-

≡ Rapid Reference 6.4

PIAT-R/NU Subtests: Appropriateness of Presentation and Response Formats for Students with Disabilities

Subtest	Presentation Format	Response Format	Use with Students with Disabilities?			
			Hearing	Speech	Vision	Physical
General Information	Verbal	Verbal responses	No	Yes	No	Yes
Reading Recognition	Visual (verbal directions)	Points to responses (items 1–16) Verbal responses (items 17–100)	No	Yes	No	Yes
Reading Comprehension	Visual (verbal directions)	Points to responses	No	Yes	No	Yes
Mathematics	Visual (verbal directions)	Points to responses	No	Yes	No	Yes
Spelling	Visual (verbal directions)	Points to responses	No	Yes	No	Yes
Written Expression	Visual (verbal directions)	Points to responses	No	Yes	No	No

dents with expressive language disabilities, all subtests are *appropriate;* responses can be written for the General Information subtest. For students with receptive language disabilities, all subtests are *appropriate* because the verbal directions are short and not overly complex.

As indicated earlier, for students who cannot point to or say the number of a multiple-choice item, the examiner may point to each response in consecutive order and elicit some indication (e.g., nodding or blinking) of the student's response.

Wechsler Individual Achievement Test

Accommodations and Modifications

Students receiving mainstream special services in school settings were not excluded from testing. As a result, 6% of the standardization sample consisted of children individually classified as learning disabled, speech/language impaired, emotionally disturbed, or physically impaired. In addition, 4.3% of the sample consisted of children in gifted and talented programs, and 1.4% of the sample were children classified as borderline or mildly mentally retarded. (The Psychological Corporation, 1992, p. 130)

The test author emphasizes that the test should be administered according to standard procedures, and that deviations from this procedure "can reduce the validity of the test results" (The Psychological Corporation, 1992, p. 10). At the same time, some guidance is presented in testing students with disabilities. Examiners are encouraged to become familiar with a student's limitations and preferred mode of communication prior to testing. It is emphasized that "some flexibility may be necessary to balance the needs of the particular child with the need to maintain standard procedures" (p. 13).

The test author states that, although

modifications of test procedures may be necessary, keep in mind that the WIAT was not standardized with such modifications. For example, if sign language and other visual aids are necessary to give instructions to a deaf child, remember that such alterations may have an impact on test scores. . . . Rely on your clinical judgment to evaluate the impact of such modified procedures on test scores. (The Psychological Corporation, 1992, p. 13)

Recommended Use of the WIAT with Students with Disabilities

The presentation and response formats and recommendations for the use of each subtest with students who have hearing, speech, visual, and physical disabilities are presented in Rapid Reference 6.5. Seven of the eight subtests utilize visual stimuli and verbal directions, with the eighth utilizing verbal stimuli only. Verbal responses are required on five subtests and paper-and-pencil responses are required on three. Pointing responses are used on initial items for Basic Reading, Mathematics Reasoning, and Listening Comprehension.

For students with hearing disabilities, the verbal directions may be problematic. Instructions could be given in sign language, provided normative comparisons are not made and the examiner is seeking information only on the presence or absence of specific skills. This procedure is in accordance with the test author's comments cited previously.

For students with visual disabilities, only the Spelling subtest is appropriate without accommodations. All other subtests are not appropriate for norm-based comparisons. No provisions are made for translating test materials into braille and many subtests utilize pictures as part of the items. If normative comparisons are not being made, the use of braille translations could be used for Basic Reading, Reading Comprehension (items 9–38), and Written Expression. Listening Comprehension can be administered as presented (the picture stimuli for Listening Comprehension are not essential to answering the test items), with cautious use of norms. Large print could also be used to facilitate administration of Reading Comprehension (items 9–38), Numerical Operations, Basic Reading, and Mathematics Reasoning. Since Oral Expression requires the student to respond to visual stimuli, it is not appropriate for students with severe visual disabilities.

For students with physical disabilities, only Spelling, Numerical Operations, and Written Expression are problematic. The student could be asked to spell the words in Spelling orally and solve the arithmetic problems in Numerical Operations orally. Unless a word processor can be used, the Written Expression subtest is not appropriate, because asking the student to respond verbally changes the construct being measured to oral expression.

Students with expressive language disabilities may have difficulties with

☰ Rapid Reference 6.5

WIAT Subtests: Appropriateness of Presentation and Response Formats for Students with Disabilities

Subtest	Presentation Format	Response Format	Hearing	Speech	Vision	Physical
			Use with Students with Disabilities?			
Basic Reading	Visual (verbal directions)	Points to responses (items 1–7); verbal responses (items 8–55)	No	—	—	Yes
Mathematics Reasoning	Visual (verbal directions)	Points to responses (items 1–4); verbal responses (items 5–49)	No	Yes	—	Yes
Spelling	Verbal	Writes responses	No	Yes	Yes	No
Reading Comprehension	Visual (verbal directions)	Verbal responses	No	—	—	Yes
Numerical Operations	Verbal (items 1–4); visual (items 5–40)	Writes responses	Yes	Yes	—	No
Listening Comprehension	Visual (verbal directions)	Points to responses (items 1–9)	Yes	—	Yes	Yes
Oral Expression	Visual (verbal directions)	Verbal responses	Yes	—	No	Yes
Written Expression	Visual (verbal directions)	Writes responses	Yes	Yes	No	No

Note. Long dash means use depends on severity of disability.

Reading Comprehension, Listening Comprehension, and Oral Expression. The other subtests are appropriate in their standardized formats.

Students with receptive language disabilities may have difficulties with Mathematics Reasoning and Listening Comprehension because both subtests involve lengthy verbal content and instructions.

Wide Range Achievement Test 3

Accommodations and Modifications

Students with disabilities were included in the standardization sample "as randomization would allow. Subjects were only excluded if they were unable to physically respond to the test items" (Wilkinson, 1993, p. 27). The issue of testing accommodations is not addressed in the test manual. Subtests may be administered in any order that is consistent with their counterbalanced administration during standardization. There are no provisions for administering subtests in sign language or another language, or by gesture. Likewise, no provisions are made for responses in a language other than English. Examiners are advised that "pronunciations due to colloquialisms, foreign accents, and defective articulation are accepted as correct if the peculiarity is consistent throughout" (Wilkinson, 1993, p. 12).

Recommended Use of the WRAT3 with Students with Disabilities

All WRAT3 subtests involve verbal directions, and two of them also include verbal stimuli (reading and arithmetic). Visual stimuli are utilized by two subtests (spelling and arithmetic). Paper-and-pencil skills are required for two of the three subtests (spelling and arithmetic). The presentation and response formats and recommendations for the use of each subtest with students who have hearing, speech, vision, and physical disabilities are presented in Rapid Reference 6.6.

Without any provisions for sign-language administration of the test or an administration in pantomime, the WRAT3 is not appropriate for students with hearing disabilities or auditory receptive difficulties. Similarly, the need for written responses on Spelling and Arithmetic and the need to pronounce words that are presented visually for the Reading subtest preclude use of the WRAT3 with students who have visual disabilities.

Two subtests, Spelling and Arithmetic, require written responses. Thus, the

⟰Rapid Reference 6.6

WRAT3 Subtests: Appropriateness of Presentation and Response Formats for Students with Disabilities

Subtest	Presentation Format	Response Format	Use with Students with Disabilities?			
			Hearing	Speech	Vision	Physical
Reading	Visual (verbal directions)	Verbal responses	No	—	No	Yes
Spelling	Verbal (name/letter writing)	Motoric (writes letters)	No	Yes	No	—
	Verbal (word spelling)	Motoric (writes words)	No	Yes	No	—
Arithmetic	Verbal and visual (oral items)	Verbal responses	No	—	No	Yes
	Visual (verbal directions)	Motoric (writes answers)	No	Yes	No	—

Note. Long dash means use depends on severity of disability.

use of these tests with students with physical disabilities is dependent on the severity of the disability. In order to complete these subtests, the examinee must write words for Spelling and numbers for Arithmetic; no provisions are made for verbal responses to these subtests.

Students with expressive language disabilities and speech disabilities may have difficulty with the Reading subtest, which requires a verbal response. Once again, use of this subtest depends on the severity of the disability.

SUMMARY AND CONCLUSIONS

The assessment of individuals with disabilities is a challenging activity. As the importance of testing accommodations in individual assessment continues to increase, we must continue to upgrade our skills in this area. Likewise, there is an increasing need for test authors to be more specific in describing the types of accommodations that are appropriate for their instruments.

 TEST YOURSELF

1. **Providing testing accommodations for individuals with disabilities is a new concept.** True or False?

2. **Testing accommodations are needed by all individuals with disabilities and are needed for all assessments.** True or False?

3. **Testing accommodations may reflect changes in the**
   (a) setting.
   (b) timing.
   (c) presentation format.
   (d) response format.
   (e) all of these.

4. **The achievement tests discussed in this chapter are all norm-based measures.** True or False?

5. **Modifications to standard testing procedures may invalidate normative scores.** True or False?

Answers: 1. False; 2. False; 3. e; 4. True; 5. True

Appendix

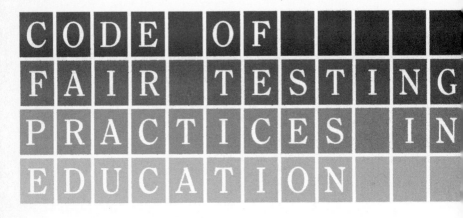

Prepared by the Joint Committee on Testing Practices

The Code of Fair Testing Practices in Education states the major obligations to test takers of professionals who develop or use educational tests. The Code is meant to apply broadly to the use of tests in education (admissions, educational assessment, educational diagnosis, and student placement). The Code is not designed to cover employment testing, licensure or certification testing, or other types of testing. Although the Code has relevance to many types of educational tests, it is directed primarily at professionally developed tests such as those sold by commercial test publishers or used in formally administered testing programs. The Code is not intended to cover tests made by individual teachers for use in their own classrooms.

The Code addresses the roles of test developers and test users separately. Test users are people who select tests, commission test development services, or make decisions on the basis of test scores. Test developers are people who actually construct tests as well as those who set policies for particular testing programs. The roles may, of course, overlap as when a state education agency commissions test development services, sets policies that control the test development process, and makes decisions on the basis of the test scores.

■   ■   ■   ■   ■   ■   ■   ■   ■   ■   ■

The Code has been developed by the Joint Committee on Testing Practices, a cooperative effort of several professional organizations, that has as its aim the advancement, in the public interest, of the quality of testing practices. The Joint Committee was initiated by the American Educational Research Association, the American Psychological Association and the National Council on Measurement in Education. In addition to these three groups, the American Association for Counseling and Development/Association for Measurement and Evaluation in Counseling and Development, and the American Speech-Language-Hearing Association are now also sponsors of the Joint Committee.

This is not copyrighted material. Reproduction and dissemination are encouraged. Please cite this document as follows:

Code of Fair Testing Practices in Education. (1988) Washington, D.C. Joint Committee on Testing Practices. (Mailing Address: Joint Committee on Testing Practices, American Psychological Association, 750 First Avenue, NE, Washington, D.C., 20002-4242.)

ode of Fair Testing Practices in Education . . . .

he Code presents standards for educational test devel-
pers and users in four areas:

    A. Developing/Selecting Tests
    B. Interpreting Scores
    C. Striving for Fairness
    D. Informing Test Takers

rganizations, institutions, and individual professionals
ho endorse the Code commit themselves to safeguard-
g the rights of test takers by following the principles
sted. The Code is intended to be consistent with the
levant parts of the *Standards for Educational and Psy-
ological Testing* (AERA, APA, NCME, 1985). However,

the Code differs from the Standards in both audience
and purpose. The Code is meant to be understood by the
general public; it is limited to educational tests; and the
primary focus is on those issues that affect the proper
use of tests. The Code is not meant to add new principles
over and above those in the Standards or to change the
meaning of the Standards. The goal is rather to represent
the spirit of a selected portion of the Standards in a way
that is meaningful to test takers and/or their parents or
guardians. It is the hope of the Joint Committee that the
Code will also be judged to be consistent with existing
codes of conduct and standards of other professional
groups who use educational tests.

A — Developing/Selecting Appropriate Tests*

Test developers should provide the information that test users need to select appropriate tests.	Test users should select tests that meet the purpose for which they are to be used and that are appropriate for the intended test-taking populations.

Test Developers Should:

1. Define what each test measures and what the test should be used for. Describe the population(s) for which the test is appropriate.

2. Accurately represent the characteristics, usefulness, and limitations of tests for their intended purposes.

3. Explain relevant measurement concepts as necessary for clarity at the level of detail that is appropriate for the intended audience(s).

4. Describe the process of test development. Explain how the content and skills to be tested were selected.

5. Provide evidence that the test meets its intended purpose(s).

6. Provide either representative samples or complete copies of test questions, directions, answer sheets, manuals, and score reports to qualified users.

7. Indicate the nature of the evidence obtained concerning the appropriateness of each test for groups of different racial, ethnic, or linguistic backgrounds who are likely to be tested.

8. Identify and publish any specialized skills needed to administer each test and to interpret scores correctly.

Test Users Should:

1. First define the purpose for testing and the population to be tested. Then, select a test for that purpose and that population based on a thorough review of the available information.

2. Investigate potentially useful sources of information, in addition to test scores, to corroborate the information provided by tests.

3. Read the materials provided by test developers and avoid using tests for which unclear or incomplete information is provided.

4. Become familiar with how and when the test was developed and tried out.

5. Read independent evaluations of a test and of possible alternative measures. Look for evidence required to support the claims of test developers.

6. Examine specimen sets, disclosed tests or samples of questions, directions, answer sheets, manuals, and score reports before selecting a test.

7. Ascertain whether the test content and norms group(s) or comparison group(s) are appropriate for the intended test takers.

8. Select and use only those tests for which the skills needed to administer the test and interpret scores correctly are available.

---

*Many of the statements in the Code refer to the selection of existing tests. However, in customized testing programs test developers are engaged to construct new tests. In those situations, the test development process should be designed to help ensure that the completed tests will be in compliance with the Code.

B   Interpreting Scores

| Test developers should help users interpret scores correctly. | Test users should interpret scores correctly. |

Test Developers Should:

9. Provide timely and easily understood score reports that describe test performance clearly and accurately. Also explain the meaning and limitations of reported scores.

10. Describe the population(s) represented by any norms or comparison group(s), the dates the data were gathered, and the process used to select the samples of test takers.

11. Warn users to avoid specific, reasonably anticipated misuses of test scores.

12. Provide information that will help users follow reasonable procedures for setting passing scores when it is appropriate to use such scores with the test.

13. Provide information that will help users gather evidence to show that the test is meeting its intended purpose(s).

Test Users Should:

9. Obtain information about the scale used for reporting scores, the characteristics of any norms or comparison group(s), and the limitations of the scores.

10. Interpret scores taking into account any major differences between the norms or comparison groups and the actual test takers. Also take into account any differences in test administration practices or familiarity with the specific questions in the test.

11. Avoid using tests for purposes not specifically recommended by the test developer unless evidence is obtained to support the intended use.

12. Explain how any passing scores were set and gather evidence to support the appropriateness of the scores.

13. Obtain evidence to help show that the test is meeting its intended purpose(s).

C   Striving for Fairness

| Test developers should strive to make tests that are as fair as possible for test takers of different races, gender, ethnic backgrounds, or handicapping conditions. | Test users should select tests that have been developed in ways that attempt to make them as fair as possible for test takers of different races, gender, ethnic backgrounds, or handicapping conditions. |

Test Developers Should:

14. Review and revise test questions and related materials to avoid potentially insensitive content or language.

15. Investigate the performance of test takers of different races, gender, and ethnic backgrounds when samples of sufficient size are available. Enact procedures that help to ensure that differences in performance are related primarily to the skills under assessment rather than to irrelevant factors.

16. When feasible, make appropriately modified forms of tests or administration procedures available for test takers with handicapping conditions. Warn test users of potential problems in using standard norms with modified tests or administration procedures that result in non-comparable scores.

Test Users Should:

14. Evaluate the procedures used by test developers to avoid potentially insensitive content or language.

15. Review the performance of test takers of different races, gender, and ethnic backgrounds when samples of sufficient size are available. Evaluate the extent to which performance differences may have been caused by inappropriate characteristics of the test.

16. When necessary and feasible, use appropriately modified forms of tests or administration procedures for test takers with handicapping conditions. Interpret standard norms with care in the light of the modifications that were made.

ode of Fair Testing Practices in Education . . . .

 D Informing Test Takers

Under some circumstances, test developers have direct communication with test takers. Under other circumstances, test users communicate directly with test takers. Whichever group communicates directly with test takers should provide the information described below.

Test Developers or Test Users Should:

17. When a test is optional, provide test takers or their parents/guardians with information to help them judge whether the test should be taken, or if an available alternative to the test should be used.

18. Provide test takers the information they need to be familiar with the coverage of the test, the types of question formats, the directions, and appropriate test-taking strategies. Strive to make such information equally available to all test takers.

Under some circumstances, test developers have direct control of tests and test scores. Under other circumstances, test users have such control. Whichever group has direct control of tests and test scores should take the steps described below.

Test Developers or Test Users Should:

19. Provide test takers or their parents/guardians with information about rights test takers may have to obtain copies of tests and completed answer sheets, retake tests, have tests rescored, or cancel scores.

20. Tell test takers or their parents/guardians how long scores will be kept on file and indicate to whom and under what circumstances test scores will or will not be released.

21. Describe the procedures that test takers or their parents/guardians may use to register complaints and have problems resolved.

■   ■   ■   ■   ■   ■   ■   ■   ■   ■   ■   ■

Note: The membership of the Working Group that developed the Code of Fair Testing Practices in Education and of the Joint Committee on Testing Practices that guided the Working Group was as follows:

Theodore P. Bartell
John R. Bergan
Esther E. Diamond
Richard P. Duran
Lorraine D. Eyde
Raymond D. Fowler
John J. Fremer
(Co-chair, JCTP and Chair,
Code Working Group)

Edmund W. Gordon
Jo-Ida C. Hansen
James B. Lingwall
George F. Madaus
(Co-chair, JCTP)
Kevin L. Moreland
Jo-Ellen V. Perez
Robert J. Solomon
John T. Stewart

Carol Kehr Tittle
(Co-chair, JCTP)
Nicholas A. Vacc
Michael J. Zieky
Debra Boltas and Wayne
Camara of the American
Psychological Association
served as staff liaisons

Additional copies of the Code may be obtained from the National Council on Measurement in Education, 1230 Seventeenth Street, NW, Washington, D.C. 20036. Single copies are free.

References

Ackerman, T. (1998). Review of the Wechsler Individual Achievement Test. In J. Impara (Ed.). *The thirteenth mental measurements yearbook* (pp. 1125–1128). Lincoln, NE: Buros Institute of Mental Measurements.

Ahrens, J. A., Evans, R. G., & Barnett, R. W. (1990). Factors related to dropping out of school in an incarcerated population. *Educational & Psychological Measurement, 50,* 611–617.

Albers, N. C. (1998). Use of the Wechsler Intelligence Scale for Children–Third Edition and the Wechsler Individual Achievement Test in the diagnosis of learning disabilities in an attention deficit disorder referred population. *Dissertation Abstracts International: Section B: The Sciences and Engineering, 58,* 3915.

Alfonso, V. C., & Tarnofsky, M. (1999). *Review of the psychometric properties of the reading component of four achievement batteries.* Paper presented at the annual meeting of the American Psychological Association, Boston, MA.

Allinder, R. M., & Fuchs, L. S. (1992). Screening academic achievement: Review of the Peabody Individual Achievement Test–Revised. *Learning Disabilities Research & Practice, 7,* 45–47.

American Educational Research Association, American Psychological Association, & National Council on Measurement in Education (AERA/APA/NCME). (1999). *Standards for educational and psychological testing.* Washington, DC: American Educational Research Association.

Archer, R. P., Maruish, M., Imhof, E. A., & Piotrowski, C. (1991). Psychological test usage with adolescent clients: 1990 findings. *Professional Psychology: Research & Practice, 22,* 247–252.

Archer, R. P., & Newsom, C. R. (1999). *Psychological test usage with adolescent clients: A survey update.* Paper presented at the annual meeting of the American Psychological Association, Boston, MA.

Bartels, D. R. (1998–1999). The Peabody Individual Achievement Test–Revised/Normative Update. *Diagnostique, 24,* 211–220.

Bell, P. F., Lentz, F. E., & Graden, J. L. (1992). Effects of curriculum-test overlap on standardized test scores: Identifying systematic confounds in educational decision making. *School Psychology Review, 21,* 644–655.

Benes, K. M. (1992). Review of Peabody Individual Achievement Test–Revised. In J. J. Kramer & J. C. Conoley (Eds.), *Eleventh mental measurements yearbook* (pp. 649–654). Lincoln, NE: Buros Institute of Mental Measurements.

Bookman, J. R., & Peach, W. J. (1988). A comparison of the standard scores obtained by special education students on the Diagnostic Achievement Battery, Kaufman Test of Educational Achievement, and the Peabody Individual Achievement Test. *Journal of Instructional Psychology, 15,* 37–39.

Chan, D. W., & Lee, H. (1995). Patterns of psychological test usage in Hong Kong in 1993. *Professional Psychology: Research and Practice, 26,* 292–297.

Clark, E. (1994). Review of the Wide Range Achievement Test–Revised. In J. C. Impara & L. L. Murphy (Eds.), *Buros desk reference: Psychological assessment in the schools* (pp. 64–68). Lincoln, NE: Buros Institute of Mental Measurements.

Code of Fair Testing Practices in Education. (1988). Washington, DC: Joint Committee on Testing Practices.

Cohen, L. G. (1993). Test review: Wechsler Individual Achievement Test. *Diagnostique, 18,* 255–268.

Costenbader, V. K., & Adams, J. W. (1991). A review of the psychometric and administrative features of the PIAT-R: Implications for the practitioner. *Journal of School Psychology, 29,* 219–228.

Demaray, M. K., & Elliot, S. N. (1999). Teachers' judgments of students' academic functioning: A comparison of actual and predicted achievement. *School Psychology Quarterly, 13,* 8–24.

Determan, D. K., Thompson, L. A., & Plomin, R. (1990). Differences in heritability across groups differing in ability. *Behavior Genetics, 20,* 369–384.

Dickenson, D. J. (1986). Test review: Kaufman Test of Educational Achievement, Brief Form. *Journal of Psychoeducational Assessment, 4,* 333–336.

Doll, E. J. (1989). Review of the Kaufman Test of Educational Achievement. In J. C. Conoley & J. J. Kramer (Eds.), *Tenth mental measurements yearbook* (pp. 411–412). Lincoln, NE: Buros Institute of Mental Measurements.

Duncan, R. D., Kennedy, W. A., & Patrick, C. J. (1995). Four-factor model of recidivism in male juvenile offenders. *Journal of Clinical Child Psychology, 24,* 250–257.

Dunn, L., & Dunn, M. (1981). The Peabody Picture Vocabulary Test–Revised. Circle Pines, MN: American Guidance Service.

Dunn, L. M., & Markwardt, F. C. (1970). Peabody Individual Achievement Test. Circle Pines, MN: American Guidance Service.

Edwards, J. (1989). Test review: Peabody Individual Achievement Test–Revised (PIAT-R). *Journal of Psychoeducational Assessment, 7,* 264–271.

Ekstrom, R. B., & Smith, D. K. (Eds.). (In press). *Assessing people with disabilities in educational, employment, and clinical settings.* Washington, DC: American Psychological Association.

Elliott, C. D. (1990). Differential Ability Scales. San Antonio, TX: The Psychological Corporation.

Ferrara, S. (1998). Review of the Wechsler Individual Achievement Test. In J. Impara (Ed.), *The thirteenth mental measurements yearbook* (1128–1132). Lincoln, NE: Buros Institute of Mental Measurements.

Flanagan, D. (1997). Review of the Wechsler Individual Achievement Test. *Journal of Psychoeducational Assessment, 15,* 82–85.

Flanagan, D. P., & Alfonso, V. C. (1993a). Differences required for significance between Wechsler Verbal and Performance IQs and WIAT subtests and composites: The predicted-achievement method. *Psychology in the Schools, 30,* 125–132.

Flanagan, D. P., & Alfonso, V. C. (1993b). WIAT subtest and composite predicted-achievement values based on WISC-III Verbal and Performance IQs. *Psychology in the Schools, 30,* 310–320.

Flanagan, D. P., McGrew, K. P., Abramowitz, E., Lehner, L., Untiedt, S., Berger, D., &

Armstrong, H. (1997). Improvement in academic screening instruments? A concurrent validity investigation of the K-FAST, MBA, and WRAT-3. *Journal of Psychoeducational Assessment, 13,* 99–112.

Gentry, N., Sapp, G. L., & Daw, J. L. (1995). Scores on the Weschler Individual Achievement Test and the Kaufman Test of Educational Achievement–Comprehensive Form for emotionally conflicted adolescents. *Psychological Reports, 76,* 607–610.

Glutting, J. J., McDermott, P. A., Prifitera, A., & McGrath, E. A. (1994). Core profile types for the WISC-III and WIAT: Their development and applications in identifying multivariate IQ-achievement discrepancies. *School Psychology Review, 23,* 619–639.

Glutting, J. J., Oakland, T., & Konold, T. R. (1994). Criterion-related bias with the Guide to the Assessment of Test Session Behavior for the WISC-III and WIAT: Possible race/ethnicity, gender, and SES effects. *Journal of School Psychology, 32,* 355–369.

Glutting, J. J., Oh, J., Ward, T., & Ward, S. (2000). Possible criterion-related bias of the WISC-III with a referral sample. *Journal of Psychoeducational Assessment, 18,* 17–26.

Glutting, J. J., Robins, P. M., & de Lancey, E. (1997). Discriminant validity of test observations for children with attention deficit/hyperactivity. *Journal of School Psychology, 35,* 391–401.

Glutting, J. J., Youngstrom, E. A., Ward, T., Ward, S., & Hale, R. J. (1997). Incremental efficacy of WISC-III factor scores in predicting achievement: What do they tell us? *Psychological Assessment, 9,* 295–302.

Hammill, D. D., Fowler, L., Bryant, B., & Dunn, C. (1992). *A survey of test usage among speech/language pathologists.* Unpublished manuscript.

Harrison, P. L. (1994). Review of the Wide Range Achievement Test–Revised. In J. C. Impara & L. L. Murphy (Eds.), *Buros desk reference: Psychological assessment in the schools.* Lincoln, NE: Buros Institute of Mental Measurements.

Harrison, P. L., Kaufman, A. S., Hickman, J. A., & Kaufman, N. L. (1988). A survey of tests used for adult assessment. *Journal of Psychoeducational Assessment, 6,* 188–198.

Henson, F. O., & Bennett, L. M. (1985). Review of the Kaufman Test of Educational Achievement. In D. J. Keyser & R. C. Sweetland (Eds.), *Test Critiques, 4,* 368–375. Kansas City, MO: Test Corporation of America.

Hewett, J. B., & Bolen, L. M. (1996). Performance changes on the K-TEA Brief Form for learning-disabled students. *Psychology in the Schools, 33,* 97–102.

Hultquist, A. M., & Metzke, L. K. (1993). Potential effects of curriculum bias in individual norm-referenced reading and spelling achievement test. *Psychoeducational Assessment, 11,* 337–344.

Hutton, J. B., Dubes, R., & Muir, S. (1992). Assessment practices of school psychologists: Ten years later. *School Psychology Review, 21,* 271–284.

Jastak, J., & Jastak, S. (1978). The Wide Range Achievement Test. Wilmington, DE: Jastak Associates.

Jastak, S., & Wilkinson, G. S. (1984). The Wide Range Achievement Test–Revised. Wilmington, DE: Jastak Associates.

Kamphaus, R. W., Schmitt, C. S., & Mings, D. R. (1986). Three studies of the validity of the Kaufman Test of Educational Achievement. *Journal of Psychoeducational Assessment, 4,* 299–305.

Kamphaus, R. W., Slotkin, J., & DeVincentis, C. (1990). Clinical assessment of children's academic achievement. In C. R. Reynolds & R. W. Kamphaus (Eds.), *Handbook of psy-*

chological & educational assessment of children: Intelligence & achievement (pp. 552–568). New York: Guilford.

Kaufman, A. S., & Kaufman, N. L. (1983). Kaufman Assessment Battery for Children. Circle Pines, MN: American Guidance Service.

Kaufman, A. S., & Kaufman, N. L. (1985). Kaufman Test of Educational Achievement. Circle Pines, MN: American Guidance Service.

Kaufman, A. S., & Kaufman, N. L. (1994). Kaufman Functional Academic Skills Test. Circle Pines, MN: American Guidance Service.

Kaufman, A. S., & Kaufman, N. L. (1997). Kaufman Test of Educational Achievement Normative Update. Circle Pines, MN: American Guidance Service.

Knapp, N. F., & Winsor, A. P. (1998). A reading apprenticeship for delayed primary readers. *Reading Research & Instruction, 38,* 13–29.

Konold, T. R. (1999). Evaluating discrepancy analysis with WISC-III and WIAT. *Journal of Psychoeducational Assessment, 17,* 24–35.

Konold, T. R., Glutting, J. J., Oakland, T., & O'Donnell, L. (1995). Congruence of test-behavior dimensions among child groups that vary in gender, race-ethnicity, and SES. *Journal of Psychoeducational Assessment, 13,* 111–119.

Lassiter, K. S., D'Amato, R. C., Raggio, D. J., & Whitten, J. C. (1994). The construct specificity of the Continuous Performance Test: Does inattention relate to behavior and achievement? *Journal of Psychoeducational Assessment, 12,* 381–392.

Laurent, J., & Swerdlik, M. (1992). *Psychological test usage: A survey of internship supervisors.* Paper presented at the annual meeting of the National Association of School Psychologists, Nashville, TN.

Lavin, C. (1996). The relationship between the Wechsler Intelligence Scale for Children–Third Edition and the Kaufman Test of Educational Achievement. *Psychology in the Schools, 33,* 119–123.

Lazarus, B. D., McKenna, M. C., & Lynch, D. (1989–1990). Peabody Individual Achievement Test–Revised (PIAT-R). *Diagnostique, 15,* 135–148.

Lennox, C., & Siegel, L. S. (1996). The development of phonological rules and visual strategies in average and poor spellers. *Journal of Experimental Child Psychology, 62,* 60–83.

Lewandowski, L. J. (1986). Test review: Kaufman Test of Educational Achievement. *Journal of Reading, 30,* 258–261.

Luther, J. B. (1992). Review of the Peabody Individual Achievement Test–Revised. *Journal of School Psychology, 30,* 31–39.

Mabry, L. (1995). Review of the Wide Range Achievement Test 3. In J. C. Conoley & J. C. Impara (Eds.), *The twelfth mental measurements yearbook* (pp. 1108–1110). Lincoln, NE: Buros Institute of Measurements.

Mahrou, M. L., Espe-Pfeifer, P., Devaraju-Backhaus, S., Dornheim, L., & Golden, C. J. (1999). *Factor structure of the WRAM-L, PIAT-R, and WISC-III.* Paper presented at the annual meeting of the American Psychological Association, Boston, MA.

Markwardt, F. C., Jr. (1989, 1990). Peabody Individual Achievement Test–Revised Normative Update. Circle Pines, MN: American Guidance Service.

Martelle, Y., & Smith, D. K. (1994). *Relationship of the WIAT and WJ-R Tests of Achievement in a sample of students referred for learning disabilities.* Paper presented at the First Annual South Padre Island International Interdisciplinary Conference on Cognitive Assessment of Children and Youth in Clinical Settings, South Padre, TX. (ERIC Document Reproduction Service no. ED 381 976).

Mason, E. M., Seese, G., & Teska, H. (2000). *A comparison of writing skills of college students using the WIAT and Woodcock-Johnson Tests of Achievement–Revised.* Paper presented at the annual meeting of the National Association of School Psychologists, New Orleans, LA.

Miller, L. J. (1998–1999). Kaufman Test of Educational Achievement/Normative Update, K-TEA/NU. *Diagnostique, 24,* 145–159.

Muenz, T. A., Ouchi, B. Y., & Cole, J. C. (1999). Item analysis of written expression scoring systems for the PIAT-R and WIAT. *Psychology in the Schools, 36,* 31–40.

Oakland, T., & Hu, S. (1992). The top 10 tests used with children and youth worldwide. *Bulletin of the International Test Commission, 19,* 99–120.

Ouchi, B. Y., Cole, J. C., Muenz, T. A., & Kaufman, A. S. (1996). Interrater reliability of the written expression subtest of the Peabody Individual Achievement Test–Revised: An adolescent and adult sample. *Psychological Reports, 79,* 1239–1247.

Peterson, R. C., Smith, G. E., Waring, S. C., Ivnik, R. J., Tangelos, E. G., & Kokmen, E. (1999). Mild cognitive impairment: Clinical characterization and outcome. *Archives of Neurology, 56,* 303–308.

Peterson, D., Stege, H., Slate, J. R., & Jones, C. H. (1991). Examiner errors on the WRAT-R. *Psychology in the Schools, 28,* 205–208.

Posey, W., Sapp, G. L., & Gladding, S. T. (1989). Validating the Kaufman Test of Educational Achievement, Brief Form with educable mentally retarded students. *Psychological Reports, 65,* 1225–1226.

Prewett, P. N., Bardos, A., & Fowler, D. B. (1991). Relationship between the KTEA Brief and Comprehensive forms and the WRAT-R Level 1 with referred elementary children. *Educational and Psychological Measurement, 51,* 729–734.

Prewett, P. N., & Giannuli, M. M. (1991). The relationship among the reading subtests of the WJ-R, PIAT-R, K-TEA, and WRAT-R. *Journal of Psychoeducational Assessment, 9,* 166–174.

Prewett, P. N., Lillis, W. T., & Bardos, A. (1991). Relationship between the Kaufman Test of Educational Achievement–Brief Form and the Wide Range Achievement Test–Revised, Level 2 with incarcerated juvenile delinquents. *Psychological Reports, 68,* 147–150.

The Psychological Corporation. (1992). Wechsler Individual Achievement Test. San Antonio, TX: Author.

Radencich, M. C. (1986). Kaufman Test of Educational Achievement (K-TEA): Test update. *Academic Therapy, 21,* 619–622.

Riccio, C. A. (1992). Wechsler Individual Achievement Test: A critical review. *Child Assessment News, 2,* 10–12.

Riccio, C. A., Boan, C. H., Staniszewski, D., & Hynd, G. W. (1997). Concurrent validity of standardized measures of written expression. *Diagnostique, 23,* 203–211.

Rogers, B. G. (1992). Review of the Peabody Individual Achievement Test–Revised. In J. J. Kramer & J. C. Conoley (Eds.), *The eleventh mental measurements yearbook* (pp. 654–657). Lincoln, NE: Buros Institute of Mental Measurements.

Ross, J. L., Roeltgen, D., Feuillan, P., Kushner, H., & Cutler, G. B. (2000). Use of estrogen in young girls with Turner syndrome: Effects on memory. *Neurology, 54,* 164–170.

Rynard, D. W., Chambers, A., Klinck, A. M., & Gray, J. D. (1998). School support programs for chronically ill children: Evaluating the adjustment of children with cancer at school. *Children's Health Care, 27,* 31–46.

Saigal, S., Szatmari, P., & Rosenbaum, P. L. (1992). Can learning disabilities in children who were extremely low birth weight be identified at school entry? *Journal of Developmental & Behavioral Pediatrics, 13,* 356–362.

Saklofske, D. H., Schwean, V. L., & O'Donnell, L. (1996). WIAT performance of children with ADHD. *Canadian Journal of School Psychology, 12,* 55–59.

Salvia, J., & Ysseldyke, J. E. (1998). *Assessment* (7th ed.). Boston: Houghton Mifflin.

Salvia, J., & Ysseldyke, J. E. (2001). *Assessment* (8th ed.). Boston: Houghton Mifflin.

Sapp, G. L., & Emens, R. (2000). Comparison of the WISC-III, WIAT, and DAB-2 scores of students assessed for exceptional class placement. Paper presented at the annual meeting of the American Psychological Association. Washington, DC.

Sattler, J. M. (1989). Review of the Kaufman Test of Educational Achievement. In J. C. Conoley & J. J. Kramer (Eds.), *Tenth mental measurements yearbook* (pp. 412–413). Lincoln, NE: Buros Institute of Mental Measurements.

Sellers, A. H., & Medler, J. D. (1992). A survey of current neuropsychological assessment procedures used for different age groups. *Psychotherapy in Private Practice, 11,* 47–57.

Shapiro, E. S., & Derr, T. F. (1987). An examination of overlap between reading curricula and standardized achievement tests. *Journal of Special Education, 2,* 59–67.

Shull-Senn, S., Weatherly, M., Morgan, S., Kanouse, K., & Bradley-Johnson, S. (1995). Stability reliability for elementary-age students on the Woodcock-Johnson Psychoeducational Battery–Revised (Achievement Section) and the Kaufman Test of Educational Achievement. *Psychology in the Schools, 32,* 86–92.

Slate, J. R. (1996). Interrelations of frequently administered achievement measures in the determination of specific learning disabilities. *Learning Disabilities Research and Practice, 11,* 86–89.

Slate, J. R. (1994). WISC-III correlations with the WIAT. *Psychology in the Schools, 3,* 278–285.

Slate, J. R., & Fawcett, J. (1995). Validity of the WISC-III for deaf and hard of hearing persons. *American Annals of the Deaf, 140,* 250–254.

Smith, D. K. (In press). The decision-making process for developing testing accommodations. In R. B. Ekstrom and D. K. Smith (Eds.), *Assessing people with disabilities in educational, employment, and clinical settings.* Washington, DC: American Psychological Association.

Smith, T. D., & Smith, B. L. (1998). Relationship between the Wide Range Achievement Test 3 and the Wechsler Individual Achievement Test. *Psychological Reports, 83,* 963–967.

Smith, T. D., & Smith, B. L., & Smithson, M. M. (1995). The relationship between the WISC-III and the WRAT3 in a sample of rural referred children. *Psychology in the Schools, 32,* 291–295.

Stinnett, T. A., Havey, J. M., & Oehler-Stinnett, J. (1994). Current test usage by practicing school psychologists: A national survey. *Journal of Psychoeducational Assessment, 12,* 331–350.

Taylor, R. L. (1998–1999). Wechsler Individual Achievement Test. *Diagnostique, 24,* 275–284.

Thurlow, M. L., Elliott, J. L., & Ysseldyke, J. E. (1998). *Testing students with disabilities: Practical strategies for complying with district and state requirements.* Thousand Oaks, CA: Corwin.

Vance, B., & Fuller, G. B. (1995). Relations of scores on WISC-III and WRAT3 for a sample of referred children and youth. *Psychological Reports, 76,* 371–374.

Ward, A. W. (1995). Review of the Wide Range Achievement Test 3. In J. C. Conoley & J. C. Impara (Eds.), *The twelfth mental measurements yearbook* (pp. 1110–1111). Lincoln, NE: Buros Institute of Mental Measurements.

Watkins, C. E., Campbell, V. I., Nieberding, R., & Hallmark, R. (1996). On Hunsley, harangue, and hoopla: Contemporary practice of psychological assessment by clinical psychologists. *Professional Psychology: Research and Practice, 27,* 316–318.

Webster, R. E., & Braswell, L. A. (1991). Curriculum bias and reading achievement test performance. *Psychology in the Schools, 28,* 193–199.

Webster, R. E., Hewett, J. B., & Crumbacker, H. M. (1989). Criterion-related validity of the WRAT-R and K-TEA with teacher estimates of actual classroom academic performance. *Psychology in the Schools, 26,* 243–248.

Weiss, L. G., & Prifitera, A. (1995). An evaluation of differential prediction of WIAT achievement scores from WISC-III FSIQ across ethnic and gender groups. *Journal of School Psychology, 33,* 297–304.

Wilkinson, G. S. (1993). Wide Range Achievement Test 3. Wilmington, DE: Wide Range, Inc.

Wilson, M. S., & Reschly, D. J. (1996). Assessment in school psychology training and practice. *School Psychology Review, 21,* 9–23.

Witt, J. C., Elliott, S. N., Kramer, J. J., & Gresham, F. M. (1994). *Assessment of children: Fundamental methods and practices.* Madison, WI: Brown & Benchmark.

Woodcock, R. W., & Johnson, M. B. (1989). Woodcock-Johnson Psychoeducational Battery–Revised. Itasca, IL: Riverside.

Woodcock, R. W., McGrew, K., & Werder, J. (1994). The Mini-Battery of Achievement. Itasca, IL: Riverside.

Worthington, C. F. (1987). Testing the test: Kaufman Test of Educational Achievement, Comprehensive Form and Brief Form. *Journal of Counseling and Development, 65,* 325–327.

Zaske, K., Hegstrom, K., & Smith, D. K. (1999). *Survey of test usage among clinical psychology and school psychology.* Paper presented at the annual meeting of the American Psychological Association, Boston, MA.

Annotated Bibliography

Alfonso, V. C., & Tarnofsky, M. (1999). *Review of the psychometric properties of the reading component of four achievement batteries.* Paper presented at the annual meeting of the American Psychological Association, Boston, MA.

The authors developed a system for evaluating the psychometric properties of reading achievement measures and applied the system to the WIAT, PIAT-R/NU, WJ-R TA, and K-TEA/NU. Psychometric properties included standardization, reliability, test floor, item gradients, and validity. For the PIAT-R/NU Reading Composite, the standardization property resulted in ratings of good on recency of standardization data and normative scores provided; adequate on age division of norms; and inadequate on sample size and number of variables used. Ratings of internal consistency were good except for sample size (inadequate). The floor for the Reading composite was deemed inadequate at ages 5 years 0 months through 5 years 11 months. Item gradients were good at all age levels. The overall rating for validity was adequate with evidence of content, construct, and criterion validity being provided. For the K-TEA/NU Reading composite the standardization property resulted in ratings of good on recency of normative data and types of scores reported; adequate on age division of norms; and inadequate on size of standardization sample and number of variables. Ratings of internal consistency were good except for sample size (inadequate) for test-retest studies. The floor for the Reading composite was deemed inadequate for ages 6 years 0 months through 6 years 2 months. Item gradients were good at all age levels. The overall rating for validity was adequate with evidence of content, construct, and criterion validity being provided. For the WIAT Reading composite, the standardization property resulted in ratings of good for sample size, recency of data, and types of scores; adequate on number of variables; and inadequate on age division of norms. Ratings on internal consistency were good except for adequate on test-retest coefficients by grade level and inadequate for test-retest sample size. The floor for the Reading composite was deemed inadequate for ages 6 years 0 months to 8 years 4 months. Item gradients were good at all levels. The overall rating for validity was adequate with evidence of content, construct, and criterion validity being provided.

Bartels, D. R. (1998–1999). The Peabody Individual Achievement Test–Revised/Normative Update. *Diagnostique, 24,* 211–220.

A thorough and in-depth review of PIAT-R/NU administration, scoring, and interpretive issues is presented. In addition, the standardization procedures, reliability, and validity of the instrument are evaluated. The author concludes that the test is well standardized and easy to use, especially with stu-

dents who have speed or motor difficulties. Caution is recommended in interpreting the Written Expression subtest.

Mabry, L. (1995). Review of the Wide Range Achievement Test 3. In J. C. Conoley & J. C. Impara (Eds.), *The twelfth mental measurements yearbook* (pp. 1108–1110). Lincoln, NE: Buros Institute of Measurements.

This critical review of the WRAT3 describes the instrument as outdated and is highly critical of both the reliability and validity data provided by the test author. In addition, weaknesses in test content, format of test items, and the basic philosophy underlying the instrument are discussed.

Mahrou, M. L., Espe-Pfeifer, P., Devaraju-Backhaus, S., Dornheim, L., & Golden, C. J. (1999). *Factor structure of the WRAM-L, PIAT-R, and WISC-III.* Paper presented at the annual meeting of the American Psychological Association, Boston, MA.

The relationship among these three tests was investigated with a sample of 326 children referred for a neuropsychological evaluation. Mean age was 9.4 years and the sample was 72 percent male. A principle components factor analysis was calculated. Factor-III was composed exclusively of PIAT-R subtests and was described by the authors as "an academic 'g' factor which is independent of general intelligence" (p. 4). The General Information subtest loaded on the g factor. The authors note that this subtest is similar to the WISC-III Information subtest, requires verbal intelligence, and differs from other PIAT-R subtests in format (not multiple choice).

Miller, L. J. (1998–1999). Kaufman Test of Educational Achievement/Normative Update, K-TEA/NU. *Diagnostique, 24,* 145–159.

An in-depth and thorough review of K-TEA/NU administration, scoring, and interpretive issues is presented. In addition, the standardization procedures, reliability, and validity of the instrument are evaluated. The author concludes that the K-TEA/NU "has several unique features which may make it the measure of choice for analyzing strengths and weaknesses" (p. 157). Caution is urged, however, in the use of this instrument with low-functioning 1st-graders.

Muenz, T. A., Ouchi, B. Y., & Cole, J. C. (1999). Item analysis of written expression scoring systems for the PIAT-R and WIAT. *Psychology in the Schools, 36,* 31–40.

Some of the difficulties in evaluating written expression skills are summarized initially; then the study is described. The sample consisted of 50 individuals, aged 13 to 46 years, who were tested individually or in small groups. Responses were scored in accordance with test manual instructions. Reliability (interrater reliability) and validity (item-total correlations) were then assessed and items were classified as reliable and valid, reliable but not valid, valid with limited reliability, or neither reliable nor valid. "Five of the WIAT items were identified as reliable and valid, and all 7 WIAT items met the validity with limited reliability criterion. Of the 24 PIAT-R items, seven were discarded because they were considered too easy, four were labeled reliable and valid, four items were considered only reliable, and three were valid with limited reliability. The remaining PIAT-R items were neither reliable nor valid" (p. 37).

Prewett, P. N., & Giannuli, M. M. (1991). The relationship among the reading subtests of the WJ-R, PIAT-R, K-TEA, and WRAT-R. *Journal of Psychoeducational Assessment, 9,* 166–174.

The reading subtests of each battery were administered to 118 students ranging in age from 6 years 5 months through 11 years 11 months. All students had been referred for evaluation due to academic difficulties. One factor resulted from the factor analysis, and all subtests loaded highly on it. Scores on the K-TEA and WJ-R were similar to one another, while scores from the PIAT-R and WRAT-R were significantly lower than those on the K-TEA and WJ-R.

Riccio, C. A., Boan, C. H., Staniszewski, D., & Hynd, G. W. (1997). Concurrent validity of standardized measures of written expression. *Diagnostique, 23,* 203–211.

This study examined the concurrent validity of the Written Expression subtests of the WIAT, PIAT-R, and TOWL-2 with 120 students who were either referred for learning disability services or receiving learning disability services; who were evaluated at an outpatient clinic; or who were nonreferrals. The WIAT and PIAT-R were administered to 45 students. Mean scores on the WIAT (77.18) were similar to those on the PIAT-R (74.73) and produced a correlation of .79. The authors concluded that the WIAT has a weaker floor in comparison to the PIAT-R and that the PIAT-R has a more restricted range of possible scores, with the highest scores in the above average range as compared to the WIAT.

Shull-Senn, S., Weatherly, M., Morgan, S., & Bradley-Johnson, S. (1995). Stability-reliability for elementary-age students on the Woodcock-Johnson Psychoeducational Battery–Revised (Achievement Section) and the Kaufman Test of Educational Achievement. *Psychology in the Schools, 32,* 86–92.

This study utilized a sample of 120 students in grades 1–6 who were tested and retested over a 2-week interval. The majority of test-retest reliability coefficients for the WJ-R were below .90. Test-retest reliability coefficients for all K-TEA subtests and composites exceeded .90. The authors speculated that this may be due to the K-TEA test items' being more age appropriate.

Smith, T. D., & Smith, B. L. (1998). Relationship between the Wide Range Achievement Test 3 and the Wechsler Individual Achievement Test. *Psychological Reports, 83,* 963–967.

In this study, the WRAT3 and the WIAT were administered to 87 students previously classified as having learning disabilities. Mean scores on the WRAT3 subtests did not differ significantly from those on the Basic Reading, Spelling, and Mathematics subtests of the WIAT. Pearson product moment correlations were significant in the moderate to high range.

Smith, T. D., Smith, B. L., & Smithson, M. M. (1995). The relationship between the WISC-III and the WRAT3 in a sample of rural referred children. *Psychology in the Schools, 32,* 291–295.

This study compared the performance of 37 rural students referred for academic problems on both the WISC-III and the WRAT3. Mean WISC-III scores ranged from 78.7 (FSIQ) to 81.1 (PIQ) and correlations with the WRAT3 subtests ranged from .45 to .65.

Taylor, R. L. (1998–1999). Wechsler Individual Achievement Test. *Diagnostique, 24,* 275–284.

A thorough examination of the administration, scoring, and interpretation of the WIAT is presented in this review. In addition, the standardization procedures, reliability, and validity of the instrument are assessed. The author emphasizes two unique features of the WIAT: measuring the achievement areas specified in IDEA (1997) and the linkage to the Wechsler scales. It is also noted that early items in Listening Comprehension and Oral Expression do not seem to be measuring those respective skills. Caution is urged in the interpretation of some subtests due to reliability issues.

Vance, B., & Fuller, G. B. (1995). Relations of scores on WISC-III and WRAT3 for a sample of referred children and youth. *Psychological Reports, 76,* 371–374.

Using a sample of 60 children and youth aged 6–25 years who were referred for special education services, the authors compared scores on the WISC-III and the WRAT3. They concluded that the significant and positive correlations between the two tests support the concurrent validity of the WRAT3.

Ward, A. W. (1995). Review of the Wide Range Achievement Test 3. In J. C. Conoley & J. C. Impara (Eds.), *The twelfth mental measurements yearbook* (pp. 1110–1111). Lincoln, NE: Buros Institute of Mental Measurements.

This review of the WRAT3 is highly critical of the test's validity and description of the norm sample. Unlike other reviews of the test, the author presents recommendations for correcting the deficiencies along with "temporary expedients" until redevelopment is completed.

Index

Acknowledgments

One's career is influenced and shaped by numerous individuals and events. This is especially true in my case. Two individuals in particular stand out: R. Wayne Jones and John W. McDavid. They served not only as advisors, but also as models of clinicians and researchers during my years at Georgia State University. I thank them for the training they provided and for their friendship. I would also like to pay tribute to my colleagues in Wisconsin and Minnesota with whom I have worked for the past 23 years. They have inspired me, motivated me, and strengthened my commitment to school psychology. Finally, I would like to thank Alan and Nadeen Kaufman for giving me the opportunity to write this book.

About the Author

Douglas K. Smith was Director of the School Psychology Program at the University of Wisconsin-River Falls for over 20 years. He obtained his Bachelor's degree in Psychology from Emory University and his Master's, Specialist, and Ph.D. degrees in School Psychology from Georgia State University. He was an active member of the American Psychological Association, Council for Exceptional Children, Joint Committee on Testing Practices, and National Association of School Psychologists. He served as a Delegate for NASP, President of the Wisconsin School Psychologists Association, and was Secretary of the Council for Educational Diagnostic Services, a division of CEC, at the time of his death. He is co-editor of *Assessing People with Disabilities in Educational, Employment, and Counseling Settings* (Ekstrom & Smith, in press) and co-author of *Psychological Testing and Assessment: An Introduction to Tests and Measurement (2nd edition)*. (Cohen, Swerdlik, & Smith, 1992). Dr. Smith is the author of numerous scholarly papers and chapters and was a frequent presenter at state, national, and international conferences on topics related to cognitive and academic assessment as well as assessment issues for individuals with disabilities.